W9-BTZ-772

Ubiquitous Computing

Ubiquitous Computing

The Universal Use of Computers on College Campuses

David G. Brown
Editor

International Center for Computer-Enhanced Learning
Wake Forest University

ANKER PUBLISHING COMPANY, INC.
BOLTON, MASSACHUSETTS

Ubiquitous Computing
The Universal Use of Computers on College Campuses

Copyright © 2003 by Anker Publishing Company, Inc. All rights reserved. Printed in the United States of America. No part of this publication may be reproduced or distributed in any form or by any means, electronic or mechanical, including photocopying, recording, or by any information storage or retrieval system, without the prior written consent of the publisher.

ISBN 1-882982-52-5

Composition by Deerfoot Studios
Cover design by Nicolazzo Productions

Anker Publishing Company, Inc.
176 Ballville Road
P.O. Box 249
Bolton, MA 01740-0249 USA

www.ankerpub.com

About the Editor

DAVID G. BROWN, a vice president at Wake Forest University in the United States, is a professor of economics and the dean of the International Center for Computer-Enhanced Learning. He has served as president of Transylvania University, chancellor of the University of North Carolina at Asheville, provost at three universities (Wake Forest, Miami of Ohio, and Drake) and chaired several national groups including the American Association for Higher Education, Higher Education Colloquium, ACE's Council of Chief Academic Officers, and NASULGC's Academic Council. He is editor-in-chief of the Gallery of Courses Taught With Technology and a member of EDUCAUSE's current issues committee. He founded the North Carolina Center for Creative Retirement, the Annual Conference on Ubiquitous Computing, and the Council of Public Liberal Arts Colleges.

As Wake Forest provost, Dr. Brown chaired the committee that brought ubiquitous laptop computing to the university. He has keynoted several conferences in the United States and at the EDUCAUSE Australasia 2001 in Brisbane, the International Conference on Improving Learning and Teaching in Johannesburg, the NACU Conference in San Juan, the ThinkTank Conference in Montréal, TechLearn workshops in London, and numerous US conferences. In addition to several hundred presentations and papers, his books include *Using Technology in Learner-Centered Education* (2002*), Teaching with Technology* (2000), *Interactive Learning* (2000), *Always in Touch* (1999), *Electronically Enhanced Education* (1999*), Leadership Roles of Chief Academic Officers* (1984), *Leadership Vitality* (1979), and *The Mobile Professors* (1967).

An active user of technology in his own classroom, he has been recognized as an "inspirational teacher of undergraduates" by the University of North Carolina at Chapel Hill. His classes have been featured on the front page of the *New York Times*, as a special on British Broadcasting Worldwide Network, as well as in *the Chronicle of Higher Education*, *USA Today*, and *Business Week*. Trained at Denison and Princeton Universities, Dr. Brown has consulted with hundreds of colleges and universities regarding their use of classroom and administrative technology.

Dr. Brown's wife of 44 years, Lin Brown, is a gerontologist and community volunteer. Both their children are married. Alison lives in Chicago (River Forest), and Dirk lives in Boone, North Carolina. More information is available at his web site, www.wfu.edu/~brown.

Table of Contents

Preface

Over 90% of American children between ages 5 and 17 have access to the computers either at school or home. Like electricity, telephones, and automobiles, the universality of computers shapes everything we do.

An increasing number of colleges and universities have recognized this universality. They have insisted that all teaching must proceed on the assumption that all students have appropriate access to the Internet. These pioneering institutions have recognized that new generations of students who insist upon Internet access for their music must capture the power of that same Internet for their education.

In this volume we attempt to share the experience of the pioneers so that the mid and late adopters of ubiquity can avoid early mistakes and advance the craft of teaching to ever higher plateaus.

Sincere thanks goes out to all our authors who have taken time from busy lives to share their experiences with others. Special thanks goes to Julie Edelson, who edited very diverse submissions toward continuity, and to Janice Schuyler, who kept the authors, editor, and publishers working together and meeting ambitious timelines. As always, the professionals at Anker Publishing—Jim Anker, Susan Anker, and Carolyn Dumore—have been a joy.

The success of our effort will ultimately be measured by the usefulness of our stories and observations to thousands of decision makers throughout the world. Let us know what you think and how we might be even more helpful to you by emailing us at brown@wfu.edu. May your study of this volume cause your students to learn better!

David G. Brown

The Ubiquitous Computing Movement

David G. Brown

TWO BASIC BENEFITS

P rofessors can teach Shakespeare even if students don't have access to a library or a textbook. They can stand and declaim the plays or recite the sonnets, lecture on historical background and criticism, or perhaps they can show a film. But what will the students retain? Options increase slightly if part of the class gains access to a library and part acquires textbooks. However, the quality of the course will be radically enhanced when teaching can proceed on the assumption that *all* students have textbooks and access to a library.

Communication among, say, five family units living in different cities is necessarily minimal without postal service, telephones, or transportation. When two units get phones, another a car, and one a post office box, communication increases. However, the quantity and quality of communication is vastly increased when all have postal service or a telephone or cars or all three. The library as a teaching tool and the telephone as a communication tool are metaphors for the fundamental precept of the Ubiquitous Computing Movement. The biggest educational advantages of the computer aren't realized until everyone has access to one. Email and asynchronous discussions can't become seamless components of courses until everyone has access. Digitized databases and Internet-dependent interactive exercises can't become integral until everyone has access. Only a small portion (about 25%) of the potential benefit from computers-in-education is gained until at least 85% of the students have access.

UBIQUITOUS COMPUTING DEFINED

In the university setting, ubiquitous computing means that all teaching and research proceed on the assumption that every student has appropriate access to the Internet, nothing more and nothing less. Ubiquitous computing in a community setting means that all person-to-person transactions proceed on the assumption that every citizen and customer has appropriate access to the Internet. It need not mean that all transactions take place over the Internet, just that the Internet is an option.

Ubiquitous computing is part of the infrastructure, like electricity and roads and telephones, that enables free markets. In the past, society provided electricity, and everything changed. Universal phone coverage was made available, and everything changed. A free, neighborhood public library changed everything. Now we can provide computer and Internet access to all, and everything will change again.

All-student access increases the quantity and quality of communication, personalization, and individual accountability. Interactions become more timely. The practice and degree of cooperative learning are enhanced, and remote resources, such as outside experts and professional databases, may be drawn on by each student. Until there is universal access, courses must be "dumbed down," just as physics courses must be dumbed down when a laboratory isn't available for all students and Shakespeare courses must be dumbed down when a reasonable library isn't available.

Dumbing down ripples. Top faculty avoid colleges that fail to provide basic teaching tools, like a good library and Internet access. Some of the brightest and most knowledgeable students likewise seek out institutions where courses don't have to be dumbed down because their professors and fellow students are limited by lack of access to effective teaching methodologies and basic communication systems.

AFFORDABLE UBIQUITOUS COMPUTING

The good news is that it doesn't cost much money to become a ubiquitous computing campus. Even third-world countries have a chance. All that's necessary is a collective faculty resolve to teach on the assumptions of threshold access to a library and the Internet.

In impecunious circumstances, avoiding expensive and exotic uses of technology is essential. Communication will be periodic, perhaps as little as twice a week, and asynchronous, since providing Internet connectivity for 20 minutes sometime during a 1000-minute week is much less expensive than trying to simultaneously connect every student during precisely the same 20 minutes. Software must be familiar or very easily learned, perhaps offering nothing more than a way to receive and send emails and to locate an Internet address. And the equipment required must be basic: a $300 computer that connects with the Internet will do. Of course, it may be necessary to support thousands of students with a few well-placed banks of three or four computers, much as books are placed on library reserve. The commercial Internet cafés springing up all over the globe show the feasibility of, and receptivity to, this approach.

Economics should not bar any college from entering the 21st century by preventing the adoption of today's most effective teaching methods—a mixture of face-to-face and Internet communication. Clearly, teaching is better backed by Harvard's library. While good teaching and learning can occur despite very small libraries, as successful graduates of small liberal arts colleges all over the United States continue to prove, making do is an immense burden and frustration. The same is true for teaching without a quality communication system enabled by the Internet.

FEATURED COLLEGES AND UNIVERSITIES

The universities and colleges featured in this volume believed in and implemented the ubiquitous computing philosophy early. They range from a public community college to very low-tuition, regional public universities in low-budget states to some of the most selective and expensive private universities in the country. Their particular models of ubiquitous computing, by world standards, are all exotic and expensive.

These 13 institutions have accommodated ubiquitous computing in very different ways at very different costs. Most, though not all, are laptop programs. Many, though a bare majority, are programs that involve a single, specified computer. All insist on a high degree of assurance that each student has convenient Internet access all of the time. We might call these campuses "superubiquitous" in that they go beyond universal access to personal convenience.

Authors have been encouraged, however, to cover common topics that caused the most concern on their own campus. For example, the chapter on the University of Hong Kong details how the high cost of real estate helped drive their decision toward ubiquity. The University of Minnesota at Crookston emphasizes the importance of computer skill sets as its graduates enter job markets. Providing maximal access to the newest learning and research tools is the Dartmouth program's motivation.

Together, these 13 institutions uphold the principle that teaching must not be dumbed down because all students do not have access to the Internet.

Because they are superubiquitous campuses, the opportunities they can pursue are more vivid, the lessons they have learned are less ambiguous, and the benefits they are achieving are more demonstrable. Therefore, these campus vignettes offer opportunities for other colleges and villages to learn from the early successes and mistakes and to plan better for the future.

Each of the campuses has many stories to tell about how ubiquity has empowered particular students and professors. Most chapters contain common success stories, background, educational rationale, governance issues, funding strategies, operational challenges, and concluding insights. Chapters may be read in any order.

THE MANY FACES OF UBIQUITY

Teaching on the assumption that all students have Internet access can be achieved in various ways. At some universities with wealthier student bodies, all students arrive at college with computers. Those few who don't probably use their roommate's computer. Some universities (for example, Sonoma State University) have made explicit their expectation that students will have appropriate access to the Internet by indicating in their admission materials that all teaching will proceed on this assumption, and it is the students' responsibility to make sure they have that access. Still other universities place pools of desktop computers throughout campus in large labs and maintain some access 24 hours per day and 7 days per week. The University of Minnesota at Duluth provides handheld personal digital assistants to its student body. At Chatham College every residence hall room has a computer. Since 1983, the US military academies have specified the type of desktop computers that new students must bring with them; in 2001, the Air Force Academy introduced laptops.

Most institutions in this volume, however, expect their students to have a specific laptop computer with a standard load. They have answered three questions: 1) Why should we insist that all students have computers? 2) Why should we insist that they all have similar computers with similar loads? 3) Why should we insist that the computer be mobile?

THE BASIC CASE FOR UBIQUITY

Why Should All Students Have Computers?
Authors cited a number of major reasons for all students having computers.

1. *For communication.* If the campus uses email as its primary communication mode, everyone must be able to readily receive messages. Otherwise,

campus-wide communication strategies must accommodate nonusers, and capturing the communication advantages of the Internet is no longer possible.

2. *For equity.* Most students already bring computers to campus. Since we can't prohibit computers, students who don't have them are at an unfair disadvantage. Computers for all is the only way to level the playing field.

3. *For recruitment.* Both students and faculty are attracted to computer-supported environments. Computerization is necessary to meet the competition, or a university's choice of students and new faculty will be limited.

4. *For advancement.* Most graduate schools and jobs require some form of computer literacy.

5. *For access to scholarly materials.* Increasingly, important data are available only in digital form. Neither scholar nor student can afford to be denied access.

6. *For customization and personalization.* Professors and administrators can treat each student as an individual, even if student-faculty ratios are high.

7. *For interactive and collaborative learning.* Computers greatly facilitate both individual responses and team projects. State-of-the-art teaching is moving toward collaboration as it recognizes individual learning modalities.

8. *For repetition and review.* Computers enable individuals to learn in their own best style, to preview and review difficult material, and to repeat learning cycles until they achieve mastery.

9. *For practical learning.* With computers connected to practitioners, often asynchronously, students gain opportunities for internships and professional interactions.

10. *For visualization.* Tapes that enable virtual learners to envision concepts and master material more quickly can be economically cut and distributed. Professors can take advantage of the Internet's unique capacity to permit visualization and manipulation of molecular models and to document procedures vital to the practice of science today.

When all students have computers, the mentality and metabolism of the community shifts. Teaching assumptions shift, from "Two or three copies of readings are on reserve in the library" to "You all have 24-7 access to your own copy of the readings." Timelines shift, from "I'll ask my question the next time class meets" to "I'll email and have my answer within the next hour or so." Students' sense of access shifts, from "My professor is my only authoritative source" to "When I want or need another opinion, I'll search reliable authorities on the Internet." Relationships shift, from a student isolated from family and friends in different states to an extended family staying connected in one virtual home. The duration and intensity of subgroups shifts, from "After the final exam, it's unlikely that I'll keep in touch with my class" to "Through group email, our class will stay connected for years." The whole mentality of students shifts! The magnitude of this shift is comparable to the transformation from a world of public telephones to custom, programmed cell phones.

Everything shifts, but not until all students and faculty have computers. An analogy may help here. Before near-universal access to cars, jobs and shopping were concentrated in central cities and along public transportation routes. When automobile ownership became standard, individual homeowners and entrepreneurs were no longer restricted to jobs, homes, and shops in specific locations. They were no longer slaves to public transportation schedules. They came to think differently about distance. Friends could be more scattered; shopping hours more varied and more frequent. Branch offices became common. Work colleagues were more likely to live in different neighborhoods. Eventually, whole cities looked different, and people took the automobile for granted. The computer, linked to the Internet, is changing the structure of lives in as many, though different, ways.

Why Should All Students Have Standard Computers With Standard Loads?

Among the major advantages cited for standardization are the following:

1. *For reliability.* Classroom time is perishable, lost forever, if nonfunctioning student computers break down or freeze during an in-class project that depends on them. The best insurance for reliability is redundant networks and identical laptop computers. When all students have the same computers, classmates and roommates can share.

2. *For training.* Computer instruction can be more focused and more accelerated when everyone in the class is starting from the same hardware and software. Classes on specific topics can be offered more frequently, and class time spent more efficiently on coursework.

3. *For solving problems.* In a ubiquitous computing environment, everyone, including office neighbors, students, faculty colleagues, secretaries, and supervisors, is a potential helper when you have a problem with your

computer. With such a large corps of volunteer helpers, fewer people must be hired to staff the computer help desk.

4. *For solving hardware/software problems.* When a problem is solved for one computer (for example, an incompatibility between a word-processing program and a printer), it can immediately be applied to all computers (for example, via an email to all users).

5. *For minimizing inventory, repair costs, and downtimes.* Maintaining a small inventory of spare parts is feasible when only one brand of computer is involved. Simple repairs can be made quickly and inexpensively. When more complex repairs involve sending the ailing computer off campus, a healthy, identical loaner can be provided.

6. *For a true equality of access.* With standardization comes an ironclad assurance to faculty that all students have identical threshold computer access and that the playing field is level.

7. *For communication.* When all have the same hardware and software, messages don't get lost or garbled.

8. *For marketing.* To outside constituencies (for example, prospective students), admissions personnel can make a fuller and more convincing case for the strength of university computing.

Why Laptops? Why Is Portability a Must?

Portability is less important than standardization, and standardization is less important than ubiquity. However, substantial advantages come with portability. Among them are the following:

1. *For collaboration.* Schedules are complex. Student-to-student collaboration is facilitated when team members may exchange emails, drafts, videos, and references asynchronously. With portability, faculty and students can keep up with the group when at home or off campus.

2. *For flexibility.* Portable computers can be taken to science lab, and the data developed there will still be available at home. Data can be collected in the field; student athletes can complete homework assignments on the road. Portable computers can be available when studying in the library, back in a dormitory room, and home on spring break. When the dorm is too noisy, portable computer users can seek quiet elsewhere.

3. *For availability.* Portable computers allow faculty to remain available to student emails at unusual hours. Communication with people in other time zones is not restricted to office hours.

4. *For communication.* With portability, everyone in the system becomes more accessible via electronic communication.

5. *For a sense of ownership.* Students will hold back on computer use if they expect that their access will be curtailed once they graduate and no longer have access to their college computer lab or because their computer can't be taken to a new job or on a trip. With portability comes a strong sense of ownership and, consequently, high motivation to use the computer comfortably in all circumstances.

6. *For marketing.* Again, the laptop provides a tangible advantage for incoming students and their parents.

7. *For saving building space otherwise committed to computer labs and classrooms.* Here, the hidden savings in infrastructure can be immense.

8. *For encouraging study abroad.* Students can stay in touch with their campus and colleagues and continue to enjoy the advantages of computing. They are both less remote and better equipped.

9. *For reliability.* Portable computers are more easily brought to a central location for repair and replacement, and borrowing an identical device is more feasible.

10. *For refreshing.* Computers can be more easily recalled in case of a system-wide software glitch. If a routine software upgrade requires a technician, students can more easily bring their computers to a common location.

LISTS OF UBIQUITOUS UNIVERSITIES

With all of these advantages, it is not surprising that more than 100 colleges and universities have adopted, either university-wide or in one or more colleges, a technology requirement. Ray Brown maintains a list of these institutions at http://www.acck.edu/%7Earayb/NoteBookList.html. A more narrow list of colleges and universities with ubiquitous laptop requirements is available from Valley City State University at http://itc.vcsu.edu/notebookinitiative/notebookcampusmap.htm. Canadian institutions committed to comprehensive laptop programs are identified by the Node Learning Technologies Network at http://node.on.ca/ltreport/. An unpublished list of institutions is available from Ron Toll at rtoll@mail.uca.edu. Links to these sites, as well as other listing efforts, are available at http://www.wfu.edu/~brown. If you know of other lists, please email brown@wfu.edu so they may be added to the list of lists.

LESSONS LEARNED

While composing their chapters, all authors were asked to generate a list of "lessons learned." The hope is that others might replicate our successes and be spared our blunders. The lessons learned below represent an overview of the themes iterated in the individual chapters. Each of the points was mentioned by multiple authors and, together, they comprise both an introduction and a checklist.

Lessons on Planning for Ubiquitous Computing

1. Don't lose sight of the ultimate goal: measurable improvement of education outcomes. Keep the focus on pedagogy, not technology. Remember that students are the center of the program: Everyone else is important, but the program serves the students directly. Stay focused on the goal of enhanced student learning.

2. Clearly defined, defensible program objectives are essential.

3. Develop a comprehensive plan first and quickly match it with a multi-year financial plan. Establish a clear financial plan and budget and a mechanism for revising the budget annually. Include adequate startup and operating funds.

4. Demand for technology will increase much faster than anticipated.

5. Most sunk costs (for example, old computers) can be ignored.

6. Getting laptops to students is only 10% of the challenge; decisions about, and implementation of, policies, training, support, networking, exposure, and motivation remain ahead.

7. Recognize that user-friendly technology in the hands of dedicated faculty is the most powerful change instrument that any academic administrator has ever had.

8. Top executive support is essential.

9. The impact of computing on teaching and learning is difficult to assess objectively.

10. Disciplines use the computer in different ways, so a broad spectrum of faculty must participate in system design decisions.

Lessons on Technology Itself

1. Reliability is crucial, especially in a robust network and trained help desk.

2. Standardize hardware, software, and ISP, at least first. Standardization pays rewards well beyond those anticipated.

3. Pay attention to the logistics of distributing equipment; it's harder than you think. Laptop distribution is a major production: Define each step and automate everything possible.

4. Don't accept the first bid from a vendor: The market is competitive, and vendors will improve their bids. Develop strategic partnerships rather than just buying from vendors. Choose a partner for the long haul.

5. Models and prices change fast; don't buy too early in the year and then be forced to deliver a discontinued model to your students, while they read ads in the newspaper for new machines at fire-sale prices.

6. Sign procurement contracts with major vendors specifying their responsibilities for delivery and for equipment that fails initially or repeatedly.

7. Technology will sometimes fail.

8. Have a structure for student repairs.

9. You can never have enough bandwidth to the Internet or network disk space.

10. One of the biggest financial challenges is what to do with laptops used for a semester or two and returned when a student withdraws or is dismissed.

11. The help desk must be close to classrooms.

12. Wireless is worth it: Don't hesitate too long, and be complete with your wireless coverage.

Lessons on Implementation and Management of Ubiquitous Computing

1. Professional project management is essential, especially during startup.

2. Be prepared to outsource challenges; consulting help is essential.

3. Use commercial course-management software.

4. Spread the gains from, and ownership of, innovation throughout all units. Identify and incorporate existing assets before creating new ones.

5. Balance central services and local control.

6. Provide academic units staff of their own and plenty of equipment without hassle.

7. Put in place an ongoing faculty and student-led oversight mechanism to monitor and to adjust the program. Place some funds under faculty control. Apply academic review structures to the program. Don't let administrators have control of faculty development.

8. Understand the role of standards in the program, and obtain agreement on them from faculty and administration.

9. Ultimate responsibility should be given to a senior administrator with the authority to set directions and settle disputes.

10. Never underestimate the power of teamwork.

11. Involve parents as early as possible.

12. Hardware and software decisions are separable.

13. Communicate, communicate, communicate frequently with all stakeholders.

14. Manage expectations; they invariably outrun the capacity to deliver. Address faculty and student concerns truthfully, adequately, and quickly in order to quell rumors. Keep your admissions office informed. Regularly reconcile program descriptions in university publications with those on the Web.

15. High percentages of faculty will use the computer if their initial introduction involves only email, URL addresses, and course materials posted by a course-management system.

Lessons on Adoption of Computer-Enhanced Learning

1. Plan a pilot year to purge bugs when stakeholders will still tolerate imperfections.

2. Provide students and faculty with just-in-time training that centers on the task-at-hand; general classes don't work well.

3. In a standardized environment, students learn basic computer skills quickly, without degree-credit incentives.

4. Standardization speeds faculty adoption and eases the pressure on support staff.

5. First encourage easily learned and administered uses of the computer by a high percentage of faculty; leave the more difficult and expensive uses of the computer until later.

6. Early academic involvement and leadership is critical to success.

7. Make use of student expertise to support peers and faculty.

8. Student access to computing can vary even in a highly standardized environment. Students aren't all computer wizards. Some can be archly conservative.

9. Coordinate the technology program with existing programs for faculty development and training.

10. Continue, long after program launch, to provide faculty training.

11. Recognize that it's quite possible to launch an online course for less than $30,000.

12. Avoid minimum expectations about the amount and character of technology to be used in individual courses.

13. Find opportunities for faculty to showcase the results of their work.

14. Develop an intellectual-property policy that benefits both individuals and the university.

Lessons on Results

1. Contact among students and between students and faculty becomes continuous.

2. Students teach faculty, and friends serve as an informal help desk.

3. Co-curricular activities thrive due to increased communication. Student groups are larger and more active.

4. Team assignments are more frequent and more easily completed.

5. Computer knowledge is a boon to student recruitment, retention, and self-confidence.

6. Computer availability throughout the student body attracts new faculty.

7. The greatest benefits are seen in what happens between classes, not during class.

8. If students are provided a standard platform with a standard software load, faculty will voluntarily and rather quickly migrate toward the same standard.

9. Student presentations are more substantive and polished.

10. Student preservation of electronic materials is greatly facilitated by writable compact discs and a program for creating portfolios.

The chapters that follow address these questions in detail and in specific instances that arose at institutions that may have much in common with your own. We hope they will prove helpful in deciding your future course.

Contact Information

David G. Brown
Vice President and Dean
International Center for Computer-Enhanced Learning
Wake Forest University
P.O. Box 7328, Reynolda Station
Winston-Salem, NC 27109
Phone: 336-758-4878
Fax: 336-758-5012
Email: brown@wfu.edu
Web Address: http://www.wfu.edu/~brown

Dartmouth College

Malcolm Brown

"Universal access to computing" is Dartmouth's translation of ubiquitous computing. Such phrases might evoke an entirely quantitative idea: that ubiquitous computing is all about providing more ports, more computers, more printers, more network bandwidth. Such arrays of equipment and usage statistics, however, merely set the stage. It's clear that the real payoff must lie elsewhere: Does an increase in the "amount" of computing result in qualitative advances? Does the investment needed to make computing truly ubiquitous really make a difference? Based on our long experience at Dartmouth, we feel the answer is decidedly "yes."

A chapter from our experience may illustrate how quantity can lead to quality. Jerry Rutter is a professor in the Classics Department, specializing in archaeology. He had been asking his students to write essays on Greek and Roman coins and signet rings. He assigned each a coin or ring in the collection of Dartmouth's Hood Museum. Students were obliged to walk over to the museum to inspect the ring or the obverse and reverse sides of the coin they had been assigned. They then left to write their essays, drawing on their notes and memories.

This system, although it worked, had clear disadvantages. Students could only view the coins when the museum was open. Because this college-level experience in Greek and Roman studies was the first for many, writing the essay entirely from memory and notes was challenging. Students found it difficult to use other coins and rings for comparison, because access to the objects was limited and it proved to be a time-consuming task to write up descriptive notes for each object. Tiny details were hard to see by simple and rapid inspection. Their essays were taken up by lengthy descriptions of the coins, rather than discussing what the coins' imagery meant.

Because every student owned a networked computer, Professor Rutter hit on the idea of making images of the coins available online. He obtained a small, internal grant to photograph a large set of the museum's coins and signet rings. These photographs were digitized, and Professor Rutter annotated each. The text and images were then placed into a database and made available via the campus information system.

Now students could view their coins at any time. They could inspect the image carefully, zooming in and out as needed. This capacity to zoom in was a great boon, as some of these coins are only a half-inch in diameter. The enlargement feature also helped them identify very small details. Students could also quickly compare their coins to others in the collection, and, working in the library, compare their object's image with photographs in books and periodicals. They could paste these images into their documents and draw arrows to point out the features under discussion. In this case, a picture truly was worth a thousand words: Students could devote the entirety of their essay to developing their ideas.

Students liked the new system, and the quality of their essays noticeably improved. Sidney Carter, class of 2000, made a significant discovery about Greek signet rings. On a surface area of perhaps two inches square, Greek artists would carve scenes of warfare, hunting, and the like. Carter's project concerned a gold signet ring, originally discovered in 1876 by the pioneering German archaeologist Heinrich Schliemann at Mycenae. This was the city that, according to Homer, was ruled by Agamemnon, who led the Greeks in the Trojan War. By carefully studying digital images of the signet ring and comparing it to others, Carter discovered shallow incisions that the Greek artists used in the preliminary stages of composing their carvings. "Such incisions," Carter wrote, "were preliminary sketch lines for the creation of deeper incisions at a later stage."[1] Carter's thesis on this ring was awarded Dartmouth's Rintels Prize in recognition of the best student thesis in the humanities and social sciences. His original discovery provided insight into the way Greek craftsmen went about their work. Carter, currently working on a National Science Foundation fellowship, is preparing his thesis for publication.

Quo Vadis?

Dartmouth has long recognized information technology's potential to encourage and to support academic innovation. This innovative capacity ties directly into one of Dartmouth's strengths: being a research university with a faculty actively engaged in undergraduate education. Dartmouth's dedication to ubiquitous computing is a direct outcome of its relentless pursuit of excellence in teaching, learning, and research.

The vision that informs Dartmouth's long-standing commitment to ubiquitous computing was first articulated by John Kemeny, a mathematics professor and Dartmouth's 13th president (from 1970 to 1981). Born in Budapest, Kemeny came to the United States in 1940 to attend Princeton University. He worked on the Manhattan Project at Los Alamos, where he was greatly influenced by John von Neumann's views on the potential of computing. He completed his doctorate at Princeton and worked for a time as one of Einstein's assistants. He came to Dartmouth in 1953, charged with developing new directions for the mathematics department.

During the 1960s, Kemeny, working with Professor Tom Kurtz and undergraduates, invented one of the first time-sharing systems and the programming language, BASIC. By 1964, the time-sharing system was in use at 20 secondary schools and 42 colleges and universities in the United States and Canada.

Of more lasting value, perhaps, was his vision of universal computer access for faculty and students. For computing to realize its full potential, Kemeny believed that access should be so universal as to be taken for granted, like access to the library or the athletic facilities. When asked about the costs associated with providing universal access, Kemeny would shrug and say that the library and athletic facilities were expensive, but nobody was suggesting that they be done away with. As he once phrased it, "Every student should have access, and every faculty member should be able to use computing in the classroom."

When he received the first Lou Robinson award from EDUCOM in 1990 for his contributions to academic computing, Kemeny related an incident that helped crystallize in his mind the importance of universal access. In 1959, Dartmouth acquired its first computer, an LPG30. Kemeny described this device as a "baby computer" with paper tape input, and "16 instructions, one of which was 'STOP.'" A group of students wanted to implement the programming language ALGOL on this computer and approached Kemeny and Kurtz. Both were convinced it was quite impossible but didn't tell the students. To their astonishment, the students succeeded. Kemeny realized "that if you only put computing in the hands of students, they're going to do incredible things."[2]

During the 1980s, as desktop computing emerged, Dartmouth had to evolve away from time-sharing. To implement Kemeny's vision on these new terms, Dartmouth made a pair of key decisions in 1983. The first was to standardize its desktop computing on a new, soon-to-be-released Apple computer called the Macintosh. Dartmouth's bet was that the innovation the Macintosh provided, especially the graphical user interface, would make computing even more accessible to a wider audience. This standardization on a single platform was a deliberate step toward the strategic goal of computing ubiquity.

The second decision was to completely network the campus, and so by 1985 every dorm room, office, and classroom had a network port. Even facilities as remote as the maintenance garages and athletic facilities had ports, and a dial-up remote access client was created so that any member of the Dartmouth community could access the network from any telephone.

The most convincing illustration of the potential of universal network access was the rapid success of Dartmouth's own email system, BlitzMail. Introduced in 1987, BlitzMail was a client-server application featuring a client fully integrated into the Macintosh user interface. BlitzMail was quickly adopted by faculty and students as a way to increase the effectiveness of their interaction, and BlitzMail is still the standard email client on campus. A name directory was created so that sending email was as simple as knowing even part of a person's name. If that person was not yet an email user, the sent message was printed and delivered as campus mail along with a brief statement on how the recipient could become an email user. Quite unexpectedly, BlitzMail became Dartmouth's "killer app."

Other innovations to promote access and increase the network's utility quickly followed. The infrastructure was developed to support free public printing, requiring Dartmouth to invent its own printer spoolers and utilities. During these pre-web days, Dartmouth wrote a more robust version of the AppleShare networked volume; christened "PUBLIC," it was an easy way for faculty to disseminate course materials, to make application software available for course assignments, and to provide drop-boxes for students to deliver assignments. PUBLIC was so widely used that it became a kind of campus portal. Running on a modern UNIX workstation, it could support many hundreds of simultaneous users, instead of the several dozen in Apple's implementation. Additional utilities, such as a better File Transfer Protocol client (Fetch), followed.

In 1989, Dartmouth was awarded a major grant from Apple Computer to build a campus-wide information system. Jointly undertaken by the Dartmouth Library and Computing Services, this project created the Dartmouth College Information System (DCIS). The project aimed to make digital resources available over the campus network. To accomplish this, Dartmouth built a sophisticated client-server structure, using off-the-shelf components when possible and building its own when not. The forerunner of the library's current digital efforts, DCIS succeeded not only in delivering networked resources, but made access easy by providing a uniform interface to a variety of online resources. Undertaking a project of this scope made sense because of the network and the fact that, at the time, nearly everyone had his or her own computer; online library resources would be just as accessible to all as other traditional library holdings.

By 1990, well over 7,000 ports on campus connected over 6,000 computers. All faculty and staff had computers in their offices, and 90% of students owned a computer. In 1991, the trustees took the final step and made ownership of a computer a requirement.

During the 1990s Dartmouth actively continued to build on Kemeny's legacy. The Academic Computing group was formed to focus on supporting curricular and research computing. In 1993, through the generosity of an alumnus who was a former student of Kemeny's, Dartmouth instituted an internal grant program called the Computing Technology Venture Fund to encourage innovation in teaching and learning. In 1995, Dartmouth's Classroom Subcommittee initiated a new effort to renovate the classrooms, with special emphasis on technology. During the late 1990s, Dartmouth extended its networking reach by securing a vBNS network connection, which subsequently became an Internet2 Abilene connection.

Dartmouth's 1999 reaccreditation effort afforded an opportunity to reexamine universal access. President James Wright identified academic computing as one of three areas for in-depth self-study. The report reaffirmed the importance of universal access as the foundation on which any innovation in teaching, learning, and research must be sustained.

While the self-study was not the sole reason Dartmouth installed a wireless network layer, or overlay, it nevertheless provided a great deal of momentum for the idea. The report had made clear that Dartmouth could ill afford to rest on any laurels, especially with technology rapidly changing the entire landscape of higher education. Our experience had shown repeatedly that innovation follows closely on the heels of increased and improved access. Accordingly, the decision to install wireless relatively quickly became obvious. Completed in April 2001, Dartmouth became the first Ivy League campus to install universal wireless coverage. Students, faculty, and staff were encouraged to consider wireless laptop use; client wireless card prices were subsidized, and a number of faculty and students began experimenting with wireless networking, including hand-held devices.

The self-study had a long-term impact as well: a call to accelerate efforts to support innovation and leadership in teaching and learning. The provost asked a committee to draw up recommendations on how to implement these findings. The committee suggested that Dartmouth establish a faculty-led central resource center, fusing traditional kinds of teaching support—workshops on methodology, assistance with course organization, course evaluation, videotaping of lectures—with new computing efforts. Program areas included an entirely new effort to support student competency in, and use of, information technology, systematic assessment of teaching methods, and rapid progress in what the self-study called "inquiry-based interactive learning." An arts and sciences faculty priorities committee came independently to a similar conclusion. It advised a more unified effort to support teaching and learning. In light of these recommendations, Dartmouth is pursuing plans for more focused support for the teaching and learning enterprise.

THE DARTMOUTH CONTEXT

Dartmouth seeks to maintain its excellence in teaching and to strengthen its growing success as a research institution. It strives to be both a college and a liberal arts university and sets for its faculty the ambitious, complementary goals of excellence in both teaching and research. Small class size, which encourages more intense and fruitful faculty-student interaction, reflects this emphasis on the curriculum. The student to faculty ratio is 8.55:1, using criteria developed in 1996 for the Common Data Set by the College Board, *U.S. News & World Report* and *Peterson's Guide to Four-Year Colleges.*

This emphasis on teaching and learning and a tradition of faculty-student interaction have informed much of Dartmouth's computing. Following the introduction of the campus network in 1984, almost all technological innovations—from email to networked storage volumes to the use of software license metering applications, like KeyServer—have been harnessed to serve the academic enterprise.

Dartmouth remains firmly dedicated to its long tradition of liberal arts education. Of the 35 courses needed for the bachelor of arts degree, students must take ten distributed across eight intellectual fields. The computing environment assists by providing a rich collection of online information and resources. It also provides both a consistent teaching and learning approach in a variety of curricular contexts as well as ways for students to work with diverse information types, from ICPSR data sets in economics to 3D modeling in architecture.

Almost all of Dartmouth's 4,300 undergraduates are housed on campus. By wiring the dorms, we provide uniform, high-speed networking for the undergraduates in a single stroke. Dartmouth is also helped by the fact that its campus is, geographically, relatively compact. This, of course, was of help to us in the installation of the wireless network; we were able to cover the campus using approximately 450 access points.

Unlike many of its peers, Dartmouth does not have an extensive graduate program: Post-bachelor degrees are awarded primarily in the sciences. Since using graduate students as a catalyst for technology adoption is not an option at Dartmouth, the faculty must be directly engaged in the use of computing technology in the teaching and learning process. These means the faculty member needs to be an active participant in the preparation of digital resources for his or her class, as well as in the maintenance of the course web site.

The Professional Schools

Dartmouth's three professional schools are similar to the undergraduate programs: relatively small student bodies in order to promote faculty-student interaction. For example, the Thayer School of Engineering has a faculty of 43, resulting in a faculty-student ratio of 3:1. The Thayer School says on its web site that its "... relatively small size is intentional. It maintains a sense of community and close student-faculty interaction, as well as facilitating quick response to new technological developments." Dartmouth undergraduates may take courses at Thayer and obtain a BS in engineering sciences. The Thayer School has been a full participant in Dartmouth's major computing initiatives, from administrative systems, such as the student information system, to the wireless project.

The Amos Tuck School of Business program involves over 400 MBA students and over 50 faculty. Like many business schools, Tuck feels that information technology is now essential in all aspects of business. To facilitate coursework, the school requires students to purchase Windows-compatible laptop computers. Laptops are used routinely for course projects both in and outside the classroom and to consult online information resources, such as Dow Jones Interactive, Lexis-Nexis, Thomson Financial Securities Data, Global Business Browser, Global Access, and Datastream. Tuck has developed its own portal, called TuckStreams, which is a role-based, "push" system that gives its community access to institutional data, web applications, and educational tools on campus and around the world. Over the past several years, Tuck has engaged in extensive building and renovation projects, all of which have promoted ubiquitous computing; data ports and power outlets are integrated into the commons, living spaces, and many classrooms.

GOING WIRELESS

When Dartmouth began to contemplate the next step in ubiquitous computing—the installation of a wireless networking layer—we returned to our roots. Our experience seemed to bear out the Kemeny idea: Innovation follows access. Our goal was for wireless to be as taken for granted as the wired network.

Dartmouth conducted its initial tests of a wireless network in 1999, using the provost in one of our very first tests. A college building was, by happy circumstance, located across the street from the provost's private home, making it easier to site an access point that would provide service to her house. She was provided with a laptop and a wireless card. It worked and worked well. Additional experimental access points were set up in locations such as the library, the student commons, the engineering school, and the computer science department. We were greatly encouraged when they all performed well, meeting expectations. The time had come to move forward.

Dartmouth didn't hesitate: Once the decision was made, in October 2000, to begin the installation of a wireless network, Dartmouth worked aggressively. This entailed extensive siting work: Given the dearth of precedents, a great deal of trial-and-error work was required to determine the best sites for the access points and to avoid complications such as "edge effects." A small team of professionals and students worked to determine access point locations. Many of the access points needed new wiring runs; current networking ports were typically located near the floor, not the ceiling, the more optimal position. Installation was completed by May 2001, deploying well over 400 access points in several months' time.

When it came time to plan the deployment of the access points, the question arose: How much wireless? Key academic buildings only? Administrative offices as well? Dartmouth decided to parallel its original networking efforts and go for 100%. The wireless network is now literally everywhere on the main campus, at all off-campus offices, and in adjacent areas like the athletic fields and the maintenance garages. Even the Dartmouth boathouse on the Connecticut River and sections of the river itself, which borders the campus, are part of the wireless overlay.

EDUCATIONAL RATIONALE

Dartmouth's goal has never been to replace or even to reduce faculty-student interaction. Technology is valued as a vehicle to leverage and expand the scope of the faculty-student interaction. A paragraph from Dartmouth's mission statement notes that "...one of Dartmouth's strengths is providing students with close contact with faculty, and an appreciation that the quality of the educational and research experiences Dartmouth offers students is one measure of its success."

Information technology provides new and sometimes better ways to fulfill this mission. Beginning with the reaccreditation report, Dartmouth sensed a need to pursue even more energetically these "new methods and new opportunities." We moved quickly to install the wireless network and to establish a digital library. The new report suggested that Dartmouth look for ways to expand the Venture Fund program so that more faculty could participate and that the institution devise "... an institutional strategy to consider distance learning techniques that can enhance our off-campus programs." Most recently, Dartmouth became a partner in the Open Knowledge Initiative, led by Stanford and MIT, to produce the next generation of course-management tools. A recent faculty report asserts, "Dartmouth has been and will remain ... dedicated to its mission of undergraduate and graduate education in a primarily residential setting." On the other hand, the report notes that "... unique technological innovations will make available both new methods and new opportunities to carry out this mission."[3] The Venture Fund grant program (http://www.dartmouth.edu/~vfund) provides a long list of examples of innovation within the Dartmouth context.

Dartmouth has elected not to mandate the use of information technology in the curriculum, either by insisting that every course have a web site or automatically generating a web site for every course. Part of the reason is our history: Faculty were distributing course materials and resources via the network long before the advent of the web, and many of these paths and resources continue to work well. More importantly, we feel that generating web sites purely for their own sake does not greatly accelerate innovation in the curriculum. We have found that the key ingredient to bringing about lasting change is the direct engagement of the faculty—with technology, technology professionals, and students—even if it means that the adoption rate is slower.

Also gone are the days when Dartmouth had a single or standard operating system: first time-sharing, then the Macintosh. Support for both Macintosh and Windows has become necessary in light of the availability of key applications on both the academic and administrative sides. It has also proved less traumatic and disruptive than initially anticipated. With the availability of Microsoft Office for both operating systems and the emergence of platform-independent options for delivering curricular resources (for example, the web and Java), we feel that sufficient cross-platform interoperability makes an operating-system mandate unnecessary.

Declining prices and rising functionality have driven up laptop owner-ship among the undergraduate students. The class of 2003 had 25% laptop ownership; the figure doubled for the class of 2004. Given the implementa-tion of the wireless network, we anticipate another major increase in laptop ownership. As of this writing, the percentage of incoming students ordering laptops has increased to over 70% for the class of 2005. While the class of 2004 was split almost 50–50 between Macintosh and Windows, the class of 2005 has shifted strongly to Windows.

INITIAL WIRELESS "STEPS"

The "paint" on the wireless network is barely dry, but already innovators are coming forward. A pair of recent developments on campus illustrate this.

Professor Chris Jernstedt of the Department of Psychological and Brain Sciences has long been studying and using interactive learning techniques. His research investigates ways to "improve the ability of students to remember and apply their knowledge to new situations," a method he calls "learning with understanding." His courses afford him the opportunity both to employ and to evaluate these techniques.

Professor Jernstedt has long been a pioneer in this area. In 1993, he was one of the first recipients of a Venture Fund grant. The project's goal was to encourage interactive student participation in a large lecture class. It enabled him to construct a multimedia teaching station that held a projector and a computer connected to standard lab test equipment. He used it in class to gather and display real-time experimental data, using a combination of graph-ical and numerical presentation methods. Professor Jernstedt's teaching sta-tion anticipated Dartmouth's classroom renovation efforts, which began sys-tematically the following year.

Professor Jernstedt has continued to experiment with computing tech-nology to further interactive learning in his courses. His class on learning the-ory seeks not only to introduce students to current learning theories, but also, by means of interactive assignments and activities, to strengthen their learn-ing capabilities. For example, he often polls the students at a lecture and is able to display the results immediately using a computer and a projector. This feedback loop allows him and his students to ask more challenging questions, based on the previous questions.

For his course on learning theory for fall 2001, Professor Jernstedt utilized the wireless network in a unique way. On the basis of an equipment grant from Handspring, Dartmouth provided students with hand-held Visors, each equipped with a Xircom 802.11b wireless module and applications written by staff in Jernstedt's Center for Educational Outcomes (http://www.dart mouth.edu/dms/koop/programs/outcomes.shtml). Students in the course used these PDAs to interact continuously in the classroom and out in a variety of ways. One example: Professor Jernstedt used the Visors to conduct more real-time experimentation during class time. In his overview of the course for his students, he wrote, "We will learn by conducting real experiments and observing their results.... Your role is to be the active learner. You must practice the material, extend it to new situations, and develop a wholistic understanding of the concepts." By conducting "instant polls" and other kinds of in-class experiments, the students got a chance to observe themselves as learners.

The installation of the wireless layer opened research opportunities for faculty and students. In 2000, faculty from computer science and the Thayer School of Engineering formed the Center for Mobile Computing (CMC; http://www.cs.dartmouth.edu/CMC/). The CMC promotes and supports "advanced research in topics related to mobile computing and distributed information resources."

Computer science Professor David Kotz is one of the faculty guiding the center's activities. He points out that the wireless network may eventually result in a radical change in the way we do computing. Instead of doing everything from a single device, like a laptop, we will use an array of devices, like our many household appliances: the equivalents of light switches, refrigerators, note pads, and lawn mowers.

Admittedly, such a development is well in the future, but it nevertheless suggests the center's conceptual framework: mobile computing. The CMC conducts research on the technical issues associated with large numbers of people each using a several wireless devices from a variety of locations. For example, one of the challenges associated with mobile computing is context awareness. Applications must be able to change their behavior, depending on a variety of contextual parameters. An application might change its behavior if it detects a slow or erratic network connection, or, if it sees that the client device is computationally weak but a hefty server is nearby and available, it might automatically shift computation to the server. Some applications might need to know if you are at home, in the office, or at the café. One student's research project was to implement a "smart-reminder" application. It issues a meeting reminder at an interval appropriate to your location: If you are across campus, it warns you 15 minutes in advance; if you are in the next building, perhaps only five.

A similar project worked on developing a "location-aware" directory service. Since the wireless protocol (802.11) is below the IP networking layer, connections break if the user roams far enough to require a new IP address. This project worked on developing a network directory service that constantly tracks your current IP address, so that a service (e.g., voice-over-IP phone call, email, instant messaging) could always find you.

The CMC will continue a usage analysis it began in spring 2001. It has been tracking certain uses of the wireless network, with a view toward identifying trends and patterns. Hopefully, this analysis will provide useful information to guide our efforts to maintain the wireless network overall and point out usage patterns that will inform future research projects.

WHO MAKES THE DECISIONS?

Governance of information technology at Dartmouth is best understood as a four-way partnership, involving the dean's office, the provost, Computing Services, and the library. Both Computing Services and the library report to the provost. We take strategic direction from that office, ensuring that computing initiatives are in sync with the overall direction of the institution. We work closely with the dean of the college for student support and with the director for alumni affairs on programs targeted to the alumni. On the administrative side, the key partnership is with the office of the vice president and treasurer.

All significant aspects of academic computing are reviewed by the Council on Computing, a body chaired by, and made up of, faculty, computarians,[4] librarians, and other senior administrators. The council formulates the purchase recommendations to the incoming first-year students and was consulted in deliberations on the wireless network.

The organization responsible for computing support is Computing Services, which has more than 140 full-time employees. Groups are dedicated to administrative and academic computing support; networking (data, voice, and coaxial video), host systems, and services; help desk and personal computing acquisitions; institutional web support; and classroom support.

Another very significant player is the library. Dartmouth has recently completed the initial phase of a two-phase library building project that, when complete, will double the amount of floor space and provide significant renovations for existing library space. This afforded Dartmouth the opportunity to co-locate much of Computing Services in the library. For example, the reference librarians and Computing Services' academic computing division are co-located on the main floor of the library. This effort also enabled the library to renew its vision to utilize information technology in support of the academic mission, and its DCIS project has now evolved into a major initiative to establish a digital library. Paralleling the Council on Computing, there is also a Council on Libraries. The directors of the library and Computing Services sit on both councils.

As always, governance is ultimately faculty driven. This means our relationship with the arts and sciences dean's office is a key one. Computing Services must be responsive to faculty needs, for as with any educational institution, the faculty are the institution. Being "responsive" is not a passive, care-taking role. Rather, Computing Services must lead by anticipating what information technology practices will ultimately best serve Dartmouth's mission. Groups like the Council on Computing are a formal expression of such governance, while an ongoing working relationship with faculty groups and individuals also creates a milieu of partnership with, and support for, all faculty.

WHO PAYS?

In minimizing barriers to universal access, Dartmouth avoids explicit charge-backs and end-user cost-recovery fees as much as possible. Whenever possible, information technology costs are centralized at the top of the budgets of major areas, so that departments do not see such costs in their budget lines. In this way, information services are taken for granted: Just as a light switch is expected to work in any room, so are network jacks (including wireless "jacks in the air") and human support. Information services are modeled after library services: Few institutions charge users explicit fees to access the library's resources.

Here is one example: covering the costs to run the campus network. A cost-per-port is calculated each year by dividing the total networking costs by the number of ports. These costs are recovered by charging campus units based on their number of ports, but the accounting is all done centrally and, to most of the Dartmouth community, invisibly. Individual accounts are not charged directly and do not have line items covering networking fees. To end users, network ports are like office desks and chairs: They are provided.

The students' price of admission is, of course, the computer they buy upon matriculation. No additional technology-access fees are currently assessed.

HOW DOES IT RUN?

History repeats itself: Sometimes this works to one's advantage. Traditions provide their own kind of momentum or inertia. We've noted how Dartmouth's tradition of universal access, initiated during the Kemeny era, has continued to exert an influence as the institution makes strategic and tactical decisions about information technology. Traditions can also gather momentum, and this is true with respect to universal access at Dartmouth. A pair of examples concern technology in the classrooms and the difficulties we have experienced with respect to modem connections.

In 1993, Dartmouth recognized that classrooms had been neglected for years. Faculty were increasingly voicing concerns; the disparity between access to, and use of, computing in the classrooms and other campus locations was apparent just as they were developing more digital resources for their curriculum. Student demand was increasing as well. The inclusion of PowerPoint on the student computers has encouraged them to use it for class presentations. A subcommittee was charged to develop and to implement a plan to renovate and maintain the classrooms, with a special emphasis on providing the full range of audio-visual and digital resources. It developed a technology standard level, dubbed smart, and renovations began in 1995. While progress was steady, the pace was slow due to the scale, expense, and complexity of the projects. Yet demand increased as the smart classroom idea took hold.

In 2000, Dartmouth commissioned a consulting firm to draw a master plan for the classrooms, informed by a variety of sources, including surveys and faculty focus groups. The demand for technology in the classroom was found to be even greater than initially thought. Since it began work, the subcommittee has "smartened" about 22% of Dartmouth's classrooms. The master plan suggests that approximately 75% of the classrooms should have at least projection and computing in the classroom.

Off-Campus Access Woes

Dartmouth's location in northern New England brings many advantages. As one of our admissions brochures phrases it, "Dartmouth's identity and strength are very much derived from its rich physical resources and natural splendor," and the mission statement asserts that its rural location "offers Dartmouth unique advantages and special traditions related to exploring and understanding of the self and society as they relate to the natural and physical environment of northern New England."

Dartmouth's location also poses challenges for ubiquitous computing, especially with respect to network access from off-campus. Demand for robust and reliable network access via modem has increased over the past years. Yet rural areas of New England are often one of the last to receive communications improvements; delivery of such services as cable modems and digital subscriber lines (DSL) lag considerably behind more urban districts. The quality of the phone lines hamper even standard modem service. The increase in demand, combined with the limitations imposed by "rural quality" of local telecommunications, have resulted in an ongoing problem. The well-established need for connectivity is forcing us to think creatively about alternatives.

One alternative may involve Internet access for the general community. When Dartmouth was the only ISP in the area, we found ourselves spending a great deal of effort and time in discussions about who should have access. To help meet the general community's growing demand for ISP services, Dartmouth helped to launch a local ISP service, called ValleyNet, some years ago. It has proved a success and helped to ease the pressure on Dartmouth's own modem pool, to some extent. The wireless layer provides some additional options. We are currently considering a variety of solutions to the off-campus problem, even becoming entrepreneurial, as we did years ago in establishing ValleyNet.

These two examples—classrooms and the challenges of off-campus network access—illustrate the ramifications of a tradition such as universal access. Increased access enables us to use computing for increasingly larger portions of our academic work: teaching and learning, research, communications, and administrative tasks. Once an institution begins to work toward the goal of ubiquitous computing, there will be a number of ramifications, one of which will be problems of success. It may prove difficult for an institution to move part way toward ubiquitous computing, due to the momentum that even a partial movement in this direction generates.

Oops

A third example will serve to emphasize this point, a case in which we underestimated the demand for access to computing. We thought we had met the student demand for access when the trustees instituted the computer ownership requirement in 1991. Surely, we thought, now that all students have their own computers, we can reduce the number of machines in public clusters. We began to scale them back, but it this proved a mistake. Student demand for public computers increased, and we've been struggling to catch up ever since.

We discovered the hard way that the student requirements for computing cannot be met solely by universal ownership and network access. Even if you have your own computer, you will need to work with other computers; these other machines might be more specialized, have more computing capability, or be more conveniently located, for example, near food! Computing has also become more a vehicle for group projects and collaborations, which requires a new set of computing locations. The dorm room is not always the place most conducive to study. Obviously, the wireless installation and the surge in laptops with wireless cards will change this landscape. However, we have learned from our mistake: We have as yet no plans to scale back our public clusters. Indeed, over the past year, with many additional locations in the new Berry Library, the size of the public computer "fleet" has more than doubled.

CONCLUSION

Ubiquitous computing is a grand enterprise. It is grand in at least a twofold sense. First is scale: Ubiquitous computing is a major, ongoing commitment. At a recent staff meeting, one administrator muttered, "Technology eats dollars." It comes, certainly, at a cost. Initial investments in the technology infrastructure put the necessary hardware and software into place. Next come the maintenance costs: As technology becomes indispensable, it must also become reliable. Technology can be cantankerous, sometimes working, sometimes not, for no discernible reason. On top of that, computing technology remains complex. Support costs include the assistance needed to educate faculty, students, and staff to be able to use computing effectively in their work, at times giving them a fish, at times teaching them to fish.

The installation of the wireless overlay is still too fresh for us to know precisely what will be involved in long-term operation and maintenance. For technology that is relatively new, improvements will arrive in a steady stream. By the time this book is published, the next round of access-point performance improvements—including a fivefold increase in connection speed (from 10 to 50 mbps)—will be available. We will also be working to implement longer-term and standard solutions to the problems of authentication and encryption.

Yet ubiquitous computing is grand, too, in the sense that the investment pays off. Recall "Kemeny's Law": "If you only put computing in the hands of students, they're going to do incredible things." The good news is that his rule applies to all user groups. We all know that each of our major constituencies—faculty, students, and administrative staff—can and do innovate, improve, and work more productively with computers. Restated, Kemeny's law holds that if you make computing available—ubiquitous—then innovation and adoption will follow. This has certainly been our experience at Dartmouth College.

LESSONS LEARNED

1. Technology will sometimes fail. Probably each of us has a favorite story about how, at a critical or conspicuous juncture, technology failed, ranging from frustrations in synchronizing a PDA to discovering that key files have been deleted from a classroom computer. Professor Jernstedt tried having students write essay exams using a web form. He had tested the form extensively and found no problems. On the day of the exam, students were given 65 minutes to write and submit their answers. Professor Jernstedt did not know that the browser had a time-out feature after 60 minutes. Many students lost their work.

The next time, he decided to use the campus email system, because it is never down. Of course, Murphy's Law struck: On the day of the test, the email system did go down in the wake of an electrical storm. Despite these setbacks, the course was able to proceed. Professor Jernstedt worked out alternative ways for students to submit their work; students were allowed to do their exams via email without a rigorous time limit. He concludes that "flexibility and willingness to make concessions are necessary components for course success."

2. Student access to computing can be uneven, even in a highly standardized environment. We are coming to rely on our computer as much as we rely on our car. The analogy to the automobile is apt: Computers can at any moment develop their own versions of flat tires, failed batteries, and getting out of tune. In the case of computers, viruses and the vagaries of Internet service providers can complicate access to computing. It is a "playing field" that is rarely completely flat or even. To conduct successful projects, we feel that you need to try to anticipate as much of the "unevenness" as you can. For example, consider the use of new media in a course web site that requires relatively high bandwidth: How will this affect students' connecting via modem? Another "unevening" factor is accessibility: Does the environment deliver all resources to all students?

3. Students aren't all computer wizards. Many faculty are under the impression that all students know all about computers and their use. We have found that assuming that the students will somehow "just know" how to perform technology-based assignments is a mistake. A certain unevenness in student competency has become a problem and is becoming even more acute as we build an increased level of interactivity into our course web sites. Don't assume your students are fully competent. At Dartmouth, faculty are increasingly requesting that our curricular support team provide instructional sessions for their students, precisely because not all students are computer wizards.

4. The bell curve of technology adoption applies to all populations. Each constituent group has its share of pioneers and those who are more cautious about adoption. They are not all Luddites. Technology adoption consumes a great deal of time and support resources. Some defer adoption not out of reluctance or skepticism, but out of a sense of the need to wait until there are sufficient resources at hand to make a successful transition.

5. *Students can be conservative.* Student reaction to computer-based learning resources and assignments can be mixed. As Professor Jernstedt points out, moving from the familiar medium of paper to electronic methods can produce anxiety, as any shift from the known to the unknown. Just because an activity involves technology doesn't guarantee that the students will think it is cool. Students, like faculty, may be reluctant to demonstrate ignorance about technology. In addition, possibly in response to the overall stress to do well in their courses, students like to keep things regular and predictable. The lesson here is to use technology judiciously and deliberately, maintaining regularity, while still encouraging interactivity.

6. *Synchronous activities, enabled by ubiquitous computing, are pedagogically useful and of interest to students.* The desktop computer was hailed as a way out of the curse of synchronicity: having to meet at the same time and the same place. Communication tools such as email make it possible to conduct business anytime, and increased access to computing makes it possible to communicate from nearly anywhere, not just near a phone. The advent of ubiquitous computing introduces the possibility of enhanced synchronous activities, supported by access to the full array of digital materials (text, images, audio, and video). New and richer possibilities open for collaborative work, a key component of a learner-based pedagogy. At Dartmouth, we have begun experimenting with synchronous systems, such as the MOO, as a first step in supporting synchronous curricular activities. Like many other schools, we are actively working on H.323 and Internet2 conferencing technologies to exploit the synchronicity that ubiquitous computing makes possible.

7. *Be complete with your wireless coverage.* In implementing wireless, Dartmouth stuck with its traditional approach: When we completely wired the campus for the data network, we made sure it went everywhere to strongly encourage and enable adoption and innovation. As Professor David Kotz points out, if coverage is spotty, people will not see its value; instead, they will think, "I'll just leave it in my room today." When the campus email system was launched in 1987, everybody automatically had an account, and even those who did not use email could get messages printed and distributed via the campus mail system. One of the reasons that the email system was successful, then, was that everybody had access, even those who were not directly participating. We feel the same will take place in the wireless era. Make sure that everybody has access from everywhere, and adoption and innovation will follow.

8. *Wireless is worth it; don't hesitate too long.* Although the installation of the wireless network took a great deal of effort and persistence, the investment will clearly pay dividends.

9. *Objectively assessing the impact of computing on teaching and learning is difficult.* You can tell when an administrative office stops using paper for some task, and you can measure campus network use. Measuring whether students are learning better is another matter altogether. A wealth of anecdotes and impressions contend that learning is improving, but demonstrating it objectively is a significant undertaking. Yet it is difficult to dispute what Lou Robinson, a champion of computing who worked at IBM for many years, said: "Information technology is a revolution of the mind, a tool for human ingenuity and creativity."

ACKNOWLEDGMENTS

I wish to thank Larry Levine, director of Dartmouth's Computing Services, for his many helpful suggestions, corrections, and additions. I would also like to thank Professors Chris Jernstedt (psychological and brain sciences), David Kotz (computer science), and Jerry Rutter (classics) for taking the time to discuss their projects with me. I'd like to thank Stan Pyc, director of computing at the Tuck School, for some helpful information about Tuck's computing program. I especially thank Sarah Horton, for her loving patience and encouragement.

Contact Information

Malcolm Brown
Director of Academic Computing
Adjunct Professor, Jewish Studies
Dartmouth College
6224 Baker/Berry
Hanover, NH 03755
Phone: 603-646-1349
Fax: 603-646-1042
Email: malcolm.brown@dartmouth.edu

Endnotes

1. Carter, S. (2000). The battle of the glen revisited: A gold signet ring (CMS I 16) of the Aegean late bronze age, Senior Honors Thesis, Dartmouth College Library, p. 17.

2. The interview with John Kemeny, produced by EDUCOM (now EDU-CAUSE) in 1991, can be viewed on the Internet at http://www.dartmouth.edu/~kemeny. Kemeny's vision and optimism about the potential of computing to transform teaching and learning are still very much relevant today.

3. Taken from the report of the ad hoc Committee on Distance Education (internal Dartmouth report).

4. Invented by Larry Levine, this term is employed at Dartmouth to avoid more cumbersome terms, such as "information technology professional" or even "information technologist."

The University of Hong Kong's Notebook Computer Program: A Glass Half-Filled

Craig Blurton
Anita Chi-Kwan Lee
Winston Kwan-Wan Ng

INTRODUCTION

This chapter describes the notebook computer program at the University of Hong Kong (HKU). Unlike most of the other notebook programs about which you'll read in this book, HKU's experience may be viewed as a glass—half-empty in some eyes, but half-full in others.

We will discuss ongoing efforts to improve and extend information technology use by students and staff, with emphasis on the notebook computer program. We explain why and how a highly successful, very traditional, and generally conservative institution has implemented an assured-access, mobile computing program and share a few of the lessons the experience taught us and what still needs to be accomplished to fill our glass to overflowing.[1]

THE UNIVERSITY OF HONG KONG: AN OVERVIEW

The University of Hong Kong, the oldest tertiary institution in Hong Kong, has a long tradition of academic excellence. Originally founded in the then-British colony of Hong Kong, the West's gateway to mainland China, HKU has become Asia's pre-eminent international university. In 2000, *AsiaWeek* magazine ranked HKU third overall among all multidisciplinary universities in Asia and first among English-language institutions.[2]

The university's foundation stone was laid on March 16, 1910. Two years later, the university officially opened with two faculties, the Faculty of Engineering and the Faculty of Medicine. In December 1916, the first class of 28 students graduated.

Since its modest origin, HKU graduates have risen to lead Hong Kong society, occupying prominent posts in business, industry, government, and academia. Today, the university has over 14,000 students (about 9,000 undergraduate, 5,000 graduate, and 650 international) and more than 1,000 full-time teaching staff. HKU has grown from two faculties to ten, with the addition of architecture, arts, business and economics, dentistry, education, law, social science, and science. In total, there are almost 100 independent academic units on campus, including departments, faculties, institutes, and centers.

The university ranks consistently among the top few research universities in Asia and compares well to the best North American institutions. In 1998–1999, more than 2,100 research projects with an overall budget of nearly HK$720 million were conducted. Academic staff were involved in a further 234 identifiable research projects that did not receive any dedicated funding. HKU has joint research laboratories located in Beijing and Shanghai and a well-respected on-campus art museum.

The bulk of the university's finances are borne by the Hong Kong Special Administrative Region. The total recurrent grants allocated to the university from 1998–2001 amount to some HK$7,649 million. The remaining major sources of recurrent income are investments and tuition fees. Academic units at HKU are normally funded by "one-line" budgets that provide individual units a fair amount of flexibility in determining how their resources will be used.

In 1997, the university began a major restructuring of its curriculum to incorporate problem-based learning, cross-curricular activity, and cross-cultural sensitivity and to ensure that all of its students achieve information technology (IT) literacy. These efforts have paid major dividends with improved student learning, a renewed atmosphere of excitement and innovation, and increasing stature among universities worldwide.

HKU is a traditional, conservative, very successful, publicly funded university, the management of which is decentralized. Few decisions affecting more than one academic unit can be implemented without widespread discussion and debate until consensus is achieved. Perhaps the most remarkable part of HKU's notebook computer story is that consensus was achieved quickly and the program launched in a little more than a year.

INFORMATION TECHNOLOGY IN LEARNING AND TEACHING

In late 1996, then Vice-Chancellor Y. C. Cheng invited the director of the Centre for the Advancement of University Teaching (CAUT) to form an Ad Hoc Group for Learning Technologies "to consider the impact of technologies on learning and to advise the Vice-Chancellor on the broad strategy and policy in respect to the implementation of learning technologies in the university" (personal communication to Professor Brian Cooke, November 1996).

The Ad Hoc Group, which began meeting in early 1997, consisted of 17 members selected by the vice-chancellor for their expertise and interest in the use of IT for teaching, learning, and scholarship. The group met frequently, publishing a web-based progress report[3] in April 1997 and its final report[4] in June 1997. The final report delineated 11 planning principles and made eight recommendations. Recommendation 2 (Section c) stated that the University of Hong Kong should require "all students to purchase a portable computer suitable for use within the university's network environment and capable of accessing networked tools and resources." With its work completed, the Ad Hoc Group was disbanded.

In October 1997, Vice-Chancellor Cheng formed an IT & Teaching Task Force, chaired by Professor Cheng Kai-ming, one of the university's pro-vice-chancellors, to implement the Ad Hoc Group's recommendations. The task force's first decision was to implement the notebook computer program. Members believed the program would serve as the "thin edge of the wedge," helping to change curriculum, instruction, management, and administrative practices.

The task force developed technical specifications and invited the 10 largest vendors of notebook computers to submit proposals for how they might work with HKU to create "an 'Assured Access Mobile Computing (AAMC)' environment on campus in which a new digital culture can be fostered."[5] Eight of the 10 corporations submitted applications. After careful consideration, IBM's proposal was selected based on several factors, including previous experience with university mobile computing programs and the potential for IT research collaboration. In August 1998, HKU and IBM signed a three-year partnership agreement.

Many other IT initiatives, some the result of the Ad Hoc Group and the IT & Teaching Task Force and some fortuitous parallel efforts by other campus groups, were introduced:

- An IT graduation requirement for all students, regardless of discipline
- A plug-and-play network (ACEnet) by the Computer Centre

- The HKU Student Computer Society (SCS) IT Student Ambassadors (ITSA) peer support program

- Cutting-edge, IT-based educational programs like the Department of Ecology and Biodiversity's "Virtual School of Biodiversity," the Department of Civil Engineering's "CIVCAL" project, the School of Architecture's "Virtual Studio," the Department of Earth Sciences' course "Geohazards," and the English Centre's "Virtual English Centre"

- WebCT as a standard platform to give instructors less experienced with IT the ability to offer courses and course content online and students the flexibility to learn at their convenience

- Student Connect, an online student information and registration system

- Over 70 teaching development grants to individuals and groups of academic staff for experimenting with and initiating new ideas and approaches with IT to achieve better quality teaching and learning

- The Centre for Information Technology in School and Teacher Education (CITE) in the Faculty of Education

- The E-Business Technology Institute (ETI) in collaboration with IBM China/Hong Kong Limited

The above list provides a sense of the range of activity on campus. More recent initiatives include installing wireless LAN capability in select areas, including the library, public podiums, and centrally time-tabled classrooms with an eye to building comprehensive wireless environments on all three campuses within the next few years. In addition, HKU has been approached by two major consortia offering online education and is currently negotiating an agreement to become the Asian focus of these efforts.

NOTEBOOK PROGRAM

If asked to explain what constitutes a digital campus or digital culture, most would agree that providing students and staff with ubiquitous access to computers, appropriate software, the campus network, and the Internet is essential.

Program Description

To achieve this objective, in 1998 HKU inaugurated Asia's first campus-wide notebook computer program. Under the terms of the agreement, IBM agreed to supply all incoming freshmen who chose to participate with a ThinkPad at a significant discount. The university agreed to provide a subsidy, making the final cost to each student for the complete notebook bundle approximately 20–25% of the retail value.[6]

This year, the complete bundle includes a choice of one of three ThinkPad models and more than 20 preloaded software packages, including Windows 98, Microsoft Office 2000 Professional Edition, Eudora Light 5.1, PC-Pine 4.33, Netscape 4.77, Explorer 5.5, Norton AntiVirus Corporate Edition 7.5, and Richwin 2000 (Chinese-language support). The bundle also includes a carrying case, Ethernet card, modem, three-year warranty, and insurance. This year, two of the models offered include integrated wireless capability, and an optional card is available for the other model.

To ensure network access, the HKU Computer Centre created ACEnet, a plug-and-play network that provides more than 10,000 access points across campus, in the library, dormitory rooms, classrooms, laboratories, hallways, and other public places. The Computer Centre also greatly enhanced the capability of the university's dial-up modem pool.

IBM has established a Service Centre on campus. Located in the same building as the campus Computer Centre, the space was renovated by IBM and is staffed by IBM employees. As part of the agreement, IBM provides loaner computers to students whose ThinkPads require more than 48 hours of service, and also provides a monthly report to the university detailing what services have been provided for which models.

After three years of the partnership, 6,799 undergraduate students (about 82%) now own a ThinkPad. In addition, about 150 second- and third-year students and staff have purchased ThinkPads but without a university subsidy. All of the partners—the university, students, and IBM—have invested significant resources in the notebook program.

As part of the notebook initiative, the IT & Teaching Group has undertaken multiple surveys of each cohort of student participants: when first entering the university, at the end of their first year, and at the end of their third year, after completing the undergraduate program. Intercohort and intracohort differences are tracked and reported to the university community.

The IT & Teaching Group has conducted a number of related studies, for example, assessing the notebook computer readiness of campus classrooms; analyzing and comparing the costs of the notebook program against open-access computer laboratories; and comparing male and female students' computer skills and attitudes.[7]

Rationale for Notebooks

Why a notebook computer program? Why not build more computer laboratories on campus?

Common Sense Reasons

Each tertiary institution that decides to start a notebook computer program usually does so for predictable, common sense reasons—the belief that 24 hour-a-day, 7 day-a-week access will enhance students' learning opportunities; that personal ownership of a notebook computer will improve students' information technology skills and knowledge; and a desire to differentiate the institution from its peers.

The University of Hong Kong is no different. In mid-1997, the Ad Hoc Group recommended that HKU implement a notebook computer program citing these same universal, common sense reasons, among others explained below.

Space: An Urban Imperative

Like other urban universities, HKU struggles with constricted space and conflicting demands for its use. Space constraints, both on campus and in students' living quarters, and the escalating costs of providing on-campus computer labs influenced the Ad Hoc Group in recommending the notebook program.

Prior to 1998, student access to computers and the campus network was only provided by means of open-access computer laboratories. Enrolled students can walk in and use them for class-related purposes. These laboratories usually have a number of workstations preloaded with a variety of general productivity or network software, including word processors, spreadsheets, web browsers, email applications, and so forth. Open-access labs are not used for instruction—that is, to host a computing class with an instructor—and they are not designed or equipped for discipline-specific purposes, for example, a GIS computer laboratory for geography.[8]

Hong Kong is one of the most expensive cities in the world. In particular, the costs related to building, buying, leasing, or renting real estate are high. Space is limited and paid for at a premium by both students and the university.

Students' Space

Individual houses are rare in Hong Kong. Most of the population live in flats in large tower blocks. Typically, a flat is about 700 square feet and costs US$630,000 (Yi-zheng, 1998). Because of these very high costs, about 50% of Hong Kong's people live in overcrowded conditions in heavily government-subsidized rental or sale units, with a median living space per person of about nine square meters (Hong Kong Housing Authority, 2000).

According to a recent survey conducted by the HKU Office of Student Affairs, new, full-time undergraduate students live in similar conditions. Only about one-third of our students (39.1%) report having their own room and desk, with almost as many (28.8%) reporting that they have neither (Office of Student Affairs, 2000).

A personal communication from a postgraduate student helps to illustrate this point:

> I plan to buy another notebook computer rather than a desktop one, although, to be sure, the former is more expensive than the latter and it may not be easily upgraded in the future. I do so wholly because my room is too small for a desktop computer. I am living with my family ... in an apartment about 70 square meters large. Apart from the living room and the dining room, there are three rooms—one for my parents, one for my sister, and one for my younger brother and me.
>
> In comparison with many others, my family is quite well off in terms of housing condition. However, to be honest, I still find difficulty in putting a desktop computer in my room ... the monitor will occupy the whole surface of my desk and I just cannot read and write at my desk anymore ... a notebook one is the only possible choice. Why do I not put a desktop computer in the living room or the dining one? As I have to work with the computer all day, putting a desktop computer outside my room will definitely obstruct my work since I will disturb or be disturbed by my *family members...*
>
> As I said that I am sharing a room with my younger brother, having a notebook computer will make my work at midnight possible—for the sake of not breaking the sleep of him, I can move to the living room to work with the computer when all others are also asleep.
>
> C. T. Chow, HKU student
> (personal communication, May 3, 1998)

The university is able to provide dormitory rooms, both on and off campus, for 21% of its students. However, about 80% of incoming students apply annually, because conditions at home are so cramped and the average one-way commute in 2000 was 76.4 minutes. The figures on commuting time have been quite consistent since 1987, with the average ranging from 71.5 to 80.3 minutes (Office of Student Affairs, 2000).

University Space

Space is not just a problem for students. The university has three campuses: the main campus in the Western District, the medical campus in the Queen Mary Hospital in Pokfulam, and the Faculty of Dentistry in the Prince Phillip Dental Hospital in Central. With increasing enrollments, the university has struggled to provide suitable teaching and learning venues, even moving some university operations, such as the Estates Office, to rented off-campus locations.

Value

As pressure for more access to computers and the network has grown, the university has been faced with the question of how best and most cost-effectively to provide such access; for example, whether to build more open-access computer laboratories or to invest instead in a notebook computer program. Space limitations have played an important role in the decision to implement the notebook computer as has an unspoken belief among some staff that this investment offers better value.

Summary of Rationale

HKU initiated the notebook computer program for five major reasons:

1. Anywhere, anytime access to a computer and the network would enhance the quality of education.

Table 3.1

Computers will make learning easier and more efficient.

	1st Cohort (98–99)	2nd Cohort (99–00)	3rd Cohort (00–01)	Changes (3rd–1st)
Agree	76.9	74.5	69.0	-7.9*
Disagree	5.3	5.3	10.1	4.8
Undecided	17.8	20.4	20.6	2.8

Note: Figures reported in percentage of valid responses. Changes between the 1st and 3rd cohorts marked with * are significant at the 0.05 level. The 1st cohort survey was of the entire population. The 3rd cohort survey was a random sample.

2. Ownership of a personal computer would improve students' information technology skills and knowledge.

3. A notebook computer program would help to differentiate HKU from other Asian tertiary institutions.

4. Space limitations made notebook computers a more attractive option than building more open-access laboratories.

5. Notebook computer programs offer better value than on-campus computer laboratories.

THE GLASS

How well has the notebook computer program met expectations?

Half-Empty

Those of us who planned and implemented the program[9] imagined a transformed educational environment, with students and staff carrying notebook computers to and from campus, plugging into the ACEnet in classrooms, hallways, lecture halls, and cafeterias—from any place on campus any time they needed to access the network for teaching, learning, and research. However, after three years and the investment of millions of dollars by parents, students, IBM, and the university, the reality is different.

Few students can be seen on campus carrying or using a ThinkPad computer. The IT & Teaching Group recently conducted a survey of students who entered HKU in September 1998.[10] They were the first to join the notebook program. When asked, "On average, how often this year did you bring your ThinkPad computer to campus," more than one-third (35.4%) replied "never." Less than 1% of students said they were bringing their ThinkPads to campus three to four times a week or more, with the median response being "very rarely" (46.5%). Surveying each cohort of students at the end of the first year for three years yielded similar results.

In addition, incoming students are becoming more skeptical about the use of computers in education. Another study compared the responses of three cohorts of incoming students to a survey administered at the beginning of the academic year (1998, 1999, 2000). Although overall agreement was still high, we found an 8 percentage point drop over the three years in the proportion who agreed with the statement, "Computers will make learning easier and more efficient" (see Table 3.1).

Also, the proportion of incoming participants who agreed with the statement, "Computers do not replace the need for lectures and discussions in class," increased from 81.1% in the 1998–1999 academic year to almost 90% in the 2000–2001 academic year (see Table 3.2).

Table 3.2

Computers do not replace the need for lectures and discussions in class.

	1st Cohort (98–99)	2nd Cohort (99–00)	3rd Cohort (00–01)	Changes (3rd–1st)
Agree	81.1	86.8	89.2	8.1*
Disagree	5.3	5.6	4.5	-0.8
Undecided	13.6	7.9	6.1	-7.5*

Note: Figures reported in percentage of valid responses. Changes marked with * are significant at the 0.05 level.

A similar trend in student expectations about computer use in education was also found in responses to the statement, "I would prefer lectures in which I get to use computers." In the 1998–1999 academic year, about 44% of incoming participants agreed; however, in the 2000–2001 academic year, the proportion agreeing dropped to about one-third (see Table 3.3).

Table 3.3

I would prefer lectures in which I get to use computers.

	1st Cohort (98–99)	2nd Cohort (99–00)	3rd Cohort (00–01)	Changes (3rd–1st)
Agree	43.2	36.5	36.8	-6.4*
Disagree	18.1	25.1	27.9	9.8*
Undecided	38.7	38.7	35.1	-3.6

Note: Figures reported in percentage of valid responses. Changes marked with * are significant at the 0.05 level.

The number of participants responding that the use of computers could make the academic climate at HKU more intellectually exciting also

decreased. In the 1998–1999 academic year, over 60% of incoming participants agreed that computers could make the academic climate more exciting;
in the 2000–2001 academic year, only about 42% agreed (see Table 3.4).

Table 3.4

**The use of computers could make the academic
climate at HKU more intellectually exciting.**

	1st Cohort (98–99)	2nd Cohort (99–00)	3rd Cohort (00–01)	Changes (3rd–1st)
Agree	61.8	50.4	41.7	-20.1*
Disagree	9.5	16.3	25.7	16.2*
Undecided	28.7	33.5	32.4	3.7

Note: Figures reported in percentage of valid responses. Changes marked with *
are significant at the 0.05 level.

Most of our students are not bringing ThinkPad computers to campus
nor are most of our instructors making use of the new educational opportunities student ownership of notebook computers are thought to provide. It
would appear that, although still generally supportive, students are increasingly skeptical about the use of computers in education. For some observers,
these results seem to support the belief that the notebook computer program
is not fulfilling its promise or realizing the planners' vision of a digital campus
and digital culture. For some, the glass is half-empty.

HALF-FULL

Nonetheless, the program has achieved some of its objectives and is making
solid progress in achieving the others. Students' information technology skills
and knowledge have significantly improved. In addition, the program has
brought widespread and mostly positive publicity that has helped to differentiate HKU from its peers. It has provided a useful alternative to building more
open-access computer laboratories, and—at least in the view of some—it has
offered better value than building more labs.

Survey Results

As noted above, the IT & Teaching Group has performed multiple surveys on each cohort of student participants in the notebook computer program. Surveys conducted at the end of each cohort's first year of study found:

1. Student self-reported IT skills grew significantly.

2. On average, students reported using their notebook computers six or more hours per week, with many students using them much more.

3. Student use of notebook computers in classes increased.

Table 3.5

Changes in Self-Reported IT Skills Over Three Years in First Cohort

Self-Rating	September 1998	June 2001	Changes (2001–1998)
Expert	2.1	21.8	+19.7
Significant	16.3	47.9	+31.6
Intermediate	30.1	24.9	-5.2[#]
Limited	44.0	5.0	-39.0
Beginner	7.4	0.3	-7.1

Note: Figures reported in percentage of valid responses. All the changes, except that marked with [#], were significant at the 0.05 level, since they were larger than the margin of error.[12]

Table 3.6

I feel comfortable using computers.

	September 1998	June 2001	Changes (2001–1998)
Agree	64.8	91.2	+26.4
Disagree	15.5	4.4	-11.1
Undecided	19.7	4.4	-15.3

Note: Figures reported in percentage of valid responses. All the changes were significant at the 0.05 level, since they were larger than the margin of error.

4. Almost all students made regular use of their notebook computers for electronic communications, that is, email, ICQ, computer conferencing.

5. Most students used their notebook computers to access network resources, including class web sites, library electronic services, and other information resources.

6. Students were satisfied with the quality of the IBM computers.

7. Students found the preloaded software useful.

8. At the end of their first year, three-quarters of students found the use of notebook computers at least somewhat important to their success in HKU classes.

9. Students were generally satisfied with IT support services provided by the university, IBM, and the peer support organized by the Student Computer Society.

10. Almost all students (95%) reported being at least somewhat satisfied with the notebook computer program.

IT Skills

Perhaps the most interesting results come from a recent study of the first cohort to participate in the notebook program. It shows a dramatic increase in students' self-reported IT skills (see Table 3.5) from September 1998, when they first entered, to the end of their undergraduate studies in June 2001.

Furthermore, these students' self-reported comfort level with computers made similar gains (see Table 3.6).

Notebook Use

Another measure of the program's success is how much students are using their ThinkPads. At the end of the first year, most of cohort one (1998) reported that they used their notebooks for 11 or more hours per week (63%); 83%[11] reported using them for six hours or more a week. The most frequent figure reported by cohort two (1999) was ten hours, and over half of all the respondents (51%) reported that they used their notebooks for six hours or more per week. The slight decrease was probably a result of changing this item in the cohort two survey to ask the number of hours of use for "school-related work." At the end of their first year, cohort three (2000) students who reported using their ThinkPads for school-related work did so an average of 11.5 hours per week (Range = 0.5 to 100; mode = 10). Thus, student use of their ThinkPad computers seems to have become a normal part of their educational practices.

Satisfaction with the Program

When asked if the notebook computer program should be discontinued, 98% of these students voted "no." At the end of three years, 92% still own their original ThinkPad, and only one-quarter (26.2%) indicated that they would rather have owned a desktop model. Only 6.2% thought that their ThinkPad had not been useful at all in their coursework and studies, while 21% thought they had been very useful. Over 70% of these students felt that ownership of a ThinkPad helped them learn more about computers. Finally, about 90% reported being at least somewhat satisfied with the notebook program.

Better Value

The question of whether the notebook program offers better value than open-access laboratories is more difficult to answer. In 2000, the IT & Teaching Group studied the costs of providing students with notebook computers and open-access computer laboratories. The study, published in the American Association of Higher Education TLT Group's *Flashlight Cost Analysis Handbook* (Ehrmann & Milam, 1999), addressed three questions:

1. How much did each of the two methods cost?

2. Who paid for which costs, for example, central budget, faculty or departmental budgets, students, other funding sources, or vendors?

3. Which method was most cost-effective from the university's perspective?

The authors found that the notebook computer program, when ignoring vendor and student costs and considering only university expenditures, was 1.3 times more expensive than the existing open-access laboratories on campus. The study also found that if the program were to be expanded to include all undergraduate students instead of the 82% it currently serves, the notebook computer program would be 1.5 times more expensive than the computer laboratories.

However, the study also found that the open-access computer laboratories offered students access to only 873 computer workstations—a 9.5:1 ratio of undergraduate students to computers—and that the access was limited to specific on-campus locations during specific hours of operation. In contrast, for 1.5 times the investment, the notebook computer program, if expanded to include all undergraduates, would offer access to 8,294 notebook computers—one computer per student—that could be used 24 hours a day, seven days a week from anywhere at any time either on or off campus.

The bottom line is that although the notebook computer program would be 1.5 times more expensive than the open-access computer laboratories in providing all undergraduate students access to a computer and the network, it would represent a better value.

In-Class Use of Notebook Computers

Although far from ubiquitous, there is a slight but discernable trend toward in-class use of ThinkPad computers by students. All three cohorts of incoming students were asked at the end of their first year in the program if they were required to use their notebook computers in class and, if so, in how many. Use has increased each of the three years of the notebook program. Forty-one percent of cohort one and 75% of cohorts two and three indicated that at least one of their courses required in-class use of their ThinkPads. Thirty-two percent of cohort one, 43% of cohort two, and 44% of cohort three indicated that one to two of their courses during the academic year required in-class use of their notebook computers. Among cohort one respondents, only 10% indicated that between three to six courses in the academic year had required in-class use of their notebooks, while 21% of cohort two and 24.7% of cohort three indicated that this had been the case (see Table 3.7).

Table 3.7

Required In-Class ThinkPad Use

	Cohort One 1998	Cohort Two 1999	Cohort Three 2000
None	58.5	24.6	25.6
1–2 Classes	31.9	43.1	44.3
3–6 Classes	9.6	20.3	24.7

Note: Figures reported in percentage of valid responses. All intercohort differences were significant at the 0.05 level.

Changes in Teaching and Learning

When conceived, the notebook program was expected to constitute the "thin edge of the wedge," driving changes in a wide variety of campus practices, most importantly in teaching and learning. This change has happened or been observed, but perhaps not on the scale originally envisaged. Many innovative educational programs have developed at the individual classroom, departmental, and university levels. Three examples out of dozens will help to illustrate these changes.

Marc Aural Schnabel in the Department of Architecture has revised his courses, Visual Communication 2 & 3, to incorporate students' ThinkPads. The courses provide a theoretical introduction to the use of digital media, computer modeling, and visualization in design and an opportunity to develop skills through intensive practical work.

A weekly lecture introduces a theoretical topic with demonstrations, followed by a hands-on laboratory session with various computer applications. Students bring their notebooks to all sessions, using their own, mostly customized tools. Assignments are submitted and published via the Internet. Feedback is given directly online. All lectures, tutorials, and materials are designed to let students take part remotely, using mobile-computing facilities. Students are expected to supplement lectures and lab sessions by completing software tutorials that they can download through the Internet. Software packages are installed on the students' laptops using network licenses offered by the department. For Mr. Schnabel's students, the notebook has become the interface between lecturer, curriculum, work assignments, and peers.

The Department of Ecology and Biodiversity has created the Virtual School of Biodiversity (VSB).[13] Billed as a "Multi-University Centre for Distributed Environmental Education," the VSB is a cooperative effort of HKU, the University of Nottingham in the United Kingdom, the London Natural History Museum, and the TLTP Biodiversity Consortium.

The department's aim in creating the VSB was to catalyze international cooperation between universities in the field of biodiversity research and education and to promote both understanding and conservation of the world's biological diversity. The VSB is currently involved in three principal areas: development of multimedia courseware materials, online Learning Support Centres (LSCs) for courses, and the delivery of shared, multimedia courses between institutions. The VSB is also now formally affiliated with the International Biodiversity Observation Year 2001–2002 (IBOY) program as a satellite project.

To supplement departmental and individual efforts, the Computer Centre has purchased a site license for WebCT and created a WebCT support unit that provides training, technical support, and advice to university academic staff. This effort has resulted in several hundred WebCT courses across the disciplines. In addition to using WebCT, other departments on campus have adopted similar packages, like Blackboard and LearningSpaces.

Gender Differences

Although not strictly related to the question of whether the HKU notebook computer program has been a success, another aspect of our investigations into student use of computers is worth mentioning. Much attention has been focused on the question of gender differences in information technology attitudes, use, and skills. We compared our male and female students on the following dimensions:

- Enrollment in computer science and IT curricula

- Self-reported IT skills and attitudes

- Taking the IT proficiency tests

- Scores on the IT proficiency tests

- Grades in the Foundations of Information Technology courses

We found that differences do exist at HKU.[13] Our results show that male students generally are much more likely to enroll in computer science and IT curricula, more confident and skillful with IT, more likely to take the IT proficiency test, and do better in the IT foundations courses. We also found that female students, given appropriate opportunities, are able to narrow this gender gap in IT.

CONCLUDING THOUGHTS

In the first three years of the program, we haven't yet reached our goal of creating a thriving and growing digital culture on campus. If individuals at HKU were asked to define these concepts, agreement as to what would constitute such an educational environment would be rare. We do know that students do not typically bring their notebook computers to class, and there still is little educational reason for them to do so. Most of the IT-based learning opportunities supplement the core curriculum, which is primarily delivered by lecture and tutorial sessions. Students use their notebook computers at home or in their dorm rooms for electronic communications, accessing class web sites, conducting research over the Internet, and writing and submitting assignments.

In the view of the authors, not promoting and investing in staff development or providing better staff access to ThinkPad computers were the two biggest mistakes made in implementing the program. The Ad Hoc Group recommended that significant new resources be devoted to staff development, technical support, and curriculum development efforts. This has not happened as the university struggled to reorganize its staff development efforts in general to be more efficient, effective, and economical. The IT & Teaching Task Force recommended that select staff be given notebook computers and encouraged to develop appropriate curricula. This recommendation was not implemented either, although IBM offered staff and academic departments a discount on ThinkPad computers. Thus far, the discount has not attracted many orders.

Despite these problems, evidence shows our students are making intensive use of their ThinkPad computers for educational purposes, albeit not on campus. Their IT skills are improving dramatically, and they are satisfied and would like the program to continue. Since the beginning of the notebook program in 1998, dozens of innovative IT-based curriculum projects have been initiated by individual academic staff, departments, and faculties. Access to the campus network has been improved, and more and more classes are incorporating ThinkPads in new ways. The IT use has become a significant component of the university's policy and planning process from curriculum reform to classroom design, and the university's international reputation as an educational leader, embracing the future while still valuing its past, has been enhanced.

For the moment, the university's glass may be viewed as either half-empty or half-full, but the water level is clearly rising. The HKU notebook computer program has made a significant and positive difference in teaching and learning and is expected to continue to do so.

REFERENCES

Ehrmann, S. C., & Milam, J. H. (1999). *Flashlight cost analysis handbook: Modeling resource use in teaching and learning with technology.* Washington, DC: The TLT Group (The Teaching, Learning, and Technology Affiliate of AAHE).

Hong Kong Housing Authority. (2000). *Housing statistics: Housing figures 2000.* http://www.info.gov.hk/hd/eng/hd/stat_00/mid_f.htm.

Office of Student Affairs. (2000). *A profile of new full-time undergraduate students 2000.* University of Hong Kong, Office of Student Affairs, Pokfulam, Hong Kong: SAR.

Yi-zheng, L. (1998). Asian Society Asian Update Series: An economic roundup of post-handover Hong Kong. In J. Fischer, H. J. Ivory, L. Yi-zheng, & J. T. H. Tang (Eds.), *Hong Kong: The challenges of change.* http://www.Asiasociety.org/publications/update_hongkong_challenges.html.

Note

Ms. Lee and Mr. Ng share equal credit for their contributions to this chapter, which is based on an ongoing research program of the IT & Teaching Group within CAUT. The group's work is wholly funded by the university.

Correspondence concerning this chapter should be addressed to Dr. Craig Blurton, CAUT, University of Hong Kong, Pokfulam, Hong Kong SAR. Electronic mail may be sent to craigb@hkucc.hku.hk.

Contact Information

Craig Blurton
Associate Professor and Head of IT and Teaching Group
Center for the Advancement of University Teaching (CAUT)
The University of Hong Kong
Pokfulam, Hong Kong SAR
Phone: + 852-2857-8528
Fax: + 852-2540-7844
Email: craigb@hkucc.hku.hk
Web Address: http://www.hku.hk/caut/Homepage/itt/index.htm

Anita Chi-Kwan Lee
Assistant Research Officer
IT and Teaching Group
Center for the Advancement of University Teaching (CAUT)
The University of Hong Kong
Room 325, Run Run Shaw Building
Pokfulam, Hong Kong SAR
Phone: + 852-2241-5272
Fax: + 852-2540-9941
Email: anitalee@hkucc.hku.hk
Web Address: http://www.hku.hk/caut/Homepage/itt/index.htm
http://mywebpage.netscape.com/anitackleehk/homepage.html

Winston Kwan-Wan Ng
Senior Research Assistant
Center for the Advancement of University Teaching (CAUT)
The University of Hong Kong
Pokfulam Road, Hong Kong, SAR
Phone: + 852-2857-8534
Fax: + 852-2540-9941
Email: wkwng@hkucc.hku.hk

Endnotes

1. The opinions expressed in this chapter are solely those of the authors and do not represent official university opinion or policy.

2. The two institutions outranking HKU, Kyoto University and Tohoku University, teach primarily in Japanese. See http://www.asiaweek.com/asiaweek/features/universities2000/schools/multi.overall.html.

3. http://nt.media.hku.hk/.

4. http://www.hku.hk/caut/Homepage/itt/5_Reports/5_1AdHoc.htm.

5. Copies of this document are available from the IT & Teaching Group.

6. Due to disclosure agreements between IBM and HKU, the IBM discount schedule and the amount of the university's subsidy to each student cannot be disclosed.

7. Most of these surveys and studies may be found on the IT & Teaching Group web site at http://www.hku.hk/caut/Homepage/itt/index.htm.

8. This distinction does not always hold. Some teaching laboratories and specialty labs are open to students at specific times for general purposes. This study asked academic units to exclude laboratories used only for such specialty computing purposes but to include laboratories that were used for such purposes but also provide open access. For the latter, academic units were asked to provide the number of hours these labs are open for general use.

9. In late 1997, the university created an IT & Teaching Taskforce under the leadership of Pro-Vice-Chancellor Cheng Kai-ming to implement the Ad Hoc Group's recommendations. The primary author of this chapter was a member of both groups.

10. The complete studies conducted by the IT & Teaching Group referred to in this chapter may be found online at http://www.hku.hk/caut/Homepage/itt/5_Reports/5_3surveys.htm.

11. Combining responses to "6–10 hours" and "11 or more hours."

12. The September 1998 survey was a census/nonsample survey, whereas that of June 2001 was a random survey. To compare differences between their findings, the margin of error (±5.2 %) at the 0.05 level of the findings of the second survey was examined. If the differences between the findings of the two surveys were larger than the margin of error, they were significant.

13. http://ecology.hku.hk/vsbhome/.

14. The complete report is online at http://www.hku.hk/caut/Homepage/itt/5_Reports/5_ 3surveys.htm.

Interactive Learning and Mobile Computing at Rensselaer

Sharon Roy

When Rensselaer Polytechnic Institute introduced a laptop computer requirement for all incoming freshmen in 1999, not everyone was delighted. In particular, students already in residence predicted dire outcomes if we were to move ahead with this "ill-considered and expensive" plan. The Student Senate solicited input from students under the rubric "Rant to the Senate," a regular weekly exercise, that featured laptops one week in the spring. Among the many outraged responses was the prediction: "Enrollment will plummet."

In fact, RPI's freshman enrollment in the fall of 1999 was the highest it had ever been. Now beginning its third year, the Mobile Computing Program is well accepted by faculty and students and quite taken for granted much of the time. Perhaps the most important reason for the program's acceptance has been the emphasis on integrating the laptop into the curriculum and the fact that the faculty were well prepared to do so. For most students, the laptop is not just a communication tool and a word processor but an integral part of the learning experience. That is not to say that we haven't encountered a few bumps along the road. We hope that others can learn from our experience.

About Rensselaer

Rensselaer Polytechnic Institute is a technological research university located in Troy, New York, a city on the Hudson River near the state capital of Albany. Our 5,200 undergraduates and 1,900 graduate students come from all 50 states and 83 countries. Our nearly 400 faculty members include a Nobel laureate, National Science Foundation Presidential Faculty Fellows, as well as members of the National Academy of Engineers, the National Academy of Science, and other eminent professional organizations. Their efforts in educational innovation have earned Rensselaer the Hesburgh, Boeing, and Pew awards for excellence in education.

TECHNOLOGY IN THE CLASSROOM

Although the Mobile Computing Program is fairly new at Rensselaer, technology in the classroom is not. Before the introduction of laptops, we had a rich history of hands-on learning, and beginning in the late 1980s, a number of learning initiatives featured classroom computing. These programs all began as faculty initiatives that were expanded with the institute's administrative, technical, and financial support. A more detailed description of these innovations can be found in Boettcher, Doyle, and Jensen, *Technology-Driven Planning: Principles to Practice.*[1]

One early example, Computer Calculus, was the work of William Boyce and Joseph Ecker. This NSF-funded program used Maple symbolic algebra software to reduce the calculation drudgery involved in learning calculus. The software allowed more class time to be devoted to learning and visualizing concepts; students could do more problems and problems of greater complexity than would have been possible relying only on paper-and-pencil calculations.[2] Students spent class time actively involved rather than passively listening and learned more as a result.

In 1991, Computer Calculus and several other technology-intensive teaching initiatives were combined in the Rensselaer Computing System (RCS), a distributed UNIX environment of more than 500 workstations. This initiative was made possible by a grant from the Kresge Foundation and partnerships with IBM and Sun Microsystems. Many of the workstations were installed in classrooms for use in large-enrollment freshman courses: calculus, physics, computer science, and engineering graphics and computer aided design (EG&CAD). In selecting software for the new system, we emphasized strategic applications—professional applications that would be taught in the freshman year, used in advanced classes, and valuable to graduates in their careers. An example of this approach was EG&CAD, a first-year course for all engineering majors, in which students learned to use a solid modeling package for engineering design. This software, ProEngineer, was used throughout the engineering curriculum and served students upon graduation, because it was widely used by practicing engineers.

Each of these initiatives fostered a hands-on, student-centered approach to learning with fewer lectures and more student participation and teamwork.

In order to facilitate this style of class, we built classrooms on the studio model pioneered by Jack Wilson and his colleagues in physics.[3] The studio classroom was designed to facilitate interaction in a technology-rich environment. It incorporated Comprehensive Unified Physics Learning Environment (CUPLE) software, which provided an interface to laboratory instruments and spreadsheet applications and used video clips and other visual materials to give students interactive models of physical problems. When it was first introduced, this program required specially designed PC classrooms. Today, faculty use student laptops and web-based course materials to create the second-generation studio, a virtual classroom environment available to students any time, any place.

By the mid-1990s, the growing use of technology was placing a heavy demand on our computer classrooms. Although we had built several new PC classrooms and were gradually converting some UNIX classrooms, the registrar's office was often hard-pressed to find appropriate rooms. Furthermore, being tethered to a classroom limited the use of technology to a specific time and place. Instructors couldn't be sure that their students would all have access to the same computing environment outside class as inside. Since freshman surveys showed that most of our students brought at least one computer with them to campus, it seemed that the best way of providing technology for the academic program was to put the computer in the hands of the students.

MOBILE COMPUTING: TAKING THE PLUNGE

We began to explore the use of laptops in a three-year pilot program beginning in 1995. Participants, both students and faculty, were self-selected. The program targeted a small number of sections of several freshman-level courses: Calculus 1 and 2, Physics, and Introduction to Engineering Analysis. From 80 to 100 students were enrolled in the pilot in each of its three years. Participants were enthusiastic about the program, and in 1998, without increasing the number of sections that integrated laptops, students were strongly recommended to purchase one. Over 300 students took our recommendation and purchased an IBM ThinkPad.

It became clear during this year that we had reached a decision point. To make the leap from a small pilot program of self-selected volunteers to a required program affecting the entire curriculum, the laptops had to be used in more than a few classes. We knew that students would object to a laptop requirement if faculty didn't use the laptop in class, but most faculty were unwilling to redesign their courses until students had laptops. In the fall of 1998, the Laptop Planning Committee, consisting of faculty and computing support staff and chaired by John Kolb, dean of Computing and Information Services (now chief information officer), decided it was time to break this log-jam. This committee, which had guided and evaluated the pilot program, made the following proposal to key campus groups:

> We should proceed with the phased implementation of a required laptop for all students beginning with the entering class in the fall of 1999. We should provide a lease to our students which will be about $100 per month. The institute will work with vendors to provide the students with exciting technology which will be "refreshed" in the junior year. Implementation of this program will be phased in over four years, i.e., in the fall of each year after 1999 freshmen will be required to have laptop computers.

By February 11, 1999, the Rensselaer Steering Committee for Academic Information Technology, Faculty of Information Technology, Faculty Senate, Information Technology Committee of the Board, Dean's Council, and President's Council had approved the laptop program. The Student Senate met on February 16, 1999. They sent out a questionnaire to students and asked additional questions, but they never took a position on the proposal.

From Decision to Program

Once the proposal was adopted, the Laptop Implementation Team was formed to launch the program. Because Mobile Computing would have wide impact on various student services, it was important for the team to include representatives of all the campus groups interacting with new students. Members were drawn from Admissions, Financial Aid, Student Life, Residence Life, faculty from all of the schools, students, and computing support staff. The team was divided into five groups: Acquisition and Affordability, Curriculum, Marketing, Students, and Technology and Facilities. The Distribution and Training Group was added later in the process and replaced the Technology and Facilities Group after it had finished most of its original tasks. The chairs of the five groups formed a Leadership Group chaired by the dean of Computing and Information Services.

Some important decisions of the Laptop Implementation Team:

1. Curriculum changes would focus on the first-year, large enrollment courses: Calculus, Chemistry, Physics, and Introduction to Engineering Analysis.

2. Classrooms would be renovated to accommodate student laptops.

3. Students would have the choice of purchasing or leasing the computer.

4. The cost of the computer would not be part of the official cost of attendance when calculating financial aid, but a number of laptops would be offered to students as need-based gifts or incentives. (Our surveys of students had shown that about 10% had never purchased computers. We wanted to make sure that students who couldn't afford the laptop would not be discouraged from coming to Rensselaer.)

5. A single system was selected: the IBM ThinkPad 600e. Students were permitted to bring their own laptop as long as it met minimum specifications for use with the required software. (In the first year, only 30 students out of 1,323 chose to bring their own laptop.)

Working through the subcommittees, the details of the IBM partnership were put into place, including the lease and purchase procedures and the selection of the IBM 600e as the first laptop model. The subcommittees also established a distribution and training schedule for students, worked with campus planning and the provost's office to plan classroom renovations, and designed a workshop for faculty on using the laptops in class and a program providing laptops to faculty of freshman courses.[4]

Faculty Responses to Mobile Computing

When the Mobile Computing requirement was introduced in 1999, technology was already widely used in the classroom as a means of increasing the students' active participation in the learning process. Standardization on a single system and student ownership of laptops gave the best possible access to computing to support this style of teaching. Faculty have found that standardization greatly simplifies using computers in class. For example, uniformity and portability made it easy for Joe Walther, associate professor of language, literature, and communications in the School of Humanities and Social Sciences, to introduce new software tools in class and have students work on assignments on their own:

> The course in which I used laptops most was an introduction
> to social impacts of the Internet for 150 first year students.
> The laptops were far more helpful on account of both their
> uniformity as well as their portability. Over the duration of
> the course, we had weekly lab sessions in which we learned
> about Usenet news, listservers, online interaction spaces such
> as MOOs and MUDs, and in which we "dissected" pornography-blocking software systems, to name a few of the labs.

In many cases students downloaded, installed, and configured special software before class began, providing a timesavings that allowed lab time to be put to better use. In other cases, labs provided enough time to cover instructions on using new software and finding critical resources. Then the students were able to master the use of a new tool before the class ended and had the tools ready to take home and continue their work. Since all students used the same systems, only one set of instructions needed to be prepared—a vast difference from the duplication of Mac and Windows instructions, and for Windows 3.1 plus WIN95 plus WIN98 or whatever, of the recent desktop days.

Harry Roy, professor of biology in the School of Science, observes, "The students are very familiar with their own machines, and so once any configuration problems are solved, the course software runs on their machine reliably. In my class, at any rate, the computing problems show up early and then go away."

With laptops in the students' hands, faculty have found countless opportunities to explore new classroom activities. John Brunski, professor of biomedical engineering, was the chair of the Curriculum Group of the Laptop Implementation Team and led planning for the Faculty Workshop on Laptops in the spring of 1999. As one of the pioneers in the Laptop Pilot Program, he had taught Introduction to Engineering Analysis with laptops for four years. In 1999, he faced the challenge of demonstrating his methods to the other instructors for the course and helping them to find their own best ways of teaching with the laptops.

He finds the laptop helps to get the students thinking about the subject:

Along with verbal and written exercises, the computer provides an additional channel for interaction between students and the instructor as well as student-to-student. Using Maple on the laptop, students set up equations that model, for example, forces in the members of a truss. Then once these equations are set up, the students can easily solve them repeatedly for different conditions, to check how a system behaves under changing conditions. This is the type of thing that engineers do a lot in their professional work—build a model of a system and then use that model to analyze system performance. Analysis of the model then

becomes a focus of the class, not just a problem for students
to work out on their own.

Debbie Kaminski, associate professor of mechanical engineering, aero-
nautical engineering, and mechanics and director of core engineering, is
equally enthusiastic about curriculum innovations made possible by mobile
computing:

> Laptops have been an absolute boon to us in teaching Ther-
> mal and Fluids Engineering I. Traditionally our students
> have spent hours looking up property values in published
> tables and incorporating them into their calculations. We
> have been using laptops to automate this process. In a pilot
> program in one section of the course, we have used Engi-
> neering Equation Solver in the classroom, for homework,
> and on exams. In many cases, using the code has cut the
> time required to perform calculations from 20 minutes to
> six or seven minutes. In addition, students can now solve
> more sophisticated and realistic problems involving iterative
> calculations. The code allows students to replace tedious
> low-level functions with higher-level engineering modeling
> and analysis. Faculty and students have both found this pro-
> gram flexible and easy to learn. This fall, based on our initial
> success, we plan to expand the use of Engineering Equation
> Solver to two sections of Thermal Fluids I and one or two
> sections of Thermal Fluids. We are also using it in the Navy
> Nuclear program in Malta.
>
> The long-range implications of the use of this code are that
> about a third of the material we now teach in Thermody-
> namics is obsolete (most of the ideal gas approximations).
> We will be able to substitute more advanced material in the
> future. None of this is possible without laptops.

Bill Siegmann, professor of mathematics, who teaches Introduction to
Differential Equations (IDE), also finds that the laptops help the students to
absorb more difficult concepts:

> The best thing for me in studio IDE with the laptops is the
> chance for students to answer what-if questions and play
> with the (sometimes fairly sophisticated) Maple worksheets
> that we use. We get pretty complicated results analytically

or numerically that can be dramatically understood by varying parameters, for example, a damped linear spring forced by a sin(omega*t) force. There is an analytically daunting formula for the amplitude of the forced oscillation, and I have never been able to present it properly in the past—students would fade in the symbol-manipulation stretch. But it's real important to engineers, part of the "Bode plot." Now I can illustrate it with a real spring-mass model in class. When students see this picture generated by Maple and are able to play around with the parameters that control it, you can see them just light up.

In the first year of the program, Introduction to Engineering Graphics and CAD was not taught on laptops. We assumed that the large screens and computing power of UNIX workstations would still be necessary to run the 3D modeling software required for this course. However, the instructor in charge of EG&CAD, Douglas Baxter, director of CAD/CAM/CAE for the School of Engineering, experimented with the laptops in some pilot sections using ProEngineer and SolidWorks. He reports:

> We were very concerned about using laptop screens for computer aided design. Normally, most designers like 21-inch screens. We were very pleased to see that the students were receptive to the laptop screen. While those that tried the larger monitors liked them, they found the ease of running CAD on their laptop far preferable to sitting around waiting for a terminal.

Doug has been one of the faculty who has made extensive use of web-based video in his course, introducing a self-paced element to replace the in-class lectures. The reaction to this aspect of the course has been mixed, depending on the students' level.

> The video lectures provide an interesting twist to the course. We now have each of the 12 one-hour lectures on video. Each lecture is divided into four segments of approximately 15 minutes each. Students watch the four segments prior to coming to laboratory. The student comments on this format fall into two categories. Older students retaking the course and transfer students like the video lectures and the freedom they provide in their schedule (no longer tying up a third hour for lecture each week at a specified time). The

freshmen disliked the video lectures, finding the teaching format was too foreign. Some disliked the inability to ask a question while watching the video. However, the end result was the failure rate for the course dropped significantly over the previous five years.

William St. John, a clinical assistant professor in Rensselaer's Lally School of Management and Technology, was one of the faculty who made innovations in the second year of the program. He requires that students use their laptop computer in two second-year courses, Accounting for Decision Making and Managerial Finance, courses he describes as "number-crunching intensive." He reports:

> In teaching either subject I present a simple example solved with paper and pencil, then move to a more realistic problem to be solved in class using Excel. The final step is an integrative multi-course project called Tech Bottling. Here the students are solving a real business problem by using skills learned in four courses. For example, in Accounting there are 22 tasks that are performed using Excel, ranging from a small 10-row by 3-column single worksheet to a 15-worksheet workbook with hundreds of rows and columns.
>
> The complexity of these problems cannot be adequately presented in any prior teaching methodology. These problems are beyond paper and pencil and if shown on the overhead would have been strictly a lecture with no real student interaction or learning.

Student Responses to Mobile Computing

We have surveyed freshmen at the end of each of the first two years of the program using an online survey constructed in WebCT. Brad Lister, director of the Anderson Center for Innovation in Undergraduate Education (CIUE) and Clinical Professor of Biology, designed and administered the survey.[5] To increase participation, he administered it during scheduled class time. Results have been consistent over the two years. More than 80% of the students surveyed expressed satisfaction with the IBM ThinkPad, and close to 70% report using the laptop in one to four of their classes. About 80% believe that using the laptop enhances their learning, and more than 75% find that it improves the quality of interaction with their instructors. Detailed results of the surveys can be found on the CIUE web site at http://www.ciue.rpi.edu/.

Students most often complain about the cost of repairs not covered under the warranty (for example, broken screens) and wish for specific software not currently provided.

Ongoing Governance

Soon after the first shipment of laptops reached campus, the Laptop Implementation Team disbanded, handing over the daily operation of the program to the departments. Managing the program, which has turned out to be a major year-round commitment, fell to Academic Computing Services, now Academic and Research Computing (ARC). A team of computing support staff meets weekly throughout the year to coordinate the program, chaired by a program manager who is responsible for coordinating with other departments, such as Enrollment Management, the Bursar's Office, Risk Management, Residence Life, Public Safety, and Student Life. ARC also works with the office of the provost and individual faculty to coordinate faculty programs and plan for classroom renovations.

However, as the program matures, we have seen a need to review a number of early decisions. To undertake this review, the chief information officer has asked the director of Academic and Research Computing to form a Mobile Computing Advisory Committee this fall with much the same representation as the original implementation team. This group will evaluate the program and make recommendations in such areas as the way the laptop is reflected in the cost of attending Rensselaer, how it affects financial aid, the need to modify campus buildings to accommodate laptops, simplification of tracking and record-keeping, and keeping the technology in step with the university's academic goals.

Financing Mobile Computing

One of the program's selling points was that it would be inexpensive to Rensselaer. We already had a faculty accustomed to using technology in the classroom and a staff to support their efforts. However, there have actually been considerable costs associated with Mobile Computing. In the first year of the program, the cost of the laptops and software was subsidized by about $500,000 and in the second year, $250,000. This year there will be no subsidy. We spent approximately $12,000 on various distribution costs, such as printing, mailing, shirts and lunches for volunteers, security, and other items.

Another major startup expense was classroom renovation. In the first year, we renovated 22 classrooms, in some cases just adding network and power connections at the desks and, in others, doing major reconstruction at a total cost of $1,365,400. In the second year, we upgraded only 12 rooms, but the construction cost was $1,131,800, reflecting the more extensive work some rooms needed. More modest work on 10 rooms in the summer of 2001 was estimated at a cost of $500,000.

To date, we have not hired additional permanent staff for the program. Instead, we hired some temporary staff for the month around the beginning of the fall semester, diverted staff from other activities, and called on volunteers from other departments to help during the staff-intensive distribution process. Additional hiring will be necessary as the program continues to grow. The effort involved in publicizing the program and tracking the decisions students make in regard to acquiring the laptop (renting, purchasing, or accepting a gift) and ending a lease (purchasing or returning) has been much greater than we anticipated. Not surprisingly, we have also seen an increase in traffic at the Help Desk and Rensselaer Computer Repair.

Successes

If we were to identify three of the most successful aspects of Mobile Computing at Rensselaer, they would be:

The program. We didn't just require a computer. We provided a complete program, including high-end IBM ThinkPads with software preloaded to customize the system for our academic needs. Then we provided instruction and support. From the computer store to the help desk to the repair service, we stand behind the program and make sure that students and faculty have a computing environment they can count on to support their academic work.

The integration. Laptop computers provide excellent communication and productivity tools, but that would not be reason enough to require all our students to have them. Rensselaer students are computer-savvy and were generally happy with our rich and diverse computing facilities before the laptop program. The fact that our faculty use the laptop extensively in the curriculum is both the justification and the greatest achievement of Mobile Computing.

Standardization. Standardizing on a single model of laptop for each new class levels the playing field for the students and provides a predictable classroom environment for the faculty.

Problems

If there is a downside to students having their own laptops, it seems to be that the computer can be a powerful distraction. Joe Walther found:

> In these labs, since students bring their own computers loaded with their own software (as opposed to desktop labs in which preloaded machines await them, with only what is

needed for class), there is a much greater tendency for students to distract themselves with applications other than those which the instructor is teaching. Often these distractions take the form of using Instant Messenger or other Chat systems. We now no longer have students passing notes to one another in the back of the classroom; they're passing notes to their "buddies" no matter where those recipients are in cyberspace. Professors know this, and we try to catch them the usual way, by calling on a student who seems not to be paying attention to the class-wide demonstration, and asking the student to repeat what the professor just said. The students have out-foxed us though: Another student in the same lab can (and does) "Instant Message" the answer to the professor's question to the prospective victim, allowing them to avoid detection yet one more time.

For some students, the course software itself can become a distraction. John Brunski says, "Sometimes students can get too lost in the programming of the computer and miss the point of the modeling exercise. Also, with web access in every room, there is always the danger of kids tuning out and browsing the web."

Not all faculty find the distraction posed by the web equally worrisome. Bill Siegmann says, "I am pretty laid back about this but I will not let others be distracted by anybody surfing; if an individual wants to waste his or her time in class, without bothering somebody else, I won't stop them."

Faculty who use the laptops for tests find that students now have a high-speed cheating mechanism: sending one another answers via Instant Messenger. Our math department gives network-based tests and, to combat cheating, is providing a CD that blocks access to all but the site where the test resides. It remains to be seen whether this will solve the problem. In any case, using the laptop does not decrease the need for monitoring exams.

In general, faculty find that they still have to work to keep students on task, just as they always did, and in some new ways as well. John Brunski reports that he needed to develop new ways to keep the class moving, with exercises bundled into small, digestible chunks of time, and clear starting and ending points. He emphasizes that it's critical for faculty to know how to do what they are asking students to do with the computer, not to delegate this aspect of the course to a TA. Not only should they not be embarrassed to make a mistake in front of the class now and then while learning to use new things on the laptop, but they should welcome it as an opportunity to show students that making mistakes is part of learning.

Brian Lonsway, associate professor of architecture, uses laptops extensively in his classes, but he raised a number of concerns about the program's impact on our students' lives. He reports, "Mobile Computing has, in my courses at the Rensselaer School of Architecture, provided an interesting context for the general evaluation of the role of advancing technologies in our everyday lives. Students and faculty are now implicitly required to complement their already cyborg existence with a padded . . . bag containing three thousand dollars' worth of fine electronics. Insurance has become of greater concern, as has personal safety, prompting an increased desire for additional coverage and additional surveillance." He also worries about the environmental impact of the increased consumption of natural resources occasioned by the program and about the marginalization of technophobic students. Many of these concerns are shared by the program administrators and have been addressed or targeted for future study.

Although we know of no cases where a laptop put a student's life in danger, we have had to deal with theft and damage and must give ongoing consideration to ergonomics. We certainly considered screen size and keyboard size in the selection of the laptop and weight-distribution in the selection of the backpack carrying case. However, we have not redesigned furniture in the residence halls, and students have been known to overload their backpacks or sling them over one shoulder. Much remains to be learned about equipment design, and we hope our students and faculty will be inspired to make contributions to this field.

Major Blunder

It remains to be seen what the Mobile Computing Advisory Group will decide, but not including the laptop in the cost of attendance gets the nod as our major blunder. Because the cost was extra and didn't figure in the calculation of financial aid, we came up with several conditions under which students received their laptops: outright purchase, lease, dean's award, or financial aid award. Although the reasoning was to provide fair access to all students, the result was confusing and frustrating. Each condition carried different implications for insurance, tracking, and record-keeping and led to different options for returning the laptop at the end of the first two years. Given the amount of paperwork, confusion, and bad feelings this created—"My roommate got a free laptop!"—it will certainly be high on the list of candidates for change.

CONCLUSION

Our faculty's enthusiasm for using the laptops in class is the strongest point of our program. John Brunski says, "I think the school is out in front of the pack on use of computers in the classroom and interactive learning. Students seem to take it in stride now and perhaps don't really appreciate how good they have it. Faculty are gradually figuring out more and better things to do in class with the laptops."

Harry Roy reports that "the laptop improves access to computing for the students, increases their sense of responsibility for their computing environment, and makes it easier for them to do their work." As for Bill Siegmann, "Great that everybody has them; would not work otherwise."

LESSONS LEARNED

Elementary

1. Anticipate theft. We didn't, because theft was not a problem in the pilot program. It seems that students who choose to participate take better care of their laptops than students who are required to participate. (We have also found fewer thefts among students who purchase than among those who lease.) We now have this problem under control through a combination of higher insurance deductibles and increased emphasis on taking reasonable precautions.

2. Damage was also far more frequent once laptops were required. Our on-campus repair shop, an authorized IBM facility, stocks extra laptops to lend to students whose machines require extensive repair work, but students are often surprised at the cost of repairs and the exclusions in their insurance policies. We have added PC Protection to address this problem.

3. Software expense can limit the program's reach. We include most of the software students need for their courses in the laptop image. However, software for some smaller programs is not included, because the cost is prohibitive. We must continue to work with software companies so that students in these programs do not bear an extra financial burden.

4. Form good partnerships. IBM and several software companies with strong ties to Rensselaer have helped us make excellent technology affordable to our students.

5. Mobile Computing is not free. We still can't say for sure how much the program costs, but it's more than we thought it would. Even though the

students bear the cost of the computer, the support and infrastructure to make the program work are not cheap.

6. Ensure sufficient campus infrastructure and staff for delivery and distribution. It takes an army, especially in the first weeks of the semester.

7. Faculty and student involvement is crucial. Technology alone can't drive the program.

8. Support of upper administration is vital. Both our provost and our president actively championed the program.

9. Phase-in presents some logistical problems. Everyone thinks of the program as done when it's still growing and needing more support resources each year. Also, in the first year, a significant number of sophomores were taking freshman-level courses and yet were not required to own laptops. We accommodated them with "hybrid" classrooms—desktop computer classrooms with laptop connections added or laptop classrooms with a few desktop computers.

10. Make sure to understand what problem you are trying to solve and take time to articulate it to the campus.

Advanced

1. The laptop can be a distraction. Computers in the classroom offer powerful competition with the instructor. Some faculty report this competition is more the case with student-owned laptops than with university-run computer labs, perhaps because students are free to install games and otherwise customize their environment. Faculty can meet this added classroom management challenge in a variety of ways, but they must be prepared for it.

2. Test security presents new challenges. Faculty will be interested in using the laptops for tests and may request special safeguards to keep students from cheating. Sometimes the only safeguard is the old-fashioned kind: proctors.

3. Despite the difficulty, the laptops should be used for giving tests to make sure that the integration is real and valued. Using the laptops for class and then giving only paper-and-pencil tests sends a confusing message.

4. Some students feel marginalized by the heavy reliance on technology. Depending on your student population, you should prepare for this problem.

5. Insurance is a time-consuming and emotional issue. We have been amazed at the variety in cost and coverage. We never expected to be in the insurance business.

6. Concerns about ergonomics must be addressed. Carrying the laptop, track point versus mouse, CRT versus LCD are all burdens that were minor when students moved from one computer classroom to another over the course of the day but now become a matter of serious concern when they use the same computer for hours each day. The laptop makes it difficult to meet some ergonomic guidelines without extra expense, for example, independent placement of the keyboard and monitor.

7. Our decisions not to include the laptop in the cost of attendance and to allow a choice between purchase and lease have made the program far more complex than it should be. At each step of the program, the details depend on method of acquisition; for example, Rensselaer provides the insurance for leased systems, while students must provide their own insurance for purchased systems.

8. Sales tax has been a vexing issue in our state. If we hadn't chosen to treat the laptop as a separate purchase, we would not have had to charge sales tax (this problem has since been resolved).

9. One of the strengths of our program is that it is built on widespread faculty interest in improving student learning. Some efforts are supported by campus departments, such as the Anderson Center for Innovation in Undergraduate Education. Others are the work of individual faculty who seek little support and may not realize that their successful innovations might benefit other courses and other curricula. Providing formal and informal means of sharing information of this kind is vital.

10. The discussion about Mobile Computing, its goals and effectiveness, is never over. Each year, the technology and the participants change. Some people who have been here all along suddenly take an interest: Rip Van Winkle lives! [6]

Contact Information

Sharon Roy
Academic and Research Computing
Rensselaer Polytechnic Institute
110 8th Street – VCC 313
Troy, NY 12180
Phone: 518-276-8124
Fax: 518-276-8109
Email: roys@rpi.edu
Web Address: http://www.rpi.edu/~roys

Endnotes

1. Kolb, J. E., Gabriele, G. A., and Roy, S. (2000). Cycles in curriculum planning. In J. V. Boettcher, M. M. Doyle, and R.W. Jensen (Eds.), *Technology-driven planning: Principles to practice* (pp. 79-86). Ann Arbor, MI: Society for College and University Planning.

2. Boyce, W., and Ecker, J. (1994). The computer-oriented calculus course at Rensselaer Polytechnic Institute. *The College Mathematics Journal, 26* (1) 45–50.

3. Wilson, J. (1994). The CUPLE physics studio. *The Physics Teacher, 32* (9) 518–523.

4. Roy, S. (2001, January) *Interactive learning and mobile computing at Rensselaer.* Paper presented at Ubiquitous Computing Conference, Seton Hall University, South Orange, NJ.

5. Lister, B. *RPI Student Laptop Survey Results.* Retrieved May, 23, 2000 from http://www.ciue.rpi.edu/laptop_evaluation.html.

6. For two web sites with additional information about the first-year implementation and current details, see a SIGUCCS 2000 presentation, www.rpi.edu/dept/acs/siguccs/mobilecomputing.ppt, and the Mobile Computing at Rensselaer Information site, www.rpi.edu/dept/cis/web/laptops/.

Case Study: The University of Strathclyde in Glasgow

Helyn Thornbury
Derek G. Law
Brian Henderson

INTRODUCTION

"I love my laptop!" No, not the impassioned ranting of a techno freak regarding his lifetime companion, but four words that made 14 months of unremitting effort seem worthwhile. This heartfelt statement was found in the very first student evaluation questionnaire examined as part of the University of Strathclyde's ubiquitous computing pilot. The student responsible could not have realized the genuine feelings of delight and relief felt by the team involved in this strategic initiative on reading such a positive response.

Much time, effort, and money had been invested in what became known colloquially around the university as the "millennium laptop pilot." Associated university academic and support staff generally felt that progress was good and that real benefit was being seen in a number of different areas. However, starting from the premise that the customer is always right, the student population's reaction was eagerly awaited to confirm or not whether the university had been correct in proceeding with a paradigm that had not been proven to work in a European, let alone a British, context.

On a personal level, for many in the laptop team, the preceding months had been an intense period of uncertainty: detailed planning; complex implementation procedures and interaction with departments; setting up administrative processes that were new to all participants. Beyond this planning stage, further effort had been necessarily directed into the support and enhancement of the sizeable 354-machine pilot. As is typical of many public institutions, the ability to dedicate staff to assignments distinct from their "normal" day-to-day work was very limited, and it became increasingly obvious that positive reinforcement was required to help staff to maintain their exceptional level of effort.

Unwittingly, then, with those four words, our 19-year-old student and many others who responded similarly helped to galvanize the university to continue this major initiative. More importantly, they made an aging project team very happy!

IN THE BEGINNING

In 1996, the British government set up the Dearing Committee on the Future of Higher Education in the UK, and its report appeared the following year. Buried in almost 2,000 pages of evidence was a prediction that by 2005 all students would have a personal portable computing device and that this would transform teaching and learning. Sir John Arbuthnott, then vice-chancellor of Strathclyde, was a member of the Dearing review group, and many of its recommendations became part of the university's strategic plan for 1997–2001. At the same time and for the same reason, Strathclyde became an early adopter of institutional information strategies. Such a strategy was drafted in 1998, and late that year, the appointment of a director of information strategy led to the development of the "Strathclyde Eye" (Figure 5.1), which

Figure 5.1

The educational vision and strategy are broken down into discrete elements aimed to transform quality without driving up cost.

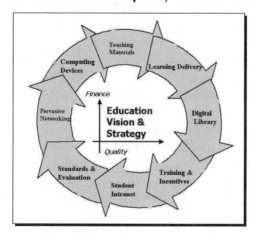

provided a holistic view of the areas to be targeted. The university would undertake activity in each of the identified areas.

Each of the areas was reviewed, and a work program attached to it. Some were funded internally, some from external gifts and research grants. There was a clear view that while each was necessary, no single element was sufficient to transform the teaching process. Thus, the decision to use ubiquitous computing (the area discussed in this essay) was made in a much wider context.

As part of the decision to make computing ubiquitous, a number of North American universities were visited to gain their experience. Many lessons were learned, but perhaps the two most important were to start with a pilot program of a few hundred machines—a lesson obeyed—and to ensure the project team was given a clear set of goals with extended and manageable timelines—a lesson ignored. Both political pressure and an ambition to take a leadership role in Europe meant that a "get-go" decision in March was coupled with a September implementation date. The plan was to pilot the program in the first year, covering some 354 incoming students in one faculty, then to extend the pilot in year two.

One crucial decision was to invite to the United Kingdom two IBM staff based at the University of North Carolina at Chapel Hill. Although attendance at the two-day seminar they ran was disappointingly small, the seminar provided extraordinarily useful insights. It gave staff confidence and kick-started the process, ensuring that its scale was understood by all the attending stakeholders and initiating a management structure and initial timelines.

BASIC CHARACTERISTICS OF
STRATHCLYDE UNIVERSITY AND THE PROGRAM TODAY

In 1796, Strathclyde University was founded as Anderson's University to be "a place of useful learning" at the wish of its founder. After over 200 years, that mission statement is still a meaningful and common point of reference that trips off the tongue of all Strathclyders in what is now a major research university with some 15,000 full-time-equivalent students and an additional 45,000 students undertaking some course of vocational study on or off campus. Traditional strengths lie in areas such as business, engineering, and education, with science and arts completing the list of five faculties. The university also has a highly rated graduate business school. In addition to the faculty body, a Central Administration Service (CAS) provides a raft of support services to both staff and students.

The primary academic department involved in the millennium laptop pilot was management science from the business faculty. Most of the resources for operational matters came from within the IT services department. The IT department reports to the head of the Information Resources Directorate and forms part of an integrated service provision system, including the university libraries, audio-visual media services, and continuing education services.

From an academic perspective, clearly technical and, more particularly, software needs vary dramatically between, say, engineers and historians. Therefore, pioneering teaching methods have been emphasized over courseware design, although over 200 degrees use some e-content. Broadly speaking, the university is following the move "from sage on the stage to guide on the side," from teaching to learning, with a special focus on group work of various sorts.

Strathclyde has a deserved reputation as an innovative, business-like organization that has continually shown itself willing to break the conventional mold in order to achieve success in diverse areas, including professional development programs, technology in teaching, and overseas partnerships (Clark, 1998).

The university was founded to meet the needs of people who had been excluded from a university education. The first intake included a majority of women—over 400—and was the first example of mass tertiary education for women in the UK. Today, as never before, it is a wider-access university. We strongly associate with the British government's commitment to social inclusion and are investing special effort in promoting opportunities for students from disadvantaged backgrounds and providing a supportive environment to help them be successful.

We realized that only if the number of students and laptops involved were sufficiently large could an attempt be made to quantify the likely impact and scale if the pilot was extended to cover most students. Fortunately, the course nominated by the business faculty involved over 350 first-year undergraduate students, thereby satisfying this requirement.

Great care was taken in the selection of the laptop, both in terms of the manufacturer and the technology specifications. A full European tender exercise was undertaken, which resulted in IBM, Ltd. being the chosen supplier. This task was time consuming and exacting but cost-effective, as it produced very aggressive competition in laptop pricing. The laptop chosen for the first-year pilot was from the ThinkPad A Series and had the following specifications:

Hardware

- Processor: Celeron 500 MHz
- Memory: 128 MB
- Hard Disk size: 6 GB
- Screen: 12.1-inch TFT
- Video: 4 MB Memory
- CD: 24x CD-ROM drive
- Modem: Integrated V90 56K
- Ethernet card: Integrated 10/100 Mbps
- Radio card: PCMCIA-based 11Mbs radio card

Default Software Load

- MS Windows 2000
- Microsoft Office 2000, Professional Edition
- Eudora Mail Client
- Web Browser: Internet Explorer 5.5
- McAfee Anti-Virus software
- Adobe Acrobat Reader, Version 4

At the pilot's inception, these specifications were relatively high in terms of what was available in the UK market. Further, they were markedly above the services required by the pilot group. The reasoning behind this choice was twofold. First, the laptop lifetime is likely to be three to four years, and by choosing a higher than required machine specification now, we hope to ensure that it will still be fully functional at the end of its life. Second, we hoped it freed the pilot to concentrate on pedagogy and not to be undermined by technology performance problems.

The inclusion of radio technology was a pivotal element of the laptop pilot. The traditional method of network provision via multiple network sockets was proving expensive and inflexible, especially in some of the university's aging buildings. A number of important areas around the campus were also kitted out with radio receivers, including the main room to be used in teaching the pilot class, four floors of the main university library, floors in the student union and the main refectory area. The pilot was then seen as a major test of the functionality and viability of large-scale radio use.

The laptops were distributed to the business students at several mandatory, two-hour training classes. It was expected, rightly so as it transpired, that student IT knowledge would vary considerably especially with respect to laptop technology. The training ensured that everyone had the basic skills to feed and care for the laptop, but it also presented a valuable opportunity for some important administrative tasks with a captive audience, for example, serial numbering to student tagging.

IT services provide the students with comprehensive support, including laptop configuration and training to help minimize help-desk calls. Loan-pool laptops, rapid software imaging, and an extended manufacturer's maintenance contract all underpin the continued operation of the pilot.

Security for students and their laptops was a major concern for the university. Having our main campus in the middle of a large city presents a number of potentially serious issues. Basic advice was given: For example, if threatened, hand over your laptop. The university also took out a comprehensive insurance policy to cover the replacement of damaged or stolen laptops.

In year one, all machines were loaned to students to test their impact, but, crucially, in year two (2001–2002), student purchasing behavior would have to be tested. Since UK government regulation means that purchasing equipment cannot be made compulsory, the students' willingness to buy the standard package will decide whether the project has a long-term future.

EDUCATIONAL RATIONALE

The rationale for introducing laptops within the institution can be categorized into two main areas: educational benefits and organizational efficiency. For Strathclyde, the decision primarily focused on the educational benefits but, for any initiative to be viable, computing provision and support also had to be efficient.

The educational benefits possible through the use of technology are well acknowledged (Laurillard, 1993; Schacter & Fagnano, 1999). A more beneficial question and one that many university staff ask is why mobile computing? Through the widespread use of laptop computing, several improvements in the educational experience for students can be achieved.

First, it removes an organizational constraint on the educational process. The traditional model of teaching in many subjects involves lectures, tutorials, and labs. The lectures and tutorials were, by necessity, held in a different location from the lab sessions. Because the use of computing within subjects is often integral to learning objectives, where not only a theoretical understanding but also a practical competency are required, this separation of lecture and lab was a constraint that mobile computing removes. The lecturer does not have to group activities to fill one-hour lab time or one-hour lecture time. They can be integrated, allowing the educational objective to dictate learning activities, rather than the physical location. The increased access to IT also allows lecturers to make more use of technology within their teaching, using educational resources and telecommunication software.

Laptops can make the process of group work more efficient. The current system of lab-based computers is not conducive to the group computer work that is a major component of many classes. Mobile computing offers much more flexibility in locations for meeting, and the smaller laptop does not impede the group dynamic to the same extent as a desktop resource, facilitating discussion. This process is much closer to the way graduates will work with colleagues in the future, better preparing them for employment. Mobile computing allows flexibility in location for work and accessing networked resources (Igbaria, 1999). Students no longer need to visit a lab; their computers can be used when and where convenient and the network and its resources accessed from various convenient locations around the campus. In addition to ready access to email, which increases communication, a student can easily access other learning resources and information available both on the university network and through the World Wide Web.

IT skills have become a requirement for graduates in most disciplines. In fact, Strathclyde is one of the few universities in the UK in the process of introducing a mandatory IT skills component to all degree courses. Mobile computing allows the students to gain computing skills and experience in a manner more closely reflecting the environment they will enter on graduation. The experience of managing their own computers in conjunction with the increased usage, which the greater flexibility of mobile computing makes possible, combine to develop IT skills and confidence.

The key elements in addressing stakeholders' concerns about Strathclyde's scheme have been evaluation and information. By exploring the benefits and costs of introducing laptops in a transparent, rigorous, and defensible manner, valuable information and experience were gained to inform discussion and future developments. The evaluation process involved close consultation with stakeholders to achieve a transparent process, ensuring that the results were not disputed on methodological grounds and that all aspects of interest to the stakeholders were investigated. Results were reported to various groups and committees, including the Student Union, providing opportunities for debate and allowing concerns to be aired and addressed.

Information is available on the university web site with a dedicated email address for questions. The web site details the university initiative, including its rationale, with links ranging from the current equipment available to the academic course site for the classes involved.

THE TEACHING AND LEARNING PILOT

The integrative core in Strathclyde Business School provides a three-year grounding in the skills that any business graduate requires regardless of principle subject discipline (Belton et al., 2001). The first year of the core focuses on five main areas: communications skills, numeracy, teamwork, problem solving, and IT skills. This class was the first to use laptop computing. Each student has a ThinkPad, and the class's organization exploits them to create a realistic business environment.

For three hours each week, the students attend group sessions in the specially designed Millennium Room. In contrast to traditional rows of desks, the room contains puddles—U-shaped desks seating six students. This design was heavily influenced by Sheridan College's work on student work environments (Smye & Greyborn, 2000). The combination of radio transmitters and power supplies underneath each desk creates a flexible work environment.

The students work in the same groups, at the same table, for each week of the course on a series of business problems. The course emphasizes using relevant resources as required rather than learning a set approach. As Granger and Lippert put it, "they need to view the software as a tool that enables them to produce useful products" (1998).

This first pilot area was the subject of considerable scrutiny that focused on the measurement of educational outcomes. Comparison was made with the same course taught the previous year, without the benefit of mobile computing. By the midpoint of the pilot year, teaching staff were struck by the marked difference in IT skill level attained by the two cohorts. The pilot class had already attained the same average skill level as the previous class had by the end of year. Staff and evaluators were unsure whether this indicated a steeper learning curve and that the skill level would plateau over the remainder of the year or heralded a higher attainment in IT skills. The students went on to finish the year showing no signs of a plateau and exceeding the skill level demonstrated by the previous group!

Governance Issues

Strathclyde has a devolved, faculty-based governance structure, so that decision making is a very consensual process. However, the vice-chancellor, who is the university's chief executive, has discretionary funds that can be used both for experiment and to guide policy formulation. In executive terms, the director of information strategy (in effect, the CIO) was charged with moving the initiative forward and enlisting support. Most financial responsibility in Year 1 also rested with the director of information strategy, and this fact coupled with the fact that only the business faculty was ready to move meant that the political environment was initially supportive. Decisions at this stage largely concerned implementation.

As the reality of the resource commitments required by the pilot took shape, the clear waters began to muddy. Choices about other, competing service areas had to be made, and external interest began to rise with the project's profile. Fortunately, because implementation was successful, the political environment calmed. The laptop team attended strategic university committee meetings and reported in detail on the project's life cycle to date.

This initial success led to a great deal of interest in the pilot's second year. Competitive bidding was used to decide who should enter the program next. The deans of each faculty were asked to rate the bids from the other faculties, ensuring both the transparency of process and the integrity of the Year 2 selection. Thus, every faculty was able to support the program, feeling that it had an equal chance of gaining access to the vice-chancellor's pump-priming funds. In Year 2, fourth- and fifth-year students of the engineering faculty are being targeted as well as a small masters course in psychology. As pilots, these programs will again rely on loaned machines.

An early decision to evaluate academic outcomes has proved significant in winning over hearts and minds to the view that the initiative is a response to educational rather than technological imperatives. The university has a small number of quasi-independent units that specialize in pedagogical issues and served as a trusted but neutral panel within the main evaluation group, chaired by a senior academic involved in the pilot. Reports were produced on estates issues, support issues, and funding models.

To set policies regarding the use of computers in instruction and further community building in this area, the university has a number of high-level committees, where the academic and administrative establishments are jointly represented. Decisions in the above areas are always made by these existing and trusted committees, which helps to ensure a properly informed and transparent process, even if the discussions do get a wee bit heated on occasion.

Financing Issues

Undoubtedly, the most vexed question has concerned funding. Since its inception, funding the pilot remains the single largest stumbling block to sustainability. An estimate of the overall cost of the technology, associated services, and staff time comes to slightly over £1,000,000, technology costs comprising more than 75% of this figure. Ultimately, over two years, this sum will have facilitated the use of ubiquitous computing in an innovative teaching and learning environment for nearly 1,000 students—a quick division, indicating that, in relative terms, exceptional value has been attained.

In absolute terms, this money has been made available primarily from the information resources budgets, with a welcome injection from the vice-chancellor's strategic initiative fund. There is no doubt that the redirection of information resources budgets for the pilot necessitated hard choices regarding other service sectors. The two-year lifetime of the pilot was underwritten but with the proviso that the experiences of the pilot would dictate a plan for either sustainability or graceful exit. The university is about to embark on a £50 million building program, and whether or not to build and wire conventional classrooms is clearly a major cost factor. More and more students arrive at the university with computers that seem always to have nonstandard software and nonstandard interfaces. They are almost impossible to support, and yet students increasingly expect such computing support.

In Year 1 of the pilot, laptops were lent free of charge to the entire pilot area. In Year 2, these laptops were then offered for sale to incoming students, who also had the option to purchase new laptops from a university-sponsored scheme. Approximately one-quarter of students are purchasing, which is encouraging and ultimately provides more cash for reinvestment into the pilot.

However, the university's political and financial environment seriously constrains the options for sustaining the pilot throughout the student population. The cost of personal devices must inevitably be passed on to the student. However, a number of issues make this difficult. University fee levels are set by the national government in the UK, which also firmly defines and prescribes the list of items for which extra charges may be made (photocopying, field trips). Therefore, the university does not have the power to make any computing device mandatory for a student's education. Persuasion and an excellent financial package are the only available tools. Even then, the university sits in a historically poor inner-city area with many local students. We are rightly proud of our inclusive and accessible educational establishment, but it does raise the question of how the less well-off are to be supported within the context of ubiquitous computing. If academic colleagues are to be presented with a student cohort who are technologically enabled, then ways must be found to increase the numbers of students purchasing technology, including those who are less well-off.

Operational Issues

The lead project manager for the ubiquitous computing pilot was also head of user services and support for the university IT department. This dual role helped ensure that one of the most vital operational areas—technical support of the pilot—could be accomplished. Right from the inception of this sizeable pilot, it was felt that as much work as possible should be subsumed into the university's normal day-to-day routines and processes to ensure that sufficient resources were available. Staffing levels would not allow for personnel dedicated to this task alone.

Nonacademic pilot support was to channel all inquiries, faults, and administration through one widely publicized service point, the student help desk. Strategically, the help desk had been upgraded with network radio access and printers specifically useful to the pilot students.

In facilitating this total service, the following points were important:

- Training all levels of technical staff
- Providing a loan pool for the temporary replacement of faulty machines
- Stipulating clear managerial policy that all support staff were involved in the laptop pilot

Ultimately, this central focusing of service proved very popular with students due to its location, approachability, and effectiveness in providing solutions. According to our surveys, less than 1% of reported calls were handled unsatisfactorily, and although improvement can be made, this structure was one of the pilot's major successes.

The most significant mistakes in Year 1 were an inappropriate budgetary structure and not delegating budgetary responsibility to a level where operational decisions could be quickly implemented. Budget for the pilot in Year 1 was not sectioned off into a separate account structure, which ultimately led to argument about the final cost. Some other projects also had difficulty in gleaning their final costs from the university financial system. This situation has been rectified in Year 2.

Further, in a project of such scale and complexity, decisions have to be taken at short notice, and monies spent to allow the purchase of services or products to facilitate progress. Budgetary responsibility for the pilot was lodged at a very high level, despite many of the project team being experienced budget holders. The unpleasant reality is that senior managers can be absent at times when operational issues come up—the technical term here being "sod's law." This structure led to unnecessary delay and had a negative impact on many occasions.

Academic Issues

A distinctive aspect of the Strathclyde Initiative has been its effect on the students' educational achievements. The evaluation process highlighted several general educational benefits linked to the use of the laptops. The IT skills level of the class showed a marked increase, a development specifically linked to the increased amount and flexibility of access to technology. The laptops generally benefited learning by increasing communication and collaboration through email, file transfer, and work management, allowing flexibility in location for work and benefits from standardization. Staff noted that the students' numeracy had been helped by being focused at a higher level: on structuring and interpreting data rather than the arithmetic of calculations.

The greater access and flexibility offered by the laptops proved beneficial to group activities. This benefit transferred to classes that the laptop students shared with others. Their group working practices became their standard way of working and were carried into all their activities.

Overall, the first year of the pilot has shown a positive impact on learning outcomes. The students themselves rated the laptop as very important to their education, both within the pilot class and in their studies generally.

The structure of the project team has been highlighted as a key aspect of the success of the Strathclyde project so far. The creation of one specific role, that of academic project manager (APM), has been particularly beneficial. The APM is a specific, academic person as opposed to a member of the IT support staff and works as part of the project team, providing an academic perspective on operations and organization. This position has been useful in maintaining the educational focus, grounding technical aspects in academic practicalities. The APM also works as a technical translator and focal point for any teaching staff involved in the project. The initial pilot had a teaching team of 10 staff. The APM is considered one of their own and trusted by the teaching team to explain technical arrangements and decisions to them. This person also acts as a filter, answering questions or redirecting inappropriate questions away from the technical team, which has freed the team from additional pressure and helped to maintain good relations between the different groups. The APM can put the technical case to the academics and the academic case to the technicians without the misunderstandings that are too often the result of different groups working closely.

The role also involved the integrated evaluation of learning outcomes, organizational infrastructure, and technical aspects. The results of this evaluation were then reported back to the academic community by an academic who had knowledge of both the teaching issues and the technical arrangements. This combination of knowledge was helpful in dealing with the variety of questions that such an exercise created.

CONCLUDING INSIGHTS

The university's ubiquitous computing pilot is a sizeable and complex project sited in a large, hierarchical, resource-constrained, and political organization. Many people reading this book will recognize this type of environment and also be skilled in steering projects through its choppy waters. Rather than repeat a list of well-known and generic project management techniques, it would perhaps be of more use to pass on two specific facts based on our experience.

First, ostensibly, such a pilot was concerned with validating the relevance of the technology to our situation, but, in the event, we discovered that technology issues became only a small portion of the task. A similar project of any size will spread through the university, requiring effort and resources from both academic and administrative stakeholders. Without exception, our pilot received a willing and helpful hand from such parties—Registry, Finance, Security, and Management Science, to name but a few. By way of a thank you and a confession, it is recognized that often little warning was given to such groups when their input was needed. The lesson learned here was to concentrate on the information flows required to sustain the use of the technology rather than the technology itself. If this concentration has implications for the project team structure, then so be it—the important result is a professional and sustainable service, not a laptop computer.

Second, it is fair to say that the divide that typifies many educational institutions is that between academia and administration. It is vital that a computing pilot be strongly backed by both. An underlying plank of the university pilot was the assembly of a multidisciplinary team that had shared responsibility for the ultimate product. The team included staff from senior management, academia, IT services, purchasing, and other departments, which helped to ensure focus and that the views and needs of all were brought to the table. While helping to ensure the healthy progress of the pilot, this team also accomplished something else—a far more enjoyable and satisfying task. Many of us gained an understanding of the work of other parts of the university and now have access to knowledge, communication lines, and friendships that will benefit further work.

One of the areas where Strathclyde has excelled is in enlisting student support. Supportive students were the best and most persuasive advocates and changed the perception from a technology-driven view to a student/customer-driven view. In reality, we believe that change is driven for sound pedagogical reasons, but perception is always more powerful than reality. In order to do this and, again, following examples seen in the United States, we sent a small group of officers from the student association and the student newspaper to North America to see the transformational effect of the ThinkPad University. The gamble paid off, and they returned as enthusiastic converts and advocates. It is simple to find examples of the devastatingly bad publicity that can occur if you neglect to get the students onside in such initiatives.

The University of Strathclyde embarked on a pilot in ubiquitous computing essentially believing in the overall benefits to staff and students across a broad range of activities. The last 14 months have taught many lessons but nothing has yet come to light that makes us question that belief. The university's strategic plan for the next four years specifically mentions the success of the pilot and its continuation. Crucially, it also indicates the need for a financially sustainable model by which the laptop pilot may be extended to all students. This level of ubiquity will be the real test.

Lessons for Beginners

- Evaluating is valuable.
- Support academic staff in developing materials.
- Schedule time for training support staff in the technology.
- The help desk is vital.
- Communication between registry and other administrators and the academics is important.
- Involve academic staff so that the program is seen as a sensible pedagogical development and not a technology-driven process.
- Use the academic project director as a trusted point of contact and interpreter for other academic staff.
- Ensure that any locations where the laptops are used, especially teaching spaces, are appropriately designed.

- The internal political process, especially that involving student officers, is important.

- Estates benefited from the lower cost of radio for networking, but a new way of working requires rooms.

- Start small and achieve success—go for the low-hanging fruit.

- Give yourself leeway on first classes and first runs; make your first training class only half capacity.

- Do have a clear, identifiable senior management sponsor; if your sponsor controls the finances, good!

- Do form a tight, multidisciplinary team for the lifetime of the pilot.

- Do embed as much of the work as possible in the core activity of the departments.

- Do get the student body involved formally.

- Do "go on the road" and sell the pilot.

- Do have a web site detailing not just the technical options but the whys.

- Do telephone us—it's good to talk.

- Don't imagine technology is the issue—total service is the issue.

- Don't imagine that everyone will like or support the pilot.

- Don't lose heart—it'll be fine!

REFERENCES

Belton, V., Johnston, B., and Walls, L. (2001). *Developing key skills at Strathclyde business school through the integrative core.* Innovations in teaching business and management. Birmingham, England: SEDA.

Clark, B. R. (1998). *Creating entrepreneurial universities: Organizational pathways of transformation.* Tarrytown, NY: Pergamon.

Granger, M. J. and Lippert, S. K. (1998). Preparing future technology users. *Journal of End User Computing, 10,* 27–31.

Igbaria, M. (1999). The driving forces in the virtual society. *Communications of the ACM, 42,* 64–70.

Laurillard, D. (1993). *Rethinking university teaching: A framework for the effective use of educational technology.* New York, NY: Routledge.

National Committee of Enquiry into Higher Education. (1997). *Higher education in the learning society (The Dearing report)*. London, England: HSMO.

Schacter, J. and Fagnano, C. (1999). Does technology improve student learning and achievement? How, when, and under what conditions? *Journal of Educational Computing Research, 20,* 329–343.

Smye, R., and Greyborn, A. (2000). *Taming the wired classroom*. Montreal, Québec, Canada: IBM ThinkTank 2000, HEC.

Contact Information

Helyn Thornbury
Academic Project Manager (Millennium Student Laptop Initiative)
and Academic Staff Member (Department of Management Science)
University of Strathclyde
40 George St., Glasgow G1 1QE, UK
Phone: + 44-141-548-4543
Fax: + 44-141-552-6686
Email: helyn@mansci.strath.ac.uk
Web Address: http://www.strath.ac.uk/projects/millennium/staff/ht_staff.htm

Professor Derek G. Law
Information Resources Directorate
Alexander Turnbull Building, 155
University of Strathclyde
155 George St., Glasgow G1 1RD UK
Phone: + 44-141-548-4997
Fax: + 44-141-553-4121
Email: d.law@strath.ac.uk
Web Address: http://www.strath.ac.uk

Brian Henderson
Head of User Services & Support, IT Services
Project Manager, Millennium Laptop Initiative
University of Strathclyde
40 George St., Glasgow G1 1QE UK
Phone: + 44-141-548-2048
Fax: + 44-141-553-4100
Email: brian.henderson@strath.ac.uk

University of Minnesota, Crookston

Donald Sargeant
Andrew Svec

IT'S THE RIGHT THING TO DO—A SUCCESS STORY

"To say we were nervous is an understatement," notes Andrew Svec, who, in 1993, was working in the Office of Admissions at the University of Minnesota, Crookston (UMC). That summer—just days before new students and their parents would arrive to register—the campus received the green light from the University of Minnesota Board of Regents to move forward with what was called the "Crookston Experiment." That experiment would put a notebook computer in the hands of every student and faculty member. According to Svec, "During our visits with prospective students, we told them we were planning this bold new technology initiative. But there were several benchmarks yet to be completed that summer: Develop the computer specifications, bid the specs, and obtain final approval of the two million dollar purchase. So we remained somewhat tentative in our promotion of it."

While there was campus-wide agreement that the notebook initiative was a move in the right direction, there was deep concern that the $700 technology fee added to student costs might turn off some students and parents. "In some people's eyes," says Svec, "it could have been perceived as a last minute tuition hike or just too much money for an undetermined outcome." Providing all full-time students with their own notebook computer was something no one had ever done before. The plan was to break the increased cost gently to the families during registration, extol the benefits of putting a computer in every backpack, and hope for a minimum of withdrawals.

Four days of registration followed, and the results surprised even the strongest advocates of UMC's notebook initiative: not one student withdrew; not one parent complained about the technology fee. UMC officials were most surprised at the reactions of parents: a general consensus that the notebook computer would be an extremely valuable tool for their sons and daughters. Svec says, "They all seemed to realize that having a personal computer and learning how to use it was going to be a tremendous benefit. We had parents thanking us!"

UMC Chancellor Don Sargeant, a strong proponent of the notebook initiative, saw it as "definitely the right thing to do. Students and families then— and throughout nine subsequent years of being a Laptop U—see this not as a gimmick, but as an important part of the educational process here at UMC." He adds, "To this day, no student or parent has ever said that they don't see a value in our technology initiatives. With the way society and the world of work are changing, it's simply the right thing to do."

Lesson Learned

Students and parents recognize the added value of the notebook computer and technology training integrated into the curriculum.

CREATING THE VISION

Back in 1992 and 1993, UMC surveyed a number of employers about the kinds of skills they sought in college graduates. They consistently ranked computer literacy and communication and human-relations skills as their primary targets in hiring. This survey encouraged the UMC initiative.

UMC is widely regarded as the first of higher education institutions pioneering the integration of ubiquitous personal computing and web-based technologies into the day-to-day activities and coursework of its students and faculty. The plan was simple. Everyone (students, faculty, counselors, coaches, administrators, and, over time, other academic and support staff) would have the same model notebook computer with a standard software load. Everyone would have 24-hour access to a notebook and the network. Everyone would use the notebook in teaching and learning and in all services on campus.

Faculty and staff have worked to create a teaching and learning environment that nurtures technological skills across every academic discipline. The goal is to empower each student and faculty and staff member with the ability to maximize the potential of the personal computer and related technologies as tools for learning, teaching, and service.

UMC faculty's main focus has been to apply existing or emerging technologies to the teaching and learning environment in meaningful ways. UMC's clear achievement is the combination of ubiquitous computing, unlimited access, and total immersion in a technology-rich environment that brings students, faculty, and academic content together in a new and pervasive way. In today's world, technology "haves" increasingly have the most options. UMC wants to ensure that its alumni fall into that category.

Lesson Learned

Committing to a campus-wide adoption of the ubiquitous computing initiative rather than phased-in adoption leaves no one behind. The total immersion atmosphere helps everyone, while hastening the acceptance and integration of all related technologies into the curriculum and the service units.

ADAPTING TO CHANGE

Since UMC began its ubiquitous computing initiative, information technology evolved. In 1993, sending an email attachment was a challenge, and the World Wide Web was a year or two away from emerging as a revolutionary cultural force. Thirty-gigabyte hard drives and rewritable CD-ROMs were almost unfathomable.

Over the history of UMC's program, students and faculty have seen yearly upgrades, if not in hardware, definitely in software. From the 486 notebook computer used in 1993, with monochrome screen, 148 MB hard drive, 4 MB of RAM, running Windows 3.1, to 2002's 1.2 GHz machine, featuring a color LCD screen, rewritable CD drive, 40 GB hard drive, 256 MB RAM, running Windows XP, faculty and students have adapted to change on a regular basis.

The first major upgrade was challenging. Faculty and students would receive it in the fall of 1994, just as they were becoming comfortable with their first notebook. As you'd expect, some liked things the way they were. This upgrade was important, however, because it set the stage for regular future upgrades, rollovers, and migrations. Continual evolution and annual migrations to new systems and software have placed institutional focus on a model of continuous improvement. Balancing the expectations of students and faculty with financial realities has resulted in a rethinking of budget priorities and reallocation.

To operate most successfully in UMC's technology-rich teaching and learning environment, faculty have had to reexamine their pedagogy within the context of student-centered learning. The "font of knowledge" and lecture approach to teaching have collided with the "faculty as facilitator" approach and more self-directed learning modules. Students respond differently when equipped with powerful tools such as a networked notebook computer. Their potential is increased, and the pressure to perform—for both students and faculty—increases as well. Education is evolving as we speak. It's very exciting yet a little intimidating to those who are less inclined to change. UMC's environment leaves no room for not rethinking past methods, since students expect to use their technological tools and to see improvements each year.

An important constant throughout these technological advances has been the standardization of the notebook computer and its software load. Not only does standardization simplify the support and repair of the computer and related classroom and network technology, but its consistency is also vital to the integration of the technology across the curriculum. It allows a common language and culture to emerge. Peer teaching and learning—an integral part of the program and the foundation for its growth—does not occur as rapidly without this consistency.

Lessons Learned

- A standardized notebook computer and multimedia software package saves money, while hastening technology adoption and integration into programs and services.

- Becoming comfortable with change and focusing on continuous improvement are important byproducts of a technology-rich environment.

THE INTEGRATION OF TEACHING AND LEARNING

From the beginning, how faculty would take to the notebook initiative was a genuine concern. During the first years, UMC faculty and staff faced a steep learning curve, heightened by a lack of peer institutions with which to share notes and discoveries. Early adopters of technology, whether they were other faculty, staff, or students quickly became information resources. Peer teaching and learning emerged as an important tool for every member of the campus, facilitated by standardization. Since everyone was dealing with essentially the same technology, new advances and techniques could be duplicated and shared quickly.

Another key factor in the acceptance of the notebook initiative by faculty, which, in turn, hastened the integration of technology across the curriculum, was the establishment of the Instructional Technology Center (ITC) in the fall of 1995. The ITC provided important technological hardware, software, and support staff to faculty who, individually, could not afford these things. It also underscored the institution's commitment to the vision of total, interactive learning and showed that the administration was sensitive to faculty needs in the technological transformation.

Incoming students enroll in Introduction to Information Technology, a required course that provides a foundation for future technological skill development and is team-taught by faculty from all programs. This interdisciplinary approach accomplished two goals: 1) It exposed faculty to the technology and its potential uses and challenges, and 2) it allowed faculty to interact on a critical level with other faculty with whom they might not regularly interact. Involving all programs was another way to hasten the integration while signaling the importance of technology within the institution.

As faculty and staff became increasingly proficient, the ITC developed a standardized training schedule and resource center, but the success of integrating technology into daily use still relies on the dissemination of information from peer contact. The ITC offers technology lunches: seminars where faculty and staff can highlight their use of technology and share best practices. These seminars foster a positive peer pressure to make the most of UMC's technologically rich learning environment and encourage those less technologically adept to develop a can-do attitude.

Lessons Learned

- A technology resource and support center for faculty and staff helps to advance the integration of technology across the curriculum.

- An interdisciplinary, shared experience for faculty to learn and to teach technological applications—such as a core course—helps to internalize the institution's goals of a fully interactive, technological, teaching and learning environment.

TEACHING AND LEARNING ANECDOTES

The proof of success in the ubiquitous teaching environment is in student learning. Faculty are continually creating more current, interactive means of teaching. For example, Steven Shirley, a marketing instructor, uses the Internet to bring the subject matter of his classes to life. During a lecture about Internet retailing, Shirley has his students use their notebook computers to search for Internet-based business articles about an actual corporation's e-commerce efforts. Students share what they've found and discuss the concepts. Then Shirley asks them to access the retailer's web site, so the class can discuss the organization's marketing strategies. This immediacy and application of marketing theories to a real-world situation make the exercise very mean-ingful. Students can see in real time that companies operate under the con-cepts being discussed.

In her early childhood education courses, Soo-Yin Lim-Thompson uses captured video clips to help students critique their own interactions with chil-dren during lab time. Lim-Thompson captures the clips into a digital file for-mat and allows the students to download the clips to their own computers. She then works with each student, analyzing the interaction and the teaching techniques. By watching themselves, the students can more objectively rein-force or correct their strategies to become more effective.

Lynnette Mullins, a humanities professor, uses the Internet to guide her students on tours of the world's great art museums. Mullins provides the URL for each museum and piece of art and leads an in-class discussion. After class, she follows up with electronic discussions on a web-based message board, a technique that draws out students who choose not to speak in class. With encouragement via email, she says many of these students eventually become more vocal in the classroom.

In his agricultural systems management courses, Paul Aakre uses geo-graphic information systems (GIS) and global positioning systems (GPS) to help students understand the concepts of precision agriculture and how it can improve crop production while using fewer herbicides and pesticides more effectively. Two miles from campus, UMC students use these technologies on the 4,000-acre farm of UMC-alum Gary Wagner and his brothers. Each acre is a farm when using precision agriculture methods.

David DeMuth's physics lab is mainly virtual. After setting up the actual lab only once for major demonstrations of physics concepts, he begins each experiment, while Tom Sondreal, a specialist in video production, captures the event from various angles on a digital video recorder. After editing, the video files are made available for download to students' individual notebook computers. Students are able to grasp the concept quickly via the video clip, leaving more class time for DeMuth to lead discussion or answer questions. The computer has allowed learning to occur faster and DeMuth to save time setting up and taking down each lab demonstration. As an added bonus, the students can call up the video clip back in their residence hall room at 1:00 a.m. and get the same experience.

Lesson Learned

Faculty most fully embrace the program when they find technological appli-cations specific to their needs and have a first success.

CONSULTATION ISSUES

In implementing the notebook computer initiative, UMC had the advantage that it was at a crossroads. Full-time student enrollment had been declining for a decade. The Regents supported our move from associate to baccalaureate degree programs, but Minnesota did not need another typical four-year college. The decision to become a baccalaureate institution and, at the same time, to provide all students with notebook computers created a bit of urgency—some would say crisis—to do something. Bolder steps are often easier to take in such an environment.

All changes in public higher education dealing with mission and program require a great deal of planning and consultation. Students, parents, legislators, other higher education institutions, faculty and staff, governing boards were all a part of the UMC change process. Often colleges implementing technological strategies focus on how to garner faculty support, but faculty support for substantive technological changes may often depend on garnering support from the larger constituent base.

The approach at UMC was simply to involve as many groups as possible in planning and improving our technological initiatives. Curriculum is the faculty's responsibility. They must be involved in discussions of not only the changes in their discipline but also the changes that are affecting higher education from technology to demographics to the nature of work. Each summer, a planning session involving faculty and administrators meets to review and discuss UMC's mission and strategic plan. Progress on past initiatives is reported and new initiatives developed. These discussions then move to unit meetings and then to program advisory committee meetings with business and industry and students. The technology initiative seems to have created more connections to employers and students and an openness and willingness to change.

Faculty governance differs from faculty consultation. The governance process is strengthened when faculty matters are respected and addressed in the faculty governance system and consultation is strengthened when program and technology initiatives are broadened to include more than faculty.

Lesson Learned
Broad representation, both on and off campus, in the development of technological initiatives is a necessity.

FINANCING ISSUES

Probably one of the first questions university top management must answer in adopting a notebook strategy is, "Are we willing to allocate significantly more funds for investments in technology and faculty development?" Significant changes in teaching, learning, and the delivery of administrative and student support services will not be made without significant investments, both personal and financial. Sustainability is paramount. Few changes in a college environment take more administrative commitment than a notebook computer strategy. Commitment must be made to finance the change and to support the faculty and staff as they make changes that affect everyone on campus.

UMC's technological investments have increased from 2% or 3% of the budget to nearly10% in the past eight years. Student investments have increased from literally nothing (no computer, printer, or software) to over $1,000 per year during the same period. The notebook computer has become very personal for everyone. It serves as the key communication tool, file cabinet, music and game box, photo shop, and the list goes on. At UMC today, students rarely talk about the cost of technology, which speaks volumes about the acceptance of the notebook in the teaching and learning environment. That attitude provides evidence that UMC has leveraged the student notebook investment into enhanced learning and improved administrative and student support services quite effectively.

How have we achieved and sustained this financial status? The first year, UMC purchased notebooks for all students and financed a loan. At the end of the first academic year (summer 1994), the notebook computer loan balance was twice the value of the computer. We exchanged the first notebook (4 MB RAM, monochrome, no modem or Ethernet card) for another model with 16 MB RAM, color screen, modem, and Ethernet card, financed by a monthly lease with the IBM Credit Corporation. At the same time, we were still under obligation to finance $600,000 from the original computers. That was our first lesson: match the student technology fee income to the notebook computer lease payment. We increased our student technology fee from $705 to $960 per year in a four-year period. Leasing matched expense payments with revenue income, while providing a predetermined refreshment date for new technology. The student technology fee finances the student notebook and software, access to the Internet campus help desk, and free printing.

In the early years, the first question was always how much would the notebooks cost? We reminded everyone that the notebook cost is less than 25% of the total cost. The other costs include building the classroom networking and infrastructure, adding technology support staff, faculty and staff training, and software investments. Without additional investments in each of these areas, the technological strategy cannot reach its potential. Table 6.1 provides a summary of UMC's investments in technology since initiating its notebook strategy in fall 1993.

Table 6.1

Summary of Technology Expenditures

	FY94		FY95	FY96	FY97		FY98		FY99		FY00
Student Investment (Hardware/ Software/LAN Access/Printing)											
Technology Access Fee	$705		$750	$780	$900		$960		$960		$960
TOTAL	$705		$750	$780	$900		$960		$960		$960
Institution Investment— Allocations											
Faculty Notebook Computers (lease)	N/A		$75,000	$107,000	$110,000		$120,000		$120,000		$138,000
Classroom Remodeling (No. and Cost)	2 $40,000		6 $120,000	6 $120,000	2 $50,000	2.0	$50,000	14	$105,700	2.0	$141,123
Faculty/Staff Development											
Training	$20,000		$25,000	$30,000	$30,000		$30,000		$30,000		$30,000
Mini Grants	N/A		$20,000	$20,000	$20,000		$20,000		$20,000		$20,000
Instructional Development— Student Employment	N/A		N/A	N/A	$20,000		$20,000		$20,000		$20,000

		$		$		$		$		$		$		$
Support Services (FTE and SEE)														
Computer Center	2	$79,496	2	$81,280	2	$83,954	2.0	$87,393	2.0	$91,286	2.0	$94,806	2.0	$117.716
Help Desk	1	$22,000	1.5	$45,000	2	$60,000	2.0	$70,000	2.0	$81,139	2.0	$83,041	2.0	$110,881
Instructional Development														
Center		N/A		N/A	1	$55,000	1.2	$72,000	1.2	$107,886	1.2	$124,474	1.2	$106,106
Webmaster		N/A		N/A	1	$6,000	1.5	$50,000	1.5	$55,552	1.5	$82,825	1.5	$85,000
Enterprise System Coordinator													1.0	$36,990
Telephone														
(Additional lines and costs)		N/A	8	$8,000	16	$12,000	24	$16,000	24	$44,000	48	$50,000	48	$50,000
Infrastructure														
NTS Support Charges												$11,272		$87,864
Servers, Routers, Software		$35,000		$109,646		$112,965		$94,564		$173,200		$163,797		$132,849
TOTAL		$196,496		$463,926		$606,919		$619,957		$793,063		$906,915		$1,076,520
Outcomes—Critical Measures														
FYE Enrollment		1,036		1,043		1,181		1,282		1,288		1,337		1,430
Institutional Technology Investment per FYE		$190		$445		$514		$484		$616		$678		$753

Lesson Learned

Technology fees assessed to students must match or slightly exceed the cost of the student notebooks and other technological services provided specifically for students.

<h2 style="text-align:center">OPERATIONAL SUCCESS</h2>

The success of the notebook computer initiative at UMC has been based on three major program aspects: portability and access, community learning, and meeting expectations.

Portability and Access

The notebook computer's inherent portability has been an asset from day one. Prior to the program's inception, the campus offered a few small desktop computer labs. Limitations included the student-to-computer ratio, access hours, and scheduling for various classes. Providing notebook computers to all students and faculty removed these limitations, making any classroom a computer lab and providing 24/7 access. Students and faculty could customize their machines, while retaining the standard software load.

As the program has evolved, the issue of access—specifically, network access—has played an increasingly prominent role. In 1993, access to the campus local area network (LAN) and the Internet were not as high a priority. As network-based tools and Internet-based course materials have proliferated, such access is now a necessity—and an expectation. UMC responded by equipping every classroom with LAN connections and then went on to wire residence hall rooms, the library, study areas, student lounges, and every office on the campus. The emergence of wireless connectivity has added a new twist, allowing even greater access and portability.

Providing access to every nook and cranny has been an integral part of the acceptance of the notebook computer initiative. The "build-it-and-they-will-come" philosophy worked. Making network connectivity easy and ubiquitous added another reason for faculty and students to make use of the computers. Increased requests by faculty for wired classrooms drove that process, and today, 100% of UMC's classrooms and labs have at least one LAN connection port, and 85% offer LAN connectivity at each student seat.

Portability and access have contributed to faculty integrating technology into their day-to-day class activities. It is no coincidence that network traffic is highest from 10:00 a.m. to 3:00 p.m., when most classes are held at UMC. At colleges where notebooks are not used in all classes, evening hours find higher network use.

The evolution followed a classic spiral: Access created opportunity; faculty used opportunity to develop web- and network-based course materials; students increasingly made use of these materials, which, in turn, created demand for expanded and faster access. In addition, increased student computer competence drove faculty to develop more sophisticated course materials. As it stands in 2002, more than 95% of UMC courses make substantial use of technology-based course materials—both primary and supplementary—with roughly 20% of all courses available entirely online.

Lesson Learned
Portability and true ubiquitous access advance technological integration into the curriculum, increase usage, and fuel the deployment of subsequent technology initiatives.

COMMUNITY LEARNING

While faculty were learning from other faculty, they were also learning from the students for whom technology was increasingly second nature. UMC successfully recognized that students had much to offer in the area of technical skills. Since hiring additional professional technology support staff had traditionally been constrained by personnel budgets, a student workforce was the logical solution. Students have become an important resource in the development and integration of technological initiatives at UMC. Many faculty have selected students within their discipline who are then further trained through the ITC in developing specialized, interactive, multimedia technologies as class resources. In a true win-win scenario, faculty benefit by obtaining materials they can use in class, and students benefit by refining their technological skills and being mentored in a specific academic area by faculty.

Lesson Learned
Students are an underutilized resource in building an interactive teaching and learning environment. Find ways to capitalize on their skills and end-user perspective.

MEETING EXPECTATIONS

Because of the ubiquitous computing environment and the unique peer and community learning processes that have resulted, the technological skill and comfort level exhibited by UMC faculty, students, and graduates is extremely high. This "techno-savvy" has been noted by employers and visitors to the campus, and enhanced the campus image. Surveys find employers eager to hire more UMC grads; surveys of graduates find a high satisfaction rate with their UMC experience; and surveys of parents reflect a confidence that UMC's technology initiatives are adding value to their students' education.

The transfer of technological skills also quickly finds its way off campus to the larger community and region through UMC graduates and current students. UMC alumni consistently comment that they have become technology experts or "go-to people" in their workplaces. Family members of current students rely on them for assistance with home or business computers. One student created and registered a web site for his family's tractor salvage company and helped improve business significantly. Another student developed a spreadsheet and database for her father's business and then tutored him in the use of the software. These grassroots examples also enhance UMC's image.

In a survey of graduating students, over 90% of respondents agreed or strongly agreed that computer access at any time, day or night, was important to them and that the technological skills they developed at UMC are essential to their future employment. In the same survey, 83% of respondents agreed or strongly agreed that having their own computer helped them assume more personal responsibility for learning. Surveys also find employers eager to hire more UMC grads, because they easily adapt to an organization's specific technological infrastructure and more quickly become productive. These responses provide strong indication that UMC's technology initiatives are adding value to student educational experiences.

Lesson Learned
For technology initiatives to be successful, institutions must meet and exceed the expectations of students, their parents, and employers. The institution's overall reputation is enhanced.

OPERATIONAL CHALLENGES

One challenge that has emerged within UMC's networked classrooms is "computer-aided distraction." When all students are logged onto the local area network or the Internet during a classroom exercise, gaming, email, instant messaging, chat rooms, and web surfing all become potential distractions from the work at hand. Faculty must find ways to deal with this. Solutions range from asking students to access the network in class only when faculty instruct them to do so to developing an individual policy on classroom distractions. At times, however, there are gray areas. Some students desire to take notes on the keyboard in class, while others in the same class will abuse their Internet access. Some even argue that their ability to multitask over-comes the potential for distraction. On the other hand, educators have always dealt with a level of student distraction in the classroom—daydreaming, doo-dling, or even sleeping. Ultimately, when the technological initiatives include course materials with highly engaging interactive multimedia, distraction is less likely to occur.

Another challenge is heightened student expectations. In the classroom, not every faculty member has the same talent and technological savvy, which can cause some frustration. Faculty are always improving, but some choose to use technology in less engaging ways. In the workplace, some graduates' expectations may come into conflict with the employers' economic realities. In both cases, the challenge is to help students understand that, within UMC and in the workplace, people operate at different levels in their acceptance and use of technology. In many cases, these high expectations can be har-nessed; the students can become agents of change to help bring up the levels of technology integration, use, and efficiency.

Lesson Learned
A wide range of student and faculty motivation and ability will always exist. Technology, while not a panacea, provides more tools to engage the learner and to enhance the educational experience.

CONCLUDING INSIGHTS—IT'S NOT IF, BUT WHEN!

Since UMC began its technology initiatives back in 1993, representatives from over 200 colleges and universities worldwide have come to see the results firsthand. Those visitors often marvel at UMC's accomplishments and try to envision such a cultural change at their home institution. Typically, they voice their reservations and fears, citing the following as reasons they could not duplicate what UMC has done:

- The initial/continuing expense is too great.
- Our campus is too big/too small to make it work.
- Our students'/faculty's technological skills vary too widely.
- We'll never get faculty buy-in.
- We don't have the infrastructure or support system.

These reasons eventually yield as individuals see that a change in culture *has* occurred at UMC and that it is the right thing to do at their respective institutions. Then discussion moved from if to how. The real question is how.

Initially, everyone at the institution undertaking the ubiquitous computing and related technological initiatives will be faced with many situations that they have never encountered before. Even at an institution where the initiative is mature, regular hardware and software upgrades and emerging technologies will present first-time situations again and again. As these situations become common, individuals become more comfortable and openness to new situations emerges. Becoming more open to new ideas and change brings students and others into the teaching and learning environment in a collaborative rather than authoritarian manner.

Individuals increasingly see the technology as what it is: a tool to solve problems and enhance learning. At this point, use begins to flower across the campus and true innovation results. Each successful use of technology lessens the fear, adds to confidence, and allows more success. Failures are often seen as lessons that perhaps the technology could be used more effectively in a different way. An environment of continual improvement becomes a part of the culture.

This notion of continual improvement causes individuals to reexamine status quo applications, processes, and services with a critical eye. With the use of technology, a better process or product may be created, whether in healthcare or agriculture or business or education. Competition begins to fuel the fire, and individuals find technological applications to enhance their personal lives as well as their careers and their businesses.

In the end, nearly all the focus is positive, and energies are devoted toward integrating technology and problem solving rather than criticizing the decision to undertake the initiative and raising discontent. A great pride results from having successfully applied technologies to improve the process and results.

The question is not whether colleges and universities should undertake these technology initiatives, but rather, when will they start? It is truly the right thing to do.

Contact Information

Donald Sargeant
Chancellor
University of Minnesota, Crookston
2900 University Ave.
Crookston, MN 56716
Phone: 218-281-8342
Fax: 218-281-8050
Email: sargeant@mail.crk.umn.edu
Web Address: http://webhome.crk.umn.edu/~sargeant/

Andrew Svec
Director of Communications
University of Minnesota, Crookston
104 Robertson Hall
2900 University Ave.
Crookston, MN 56716
Phone: 218-281-8435
Fax: 218-281-8440
Email: asvec@mail.crk.umn.edu
Web Address: http://www.crk.umn.edu/faculty/S/Andrew_Svec.htm

Wake Forest University

David G. Brown

Our "computer utility" is a powerful communication system that is universally accessible and universally used. Like driving a car or using a telephone, most of us can't envision life without connectivity. Most of us no longer think much about the computer itself; our focus is on our subject matter or the task. We stay in touch with committees, colleagues, and classmates for longer periods of time, even when distance separates us at holidays or when studying abroad or after graduation. We are a community now, dependent on a very sophisticated communication system, yet we expect it to operate and think little about it.

HISTORY AND VISION

In 1995, the Wake Forest undergraduate faculty voted to phase in a program that would eventually provide a new laptop computer and printer every two years to every student and faculty member as well as most administrators, beginning with entering freshman. Comparable programs now exist for our medical school, graduate management school, and divinity school. By the fall of 1999, we were fully computerized. We estimate that our laptops-for-all program cost us about $500 per year per student: $500 more, that is, than we would be spending on computer support, computers, computer labs, and training if we had pursued a more conventional program. By spending the extra $500, we believe that we are achieving immense educational gains, while saving big dollars on training and computer lab space. And we are sending our students off with the learning tool that they successfully used in college still available to them.

For over 150 years, Wake Forest has sought to emphasize personal (students and professors know each other) and individual (customized) education.

Our specialty is a rigorous liberal arts curriculum, enhanced by close student-faculty relationships. Maintaining intimacy and customization, while affording the specialized resources available in a large research university in a wide spectrum of disciplines, is truly a challenge. In the computer, we saw a means of staying connected and collaborative, even while growing more complex.

We identified four primary computer advantages: for communication, access to experts and databases, analysis, and presentation. Our choices on where to spend our money were driven by a desire to maximize communication and interaction within the community and with the outside world. Pursuit of the other three objectives—access, analysis, and presentation—would be through a computer system that was designed to maximize communication and interaction. When compromises had to be made, they would favor enhancing the communication capacities of the computer system.

As we look to the future, we continue to emphasize rigorous, personal, and individual education in the liberal arts. If this emphasis means providing even more sophisticated communication systems, we should do it. If a sophisticated computer utility is the most effective way to support learning strategies, such as collaboration, cooperation, team projects, and real-world practice; and if these developing educational strategies prove most effective in supporting learning, we should invest. If, on the other hand, additional investment in technology is less productive than investing in additional people, we should let others be the technology pioneers. Our strategy has been and should be to provide a rigorous, personal, and individual liberal arts education at a responsible cost.

Wireless communication via handheld devices has much to offer, especially for students studying abroad and working collaboratively. E-journals, alumni clusters, asynchronous communication strategies, just-in-time teaching, courses built from chunks, multimedia demonstrations, interactive exercises, search protocols designed by scholars, databases, and ownership policies are evolving rapidly. Our responsibility is to monitor these developments and to adopt them if and when they are proven reliable and effective. Computer-enhanced education is in its infancy. Many opportunities will ripen over the next two decades.

GUIDING CONCEPTS

Wake Forest's bold leap to become one of the most computerized campuses in the country was structured by a few specific guiding concepts. These concepts allowed us to determine where our dollars might most effectively be deployed.

The principles of 1995 have stood the test of time well and are essentially the same today.

Concept 1: Students First. Students were likely to be the most eager and, in many cases, the most knowledgeable computer users. In a reversal of their typical roles, students will introduce faculty to the advantages of electronic communication. If we expect students to use computers, they must be available when students are in the classroom, studying abroad, home for vacation, and researching in off-campus libraries and laboratories. Students must feel that they have full access to the best computing facilities on campus. Faculty computing power is a second priority. Staff computing power is a distant third.

Concept 2: Academic Freedom. Copyright, security, and privacy are elements in our decision to adopt a system with extraordinary password protections. We believe that the communication between and among students and faculty must be private. We must avoid establishing open records that haunt individual students and scholars for the rest of their careers.

Concept 3: Communication and Community. Our emphasis is upon access, communication, and the building and maintaining of community. Entry into distance-learning programs, production of elaborate multimedia chunks, extensive use of presentation software, and access to new digital materials are desirable but secondary to our primary focus on providing all students and faculty more opportunities to interact with each other and with people beyond the campus in ways that support and enhance learning and discovery.

Concept 4: Standardization. Early on, we decided to standardize the computer provided to all students, the software load, the campus-wide introductory instruction, and the course management system. Clearly, there are cost savings and maintenance advantages to standardization. The driving force in our decision, however, was educational.

Our community must have a common language, "tracks with a common gauge." Standardization means that students can help each other learn. With common systems, professors and students can exchange documents in the format and aesthetics that were intended. Standardization means that how-to classes on computer usage can be taught more frequently and in greater depth by computer consultants, trained in the applications within a single system, who can be hired more readily than more general consultants. Taking two early class periods to explain how the computer will be used in each course is no longer necessary; class periods can be devoted to teaching English literature, instead of how to use the computer to learn about English literature. Standardization means that when a computer breaks down in the middle of a class, a loaner can be checked out from the departmental secretary with minimal disruption. Standardization means that students having problems with their computers can submit an assignment through a roommate's computer.

In recent years, the standardization principle has led us to adopt a common course management system (Blackboard) and to encourage the development of course chunks in accordance with emerging worldwide IMS standards.

Concept 5: After College. Decisions concerning hardware and software were made more easily when we emphasized the criterion: What systems will students most likely be using after they graduate? Once we identified the market leader, we sought that standard. Although most of our students used Apple Macintoshes in high school and brought Macs for college, most of our graduates were using PCs in their life beyond college. In software, Microsoft Windows and Microsoft Office are dominant, so that's what we adopted.

We switched from a locally designed course management system to one that would still be accessible to students after college. We switched from a proprietary email system to Netscape Mail so that students could easily continue with it after college. We switched from emphasizing an intranet to almost exclusive use of a standard web browser (Netscape, a registered trademark of Netscape Communications Corporation), because most students were already familiar with web browsing, and web-browsing skills enhanced in college would be used after college.

Concept 6: Basic Use. We have emphasized providing a basic level of service to every member of the community, encouraging 85% of the faculty to use some minimal technology, perhaps only group email, even if it means shifting attention from the most eager 15% of the faculty.

Hardware, software, and educational programming have been designed so that every user can achieve a basic level of proficiency and use. The system is designed first to serve every student, with the presumption that the more expert can better take care of themselves.

Concept 7: Empowerment of Existing Units. For both political and operational reasons, many faculty and offices are involved in our community commitment to technology. An elected committee of the faculty determines the standard load on student computers and sets myriad policies. The computer center decides on networks, distributes and maintains computers, and advises administrative offices. Academic computer specialists formally report to the dean and are assigned to clusters of departments, defined by location, to assist faculty and student adoption and instruct them in specialized uses. The bookstore operates the computer store, which sells add-on capacities. The library, which has traditionally provided access to information, is responsible for choosing the electronic database and for students' basic computer training. Deans and department chairs allocate funds for nonstandard software purchases, nonstandard computer peripherals (for example, laser color printers), and external training fees. Individual faculty members are responsible for actually adopting technology in their teaching and in their classrooms. Our computing initiative is therefore a total campus affair, not in the sole domain of the IS Department.

Concept 8: Exposure, Not Mandated Adoption. With time, the power of the technology itself will sell its use. Faculty are curious about the potential of computers. Students reared on computers will, with time, push faculty to experiment. To insist that every faculty member adopt computer methodologies is neither wise nor necessary. Our obligation is to enable faculty, without risk or extraordinary inconvenience, to explore the advantages of teaching with technology. Our corps of student designers is part of this strategy. We also send faculty delegations to visit other campuses, host symposia examining specific applications in use at other universities, subsidize trips to workshops, purchase software for particular purposes or equip laboratories in special-purpose classrooms. We hold training sessions on how to maximize our course management system and maintain a very active listserv among Blackboard users.

Concept 9: Rapid Change. Information technology is a fast-moving field. Both equipment and knowledge obsolesce rapidly, and our system, with its complete turnover of hardware every two years, is built to anticipate this rapid change. Things may settle down in the distant future, but, for now, our policy committees, computer staff, and individual faculty members reevaluate what we are doing each year and make changes as necessary.

Concept 10: Pilot Year. Since virtually every system on campus had to be changed, never before had we so vigorously, so constantly, discussed our teaching goals and how best to reach them. This ferment needed time. Many false starts were made. The student and faculty forgiveness that naturally accompanies a pilot year and disappears when implementation has been announced as robust and dependable was essential. Therefore, we piloted our various programs with roughly 20% of our first class and a few volunteer faculty. In retrospect, that decision was absolutely critical to our success.

Concept 11: Marketable Difference. Our early adoption of ubiquitous, mobile computing allowed us to market the difference among prospective students. Financing this bold move required a tuition increase of $3,000 per year, to be paid, at first, only by the incoming freshmen. The benefits from this much higher tuition had to be visible to be credible. Although it was only one component of the total plan, the computer provided that visibility. In the first years after introducing our Technology Plan, admission applications and acceptance were up in both numbers and quality. Now that many other campuses have adopted similar plans, the advantage is not as great.

Concept 12. Partnership. In implementing a change of this magnitude, a university of our size required immediate and ready access to consulting expertise. We also needed a relationship with a vendor that would allow modifications of the available equipment and the delivery and maintenance systems. Our long-term partnership with IBM provided that depth of capacity. On several occasions, when IBM would have liked us to adopt its software and operating systems, we said, "No, there's a better way for us." At the same time, IBM has often said, "At least try this," and we found that their suggestion worked well. While retaining the autonomy and academic freedom of the university, partnerships are essential in business ventures of this magnitude.

BASIC CHARACTERISTICS OF THE PROGRAM TODAY

Each August, 1,000 Wake Forest freshmen receive, as part of their tuition, a new printer and a laptop computer with the campus software load. Two years later, they trade in their freshman computers for new ones, which they take with them upon graduation, and the two-year old computers are sold as a lot to our local school system. Faculty, staff, and almost everyone on campus who needs a computer are also on two-year refreshment cycles, with the same computers and loads. With a few special exceptions, therefore, only two types of computer are on campus at any time; for example, those issued in August 2001 and those issued in August 2000.

The August 2001 computer is an IBM A21m ThinkPad. This laptop includes Pentium III; 800 MHz; 14.1-inch active matrix screen; 192 mb of RAM; a rewritable CD; 56K modem; 8 mb video RAM; 10/100 ethernet; floppy; lithium-ion battery; 12 Mbps USB; and serial, parallel, and infrared ports. It weighs 6.7 pounds. The software load includes Windows98; Netscape Communicator 4.77; MS Office Pro 2000; Macromedia Dreamweaver 4; Shockwave and Flash; Apple Quick Time 4.1.1; Waterloo Maple V 6.0; SPSS 10.1; Real Player and Producer; Adaptec Easy CD; Norton Antivirus; and Remedy AR Client 4.05/01. The printer is a Lexmark inkjet.

For our 3,700 undergraduates, 92% of whom live in residence halls, there are 31,000 active ethernet connections. Roughly one-fourth of campus computers are wireless. An Internet provider is subsidized for faculty homes.

One hundred and twenty classrooms are equipped with identical presentation consoles that include Super VGA projectors, VCRs, opaque projectors, and overhead transparency projectors. Like the computers, this projection equipment is standard and on rotation.

Staffing our program is an IS department of 70, which includes telephone and cable; 22 academic computer specialists hired by the academic departments; and three librarians responsible for student training and maintaining a multimedia lab. Twenty-five student technology assistants have assignments with individual professors for a semester to add computer enhancements to particular courses. The help desk and loaner pool are run by IS.

Academic computer policy is set by an elected committee of faculty, with the CIO and the library director serving ex officio. This committee selected Netscape as our mail system and Blackboard for course management. Our highly developed Administrative Computing System has been created locally, within IS.

At the moment, all stakeholders seem pleased with what we are doing. Assessment studies reveal that both faculty and students believe they are learning more. Acceptance rates have increased. Retention and graduation rates have increased. Faculty recruitment success has increased. Some use of the computer is almost universal.

REACHING A CONSENSUS

In 1995, Wake Forest's Strategic Planning Committee proposed a 37-point program for upgrading the undergraduate liberal arts education. It advised reducing the student-faculty ratio by 15%; junior scholarships for high-performing students; study-abroad subsidies for 20% of all undergraduates; a $1 million supplement to the library acquisition budget; competitive salaries for faculty; a new program of freshman seminars; and powerful laptop computers for all. To implement this ambitious program, a 15% increase in tuition and substantial administrative savings were needed. The IS staff had to be doubled. Nearly every department of the university had to take on additional work.

The lures of the 37-point program, called the Plan for the Class of 2000, were a reaffirmation of Wake Forest's emphasis on personal and individualized learning, more and better faculty, and a more honest approach to solving the digital divide. Yet a 15% tuition increase would almost wipe out the $3,000-per-year tuition advantage Wake Forest had held over its competitors. The higher tuition could undesirably affect the university's commitment to diversity, and each university subgroup had a special project whose funding, in their minds, took precedence over more fundamental changes in student-faculty ratios and academic infrastructure.

Issues were debated over four months in well-attended weekly faculty meetings. Eventually, both the faculty and trustees came to believe that if the entire package could be implemented, the gains would offset the sacrifices. The trustees were inclined to emphasize the increase in technology; the faculty, the increase in professors and more competitive pay. The ultimate plan spent about one-third of new monies on technology, one-third on new faculty, and one-third on scholarships to offset the potential demographic impact of higher tuitions.

Key to the acceptance of the plan was a strong group of computer-knowledgeable faculty who at first rejected the technology portion of the plan and later—after the plan was substantially improved by shortening the refreshment cycle and adding computer-related staff throughout the university—sold it to their faculty colleagues. Under the improved plan, faculty could keep their nonstandard computers, which often housed research data that would be too expensive to migrate. An elected faculty committee determined the choice of software on the standard computer.

Soon after the votes, I articulated, in *The Future Compatible Campus*, the benefits anticipated as follows:

> Often I am asked, why would a selective, private liberal arts college such as Wake Forest invest in so much technology? Aren't you emphasizing the wrong thing?
>
> Clearly, there are dangers. Much like a group of teenagers first learning how to drive or a group of octogenarians sharing information on ailments, we are currently spending too much time evolving new strategies and learning new programs. The means to learning is temporarily too prominent. The substance of learning must soon, and once again, become primary. The infatuation with our new utility will end soon. Our willingness to endure the learning curve is explained by the following five benefits.
>
> **First Benefit: Personal and Individual**
> Wake Forest's comparative advantage rests with providing education that is both personal and individual. Before the computer revolution, the way to personalize education was to focus vast quantities of faculty time upon teaching and students. Individualization and customization was achieved

by the same means. Suddenly, with the advent of computers, a student's education can be individualized and customized through computer access. Corps of graduate students can answer individual e-mails, even when students are
in very large organic chemistry classes. Assignments can be
individualized, even when large numbers are involved.

If Wake Forest is to maintain its comparative advantage in
both personal and individual education, it must strengthen
its means to personalize (which means more faculty) and
strengthen its capacity to individualize (which means more
computers). A few well-funded universities will have an
opportunity to be both personal and individual. We are not
computerizing for the age of distance learning. We are computerizing for the sake of individualization while preserving
personalization.

Second Benefit: Technological Transformation

Suddenly the computer has become a basic tool of scholarship in every discipline. Like the newly powerful telescopes,
which are drawing many research programs to reanalyze ear-
lier hypotheses with never-before-available evidence, and
like new scholarly theories about the relevance of gender
and ethnicity of the authors and readers when analyzing literature, the ability of the computer to dig more deeply and
to analyze larger and more complex data sets means that
most of the dissertations over the next decade or so, in virtually all disciplines, will draw heavily upon possibilities
presented by the computer. Old hypotheses will be retested
using new powerful techniques of analysis.

In turn, this means that prospective faculty seeking first jobs
will cherish those positions accompanied by adequate computer facilities and computer literate colleagues and students. Our capacity to attract the best and brightest faculty
over the next decade is dependent upon our capacity to provide for them a computer environment where they may
practice their profession.

Third Benefit: Nomadic Learners

Students are a privileged class in our society, yet they are
without home or office. They are intellectual nomads,

spending part of each year in a residence hall, a family bed-room, traveling abroad, and visiting friends. Wherever they are, students need access to the instruments of learning and scholarship. The instruments they learned to use while in school need to continue to be available to them upon grad-uation. The solution is a personally owned mobile com-puter.

Fourth Benefit: Access Information

Much like the telephone and the public library, the com-puter has become a common utility for communication and the access highway to information. In the information age our graduates will be greatly disadvantaged if they do not have access to a primary means of communication.

Fifth Benefit: Level Playing Field

We sensed that we were rapidly moving toward a two-class society, those students with computers and those who could not afford them. To level the playing field, we felt we could not deny computer access to students who could afford them, and yet, we could not afford to support this disparity. Universal ownership of computers seemed to be the only solution.[1]

EXAMPLES OF COMPUTER-ENHANCED TEACHING

Today, it is most gratifying to observe how many professors are using the technology infrastructure.

- Rick Matthews, professor and chair of our Physics Department, posts 30-second digital videos of each of his classroom demonstrations. Stu-dents can anticipate and review what happens at their convenience.

- In my economics class, I have fellow students and volunteer alumni com-ment on rough draft student essays over the Internet.

- Bob Swofford, professor and former Chemistry Department chair, has developed a set of simulations that allow students to understand chemi-cal reactions, while Angela King, senior lecturer in chemistry, uses before-class, just-in-time quizzing to grasp the level at which she should aim class activity.

- Law Professor Steve Nickels encourages students to view lectures from other campuses and has recruited Supreme Court justices from several states to comment on the casework of student teams.

- Students come to my office with their computers so they can ask for help exactly at the point they got stuck.

- Students abroad keep in touch with on-campus courses.

- Students in the field support their work with their portable computers.

- Students often first learn new computer techniques when serving their athletic team or social fraternity and subsequently transfer this knowledge to the classroom.

In our environment, computer use is universal and taken for granted.

WAKE FOREST'S GREATEST SUCCESSES

Each stage in the adoption process seems to carry its own challenge. Our toughest and probably most important and best decision was to standardize. By providing every student and every faculty member with the same software loaded on identical computers, issues of training, support, and reliability have almost disappeared. Professors needn't take time away from teaching Shakespeare or Einstein to teach their students how to use the computer. Collaboration becomes natural and easy. Sharing is simplified and, therefore, encouraged. Breakdowns are fixed faster and are less important, because borrowing an identical computer is easy. Instead of arguing over which computer is best, our community focuses on how best to use the computers we have to advance learning. Computer access for all students is predictable and reliable, so professors find it easier to make, in good conscience, assignments that involve computers. Just as teaching is simplified by a common language, a common library, equal access to science labs, and the same textbooks, a standard computer allows the university to focus on central purposes.

Moving from a free-for-all computer environment to a truly reliable, standardized environment involved changes in every domain of the university. These changes, from the delivery of new computers on the first day of classes to the resale of two-year old computers, required funding, sequencing, and punctual completion. With over 200 specific sub-projects associated with implementing a ubiquitous laptop program, a professional project manager with credentials similar to a general contractor's, was hired. Looking back, we are convinced that without such a taskmaster, minor glitches could have turned a portion of our community against computerization.

We also think we picked the right target: basic communication. We emphasized improved communication, especially between professor and student and among students. Simple uses of the computer, like email, were stressed, while more difficult and complicated uses were left for a small core of enthusiastic "computer eagles." By keeping it simple, almost all members of the community were quick to embrace the new technology.

Finally, great care was taken to stress with all faculty and students that the computer is a means to an end, not an end in itself. Faculty were encouraged to consider adopting computer enhancements in their teaching and given many opportunities to seek help, even 18 hours per week with a knowledgeable student who might help them augment their course with computer enhancements. Faculty in each department had access to their own full-time academic computer specialist, trained in the discipline and assigned to help faculty and students in the discipline. The computer was initially compared to the library. The university is obliged to provide the means to reach the Internet, but individual professors must determine whether using the Internet is the best expenditure of time and effort for their course. Those professors who choose not to use the Internet are to be valued every bit as highly as those who do.

Perhaps the most gratifying aspect of our venture into technology is the way we now take it for granted. The library is available if we need it. Classrooms are available if we need them. Now the Internet has fallen into that category, the domain of the expected and the ordinary.

Contact Information

David G. Brown
Vice President and Dean
International Center for Computer-Enhanced Learning
Wake Forest University
P.O. Box 7328, Reynolda Station
Winston-Salem, NC 27109
Phone: 336-758-4878
Fax: 336-758-5012
Email: brown@wfu.edu
Web Address: http://www.wfu.edu/~brown

Endnote

1. See David G. Brown, Ed., *Electronically Enhanced Education: A Case Study of Wake Forest University* (Winston-Salem, NC: Wake Forest University Press/Scientific Division, 1999) for 17 chapters by the leaders of Wake Forest's implementation. The book may be ordered from Box 7328, Winston-Salem, NC 27109. Portions of this chapter have been adapted from Chapter 2 of that book, which was first published in *The Future Compatible Campus*, Eds. Diana C. Oblinger and Sean C. Rush, (Bolton, MA: Anker Publishing, 1998).

The Acadia Advantage

Jennifer Bolt

A cadia University, in Nova Scotia, Canada, calls its mobile computing program Acadia Advantage. Like many institutions of higher education, Acadia believes that providing students with anywhere, anytime access to technology improves learning. Extensive resources and energies have been dedicated to helping faculty, in particular, discover just how to do this.

In January 2001, an Acadia student, Allison Randall, wrote a letter to the Acadia Institute for Teaching and Technology (AITT), the department responsible for assisting faculty in using technology. Allison was a fourth-year student, a member of the first class to graduate from the Acadia Advantage environment. Her letter was written to outline the advantages of Acadia's Course Management Environment (ACME) and to request that faculty use it more extensively. In her words, the "advantage" of Acadia Advantage is communication. The program "provide(s) the framework for instant and uninterrupted sharing of resources." Her letter describes two scenarios. In the first, a student, struggling with a last-minute assignment late at night, finds the direction and help they need on ACME to successfully complete the paper. In the second more traditional scenario, the student flounders without help and does not get the paper done. The letter goes on to request that the AITT make the use of ACME mandatory for all professors, a request that is not granted.

Just over 75% of Acadia's 200 faculty use ACME. When the student wrote this letter, 900 full-time ACME course sections supported in-class activities. These were not distance education courses. In the 2000–2001 academic year, over 214,000 online tests were written on the ACME system, and over 3,000 online discussion groups were conducted. ACME use has increased by 15% to 20% in each of the last two years. Studies show that at most campuses where course management systems are used, faculty use hovers at just under 20%.[1] ACME is the most-used academic application at Acadia and there is a desire for more.

When Acadia Advantage was first implemented in 1995, the university considered purchasing a course management system. Commercial products were in their infancy and, without any significant experience with such systems, we had difficulty knowing which features would be useful and finally chose none. AITT staff began to offer professors workshops in HTML, and the keen and brave-of-heart began to code their own web pages. The AITT then, as today, also made great use of technically savvy students, hiring them as programmers, trainers, and graphic artists. AITT students saw early on, back in 1996, that the faculty needed an easier way to build web pages than learning HTML. They suggested that a template system would reduce frustrations and save time, but, as is so often the case, the AITT's preoccupation with the task at hand did not allow it to see the wisdom of its students' advice. Students were asked to prioritize and to focus on their current projects. Thankfully, they developed their template system anyway, and ACME was born, built late at night with the help of gallons of coffee.

What is evident in both the student letter and the ACME story is the single most important result of the mobile computing initiative at Acadia, one that is both a difficult and ongoing challenge and a significant and compelling opportunity. This result is student empowerment.

As technology and the world's resources are wired into the classroom, a not-so-subtle power shift takes place. Content expertise is found not only at the lecture podium but also at the well-searched web site. Technical expertise can be found anywhere. The quiet student previously unnoticed in the second-to-last row suddenly creates new learning possibilities by programming an animation or building an interactive spreadsheet or helping to fix the technical glitch that has stalled class.

Student empowerment is difficult for the holders of traditional power. It grows as students understand their ability to provide technical leadership and as their access to tools allows them to solve their own problems. It also creates very high expectations about how technology should be used, which are difficult and costly for administrators and faculty to meet.

At Acadia, students wanted to publish the ranking and results of course and professor evaluations. The faculty union and university administration did not react quickly in granting the students this request, so they created their own online surveys on the Student Union server at www.courseval.com. They surveyed the campus, tabulated their results, and ran their own Faculty

Teaching Award at the on-campus pub. It was one of the best-attended events that year, by students and faculty alike.

Student empowerment is a little bit scary, but it is, after all, what universities are all about. A university can teach no better lifelong skill than the ability to solve personal or professional challenges and problems. The power shift, created by wired classrooms and access to technical resources, has helped create a new kind of student.

Mandate and Context

The mandate of Acadia Advantage was and continues to be providing anywhere, anytime access to information technology to assist teaching, studying, research, and learning. The program's most important elements follow:

- *Academic Focus.* The main intent of the program is to support the academic endeavors of teaching, studying, research, and learning.

- *Mobility.* Anywhere, anytime is facilitated through notebook computers.

- *Universal Access.* The program is intended for all students and all faculty.

Understanding the mandate requires an appreciation of Acadia University's demographic profile and Nova Scotia's provincial education environment.

Acadia University is Canada's second oldest, dating back to 1832. It is a traditional, small, liberal arts institution with approximately 3,700 students and 200 faculty. Situated in a small town, Wolfville (population 4,000), in the small province of Nova Scotia (population one million), Acadia is easily overlooked, despite its outstanding academic history.

Nova Scotia, notwithstanding its rural character and small population, is home to 13 postsecondary institutions, second only in its enrollments per capita to Boston, Massachusetts. Competition for students, therefore, is fierce. All universities in Canada, to date, are public institutions with regulated tuition fees. Restrictions on tuition add to competitive pressures.

In the late 1980s and early 1990s, Acadia administrators, like many others, faced two trends that compelled them to consider mobile computing. First, the use of computer labs on campus was rapidly increasing. To satisfy student demand for computing facilities would require a significant investment of both capital resources, to build new labs, and operating resources, to staff and outfit them. Second, the fear of graduating from a social science or arts program with only a "McJob" awaiting contributed to an enormous demand for business and computer science programs at all institutions in North America. Yet the business community itself bemoaned the lack of team building, critical thinking, and communication skills, skills that are the hall-marks of solid liberal arts education.

Mobile computing addressed both issues. It could restructure the costs associated with providing technology to students by reducing the need to build new labs. It could also ensure that students from all programs graduated with career skills. Acadia graduates would not only benefit from the tradition-al excellence of liberal arts programs but also be technologically equipped to perform in the modern workplace, proficient with web resources and applica-tions and ways to put them to work. The program would help to differentiate Acadia University from its many neighboring universities. In fact, as the first such program in Canada, Acadia would create a national reputation as a leader in teaching and technology.

Acadia is a university that takes pride in its concern for effective teaching. Classes are small, averaging approximately 30 to 40 students. Professors know their students by name, believing that a personal connection facilitates the learning process. Added to these compelling conditions, a faculty group of innovators had begun to experiment with on-campus technology resources. These early adapters would play a critical role as the Acadia Advantage pro-gram was rolled out.

Implementation and Program Today

In 1989, Dr. Kelvin Ogilvie, today Acadia's president, sent the university librarian and director of computing services on an exploration of North America's most innovative learning organizations. They were to gather the best ideas and recommend a course of action that would help the university chart a new direction in technology and teaching. From the white paper they produced came the mobile computing concept and the mandate for Acadia Advantage. The program was not launched until six years later, however, pri-marily due to the prohibitive costs of building the required technology infra-structure in those early days.

The program was rolled out in stages, first with a volunteer pilot group consisting of 350 students from business, computer science, physics, and arts and 43 faculty. The faculty represented the early adopters, who broke out of their traditional academic silos to work together to find new opportunities to use the technology to support their course work. Studio Physics, a concept borrowed from Rensselaer Polytechnic Institute, was one of the first academic initiatives that demonstrated improvements in student learning.

In the second year of the program, all first-year students and all faculty received notebook computers. Every subsequent year, from 1996 to 1999, the entering class joined the program. By the time the first-, second-, and third-year students all had notebooks, the fourth years were calling the program "The Acadia Disadvantage," for they recognized that they had been denied an essential learning and communication tool. Universal access proved a worthy objective.

Acadia Advantage today, as the program enters its seventh year, has some well-established characteristics that have proven successful for Acadia. These include:

- *Standardization.* All students and faculty have the same notebook with the same template offering a standard set of software licenses. This high degree of standardization has allowed the User Support Centre (USC) to offer one- to two-hour turn-around time on any technical problem or repair. Faculty can plan learning activities knowing that all students have access to required tools and will not encounter significant downtime.

- *Evergreen Technology.* Notebooks are leased and upgraded every one to two years, ensuring that students and faculty have access to the latest available technologies. Software licenses are also upgraded as notebooks are rolled. Students can purchase their notebooks for the residual value upon graduation.

- *Integrated Fees.* All fees associated with Acadia Advantage are integrated into the tuition fee. The combined fee becomes a component of the needed calculation for financial aid and is tax deductible.

- *Mandatory Training.* All students receive their notebooks at a "Care and Feeding" session, where basic use, care, file structure, standard applications, and computing policies are reviewed. Additional training and one-on-one help are available at no cost throughout the year.

- *Multimedia Resources.* Students and faculty can signout multimedia equipment (digital cameras, videocameras, tablets) and have access to MIDI and digital recording equipment, scanners, CD burners, and color printing.

More important than the equipment, however, are the human resources dedicated to making Advantage work. Two new technology support departments were created upon the implementation of the program. The USC is the front-line help desk and call-center operation. It provides repair services, notebook training, and classroom support; phone lines in Acadia's wired classrooms are connected directly to USC staff.

The AITT helps faculty to use the technology and develop new teaching methods and applications. This mandate is carried out by providing training and consulting services and by building learning applications and digital content. The AITT also provides a central gathering point for pedagogical discussions and research that focuses on the integration of technology in learning.

As at any university, Computing Services runs the technical infrastructure. Its resources and expertise have grown to support the significantly increased web services, academic applications, and bandwidth appetites that have resulted from Acadia Advantage. The centralization of technology support is efficient not only in providing technology and human resources but also in moving innovations from one discipline to another. As a focal point for technology innovation on campus, the AITT can ensure that an activity or application created for one course can affect another. It also gives the institution a comprehensive view of the use of technology across campus.

The results of this technical and human investment are measured in several ways: the growth of the technical environment itself (almost 7,000 network drops on campus and 50 classrooms with Internet access at each seat); the use of technology on campus (ACME usage statistics, creation of digital learning content); the innovation of new projects and applications (the AITT worked with 67 faculty on projects last year); and the attitudes about, and attainment of, learning using technology reported by students (measured each year in the Campus Computing Survey). Most compelling of all, however, are the inspiring stories of those teachers and students who are making new learning possibilities a reality.

Perhaps the most difficult challenge in bringing technology into the classroom is the opportunity for distraction. Teachers for decades have dealt with student distractions, but technology makes electronic note-passing or drifting off to beckoning cyberworlds fast, silent, and limitless. Further, students are outstanding multitaskers; many argue, along with the members of Parliament in Nova Scotia, that they should be allowed to handle their email in class (or the Legislature). In addressing this particular challenge, some of Acadia's faculty have adopted the "if you can't beat 'em, join 'em" approach. It makes sense, after all, to use the students' technical expertise in Internet searching and communication to support the learning tasks, if possible.

It is 8:30 a.m., and students are already plugged into the network, as Professor Conor Vibert of Acadia's School of Business enters his class. His area of expertise is Competitive Intelligence. He attempts to develop in his students the analytical skills to understand industries, their competitive players and suppliers, their interactions and interdependencies, and the impact they have on organizational strategies and investor markets. In today's business world, the analytical tools of Competitive Intelligence are found on the Internet, so it is important that his students learn to use them.

Conor's class of 40 students is divided into industry teams. Today, one team will present their PowerPoint slides with embedded links that launch the web sites that were critical to their analysis. While this presentation takes place, the audience teams are also at work, checking the validity of the Internet sources, even searching out critical ones that were missed. The audience teams communicate their findings to each other using ICQ, an instant messaging application that allows for the silent note passing. The silent conversation is important, for a rebuttal team will be asked to present their feedback five minutes after the presenting team is done. The activity is designed to encourage informed articulation of quick thinking. By the end of the semester, Conor's students will be comfortable presenting material that integrates electronic presentation tools, spreadsheets, online stock analysis, and company web sites. They will also have learned to work in virtual teams, to search and to validate Internet sources, and to identify the best online investigative tools for industry analysis.

If you were to visit Dr. Vibert's class, you would see him sitting at the back overseeing activities that are clearly in the hands of his students. You would also see screens flashing a variety of web sites and rolling scripts of conversations that thread through the class—the very things that irk so many teachers. Here, however, the students are engaged in the learning task at hand, and the cyberworlds they visit are the boardrooms and trading floors of their extended classroom.

Governance Issues

Despite the success of Conor Vibert's class, some faculty at Acadia, like faculty everywhere at work in wired classrooms, have requested that networks be switched off at their discretion. This seemingly simple request triggers a variety of responses among the major stakeholders who must be involved in governance and policy setting. Students, not surprisingly, behave increasingly as consumers at our institutions, often believing that the tuition they pay comes with rights to demand things of us that begin to encroach upon the teaching environment. (It is that old student empowerment challenge one more time.) Students want access to the network with all of its resources and distractions "anytime, anyplace." Sound familiar?

Faculty, quite rightly, feel they deserve some control over the classroom environment. Though new presentation methods and teaching strategies abound, they do not imply that traditional methods and materials, particularly the lecture, are no longer useful. Administrators, caught somewhere in the middle, also have to be concerned with the efficient use of the technology resources. They, more than anyone, must show that the incredible resources invested in technology are having a meaningful impact on the institution and providing a positive return on investment.

These three stakeholder groups are at the heart of every policy and procedure decision concerning Acadia Advantage. They come together in various groups: the Information Resource Advisory Committee, the High-Quality Learning Task Force, the Information Technology Managers Group, and the University Web Committee, to name a few. Each has a specific mandate, but together they shape the policies, practices, and strategies that make Advantage work. Collaboration, inclusion, and communication are key to creating policies that not only consider all stakeholders, but also prove effective in their implementation.

In the early days, many faculty and alumni voiced concern about the implementation of the mobile computing program at Acadia. Acadia alumni are a close-knit family group with a strong love for the long-standing traditions of their very traditional university. Some found it difficult to imagine how computers and wires would fit in the sweeping green spaces of the residence quads or the quiet tranquillity of the library stacks. Many feared that computers would isolate people and break down personal relationships and communication, particularly between faculty and students. Faculty had valid concerns about their intellectual property rights and added time pressures to use technology that were not adequately defined in the early days.

As with any fundamental change, education and time were needed to demonstrate that the fears were, for the most part, unjustified. In fact, technology has dramatically increased communication between people, especially between faculty and students. Intellectual property rights were clearly outlined in the last collective agreement, and while faculty certainly do take more time to use technology, many who have made the investment are finding rewards. They are also getting significant help from the technical support groups and their students.

Cataloging experiences and communicating them to the anxious are particularly important activities that can address concerns brought about by any significant change to an already successful institution. Sharing the program's successes is equally important. Acadia University has been ranked as Canada's most innovative liberal arts university for the past four years. Enrollments have increased, and student surveys strongly support the use of technology in academic life. The results are beginning to speak for themselves.

Financing Issues

It is expensive, exponentially expensive, for as we succeed in discovering more and better uses for the technology and more students and faculty actively participate, the costs increase. Since music and video are particular student favorites, new media applications create unending demands for bandwidth. Academic applications that are integrated into courses have become increasingly complex and now require servers, backup space, and the technical expertise to administer them. The need for training workshops, where 20 can learn at one time, has, for the most part, been replaced by a need for individual consulting, where faculty require a development team to help bring their innovations to life. The early adopters, who lead the way, can exhibit a tendency toward gadgetry, a desire to play with the latest techno-toy. Some of this play must be tolerated, for without experimentation and exploration, we would not benefit from innovation at all. Hence, the fond name for the AITT: the Sandbox. However, too much is too expensive.

In a country with regulated tuition and a province with one of the poorest economies, financing a program like Acadia Advantage is a significant challenge. To gain support for the program, administration promised that Advantage would be funded outside of the operating budget, and a significant fund-raising initiative began. To its credit, Acadia raised more than $12 million to cover the installation of the infrastructure and has not increased the program fee for students in the past four years. In addition, the AITT's programs have contributed over $4 million to support teaching and technology on campus. Their $1.2 million annual budget is generated entirely from external funds. Being first in Canada has afforded the university important fund-raising and program-development opportunities. However, the program fees charged to students today for Acadia Advantage do not cover the costs of running it. This financial shortfall continues to be one of the biggest challenges that Acadia faces, particularly as technology use increases in all departments on campus.

Operational Issues

Not all ubiquitous computing programs have the academic focus of Acadia Advantage, nor have they attempted to fundamentally change the classroom environment to the same extent. The focus, not surprisingly, has resulted in one of the most successful aspects of the program: the breadth and depth of innovative learning projects across campus.

Each spring, the AITT invites faculty to present a project that they would like to implement in their course or program. The project is articulated first as a learning challenge. It might involve providing remedial resources to students, increasing attention and activity in class, or communicating difficult concepts. The faculty might or might not describe a solution to the challenge that might or might not use technology. The AITT's role is to consider how technology might solve the challenge.

Each summer, the AITT hires 30 to 40 students who are paired with a faculty member who has submitted a project in their program area. Students are hired, in fact, to match the profiles of projects presented, both in terms of disciplinary focus and technological skills required. The student provides the technical expertise to build the project, assisted by the training, resources, and project management of the AITT's full-time staff, and the faculty member provides the vision, the concept, and the content expertise.

Building projects, rather than purchasing commercial solutions, has many benefits. Most important, faculty are much more likely to use a product or tool that is created with their input and time than one acquired off the shelf. Acadia often purchases software and uses commercial applications extensively, but we also do not hesitate to customize products, build applications within commercial products, or create tools from scratch, if market-ready products are not available or affordable.

Building projects not only increases faculty buy-in and use but also allows for continued customization and integration into other campus applications. At Acadia, ACME is the best example. The course management tool automatically integrates class lists and email addresses from the registration system and reserve readings from the library to present students with a customized menu of courses and learning materials that requires no data input from faculty. Building projects also greatly enhances learning and employment opportunities for students. AITT students from all program areas are hired regularly as instructional designers or programmers by eLearning companies.

Another result of the academic focus of Acadia Advantage is the growth of external partnerships and programs. As Acadia becomes known for technology innovation and training expertise in the use of technology, opportunities to form new relationships and programs increase. The AITT has received funding to run provincial and national training programs for teachers and students. It has also taken on development projects, as have several early adapters on the faculty, to build corporate training tools and learning portals. Making a ubiquitous computing program run successfully requires close relationships with industry partners. Learning how to bring industry players into the academic world has presented numerous opportunities to extend the learning environment at Acadia and the impact that Acadia can make on other educational institutions.

The program's most gratifying result is the focus on teaching. Technology is a challenge that all faculty members share. Because figuring out how to use technology to support learning takes time and energy, questions of pedagogy naturally arise: "Did that work?" or "Was it worth the effort for me or my students?" After attending technology-driven workshops for the past several years, Acadia faculty are now asking for help with the teaching strategies that they recognize are needed alongside the tools. Such discussions benefit learning institutions the most.

Looking back, perhaps this lesson was lost in the early days of Acadia Advantage or, if not lost, was not put forth to its proper prominence. Focusing a ubiquitous computing program on the technology is very easy. Students will identify the program very quickly with the box that is the notebook computer. Administrators and technology-support groups like the AITT encouraged any early effort that made use of the technology and made promises to students that created visions of wired classrooms filled with multimedia extravaganzas and technology fireworks. Students brought expectations to class that were difficult, if not impossible, to meet. A more balanced approach is called for. Neither the lecture nor the lecturer is obsolete. In fact, good teaching remains remarkably the same, though the tools, delivery methods, and student-teacher relationships have expanded and changed.

Acadia University's ubiquitous computing program focuses on learning and all activities that support learning. If the focus is understood and accepted, decisions are much easier to make and are more easily accepted.

Contact Information

Jennifer Bolt
Director, Acadia Institute for Teaching and Technology
Acadia University
Box 18
Wolfville, Nova Scotia, Canada B0P 1X0
Phone: 902-585-1006
Fax: 902-585-1050
Email: jennifer.bolt@acadiau.ca
Web Address: http://aitt.acadiau.ca

Endnote

1. McGraw-Hill Ryerson, Limited. (2000, January). *Student success and the use of new technology in education,* A McGraw-Hill Ryerson Survey of Higher Education Teachers in Canada, McGraw-Hill, New York, NY.

Drexel University

Janice Biros

IT STARTED WITH AN APPLE

In the spring of 1983, just a few years after the microcomputer became a commercial product, Drexel University required all incoming freshmen to have personal access to a microcomputer—not just the engineers, not just the computing science majors, but all students in all majors. After a careful review of the few microcomputer brands and models available, the university decided to standardize on a new model introduced by Apple Computer, Inc. The Macintosh had 128 K of RAM, no hard drive, a floppy disk holding 400 K of information, and a Motorola 68000 processor. It had all anyone could need to transform an academic program!

A faculty review group went out to Cupertino, California, to meet with Apple technicians and returned with a Macintosh prototype—the final version. Everyone was sworn to secrecy, and the machine was locked away in a secret room in the basement of what would soon become the Korman Computing Center. Here, select faculty and technical staff, sworn to nondisclosure, tested and worked with the machine. In March 1984, 2,800 Macintosh computers arrived on campus—several months late but amid a flurry of excitement nonetheless. Drexel made national news, was featured in national and new computing publications, and quickly moved from a regional technical school to a university with a national draw.

The university sold those first 2,800 computers directly to students, distributing them in a large warehouse on campus. Students shared the excitement over the promise this new technology held for their academic experience. Faculty and staff shared their anxieties about what they were going to do with this new technology. They wondered how they were going to use computing in their teaching to justify the $1,000 that each student had just spent on a computer. After all, no academic courseware was available, and the machine came with only two applications—MacWrite 1.0 , a word processor, and Multiplan 1.0, a limited spreadsheet program.

What transpired over the next couple of years was impressive. The university received a significant grant from the Pew Charitable Trust Foundation for the development of microcomputer-based academic programs, and faculty creativity reached new heights. They developed over 65 courseware applications for use in Drexel classes and for dissemination, through Intellimation, to other colleges and universities throughout the world. Drexel assumed a leadership position in academic technology integration.

THE NEXT STEPS

Many details have changed since 1983, but Drexel's commitment to technological integration and "being there first" have not changed. We no longer standardize on the Macintosh. In fact, since 1996, support has overwhelmingly moved to the Windows platform, based on what students are bringing to campus. Progress was evolutionary, responsive to, and affected by, organizational changes, technology changes, and changes in the demographics of the potential student population.

Our original microcomputing initiative was the work of then-President William Hagerty. Dr. Hagerty was visionary in conceiving such a program at that time and daring as well, but the university quickly realized that his revolutionary concept was nothing short of brilliant. As a result, the university would reach new levels of academic leadership and national and international recognition. That was one of Dr. Hagerty's goals—to attract students from across the nation and around the world, not just from the region.

The Macintosh computer was originally chosen as the hardware standard for everyone. It had a graphical user interface, making it extremely intuitive and easy to use, which was important, given the intent to equip all students, not just technical students, with this new tool. The program also included universal site licenses for productivity software for many years, first through Apple and then Claris. More recently, our site licenses have been for Microsoft Office.

The stated policy translated into each student purchasing a computer when entering Drexel. While it was not mandatory—that is, no one would be refused admission without one—it was presented and accepted as an integral part of the institutional culture. To launch the microcomputer program, the university sold computers directly to the students. While the bill for the computer was sent to each student along with the tuition bill, it was an additional cost.

This factor has been debated over the years, especially at a time when enrollments were declining, and our institutional health and stability were in danger. Many argued that being asked to purchase a computer upon entering the university would be a financial hardship and a deterrent for students, rather than an attractive unique opportunity. Each year, two or three Macintosh models were chosen as recommended machines, and for many years a low-end model, priced under $1,000, was included as an option. Over time, the microcomputer became more prevalent, and students were inclined to bring a computer to school regardless of any requirement.

Since we were the computer vendor, we established our own repair center and performed virtually all repairs on all Apple equipment. We also assisted departments with institutional purchases and faculty and staff with personal purchases. After about 10 years of supporting this model, the growing preference for "Wintel" computers made the standardized single platform impractical. A new president and a new CIO decided that Drexel would support both Macintosh and Wintel platforms and that we would no longer be in the computer sales and service business.

Now we have clicks from our web site to several national vendors who provide preferential student pricing. Minimal and optimal specifications both for new computers and existing home computers students may wish to bring with them are published each spring to guide student decisions. No longer our own repair center, we contract with a local vendor to provide repair service in the basement of our computing center. This arrangement has proved to be more cost effective and easier to manage. Faculty, staff, and students can bring in personal computers and printers for repair. Most national brands are serviced and their warranties honored. Institutionally owned equipment receives onsite service in the office or classroom.

Early in our microcomputer requirement initiative, there was a need to provide training and motivation for faculty. The administration was eager to ensure that students would use their computers in their classes, not just as personal productivity tools but as tools for learning, discovery, and research in projects assigned by faculty. In those days, very few productivity applications and even fewer academic courseware projects were available commercially. Drexel provided programming support for faculty to develop tools to use in class. Faculty submitted proposals for academic courseware projects that were reviewed by a faculty committee. Proposals selected for support were assigned a percentage of a programmer, who would work with the faculty member on the proposed application. The faculty member was the content expert, while the programmer provided the technical development skills.

Drexel's vision for technology has remained fairly constant, despite changes in the way it has been implemented and translated. It is to provide the entire community with current and developing technologies so as to improve the academic program. While the program has changed from distributed computing on personal computers to high-speed networked computing, the goal remains the same: to provide students, faculty, and staff with the technological tools and infrastructure and the training and support necessary to use those resources. The key is to remain just ahead of the curve, knowledgeable about emerging technologies, willing to take studied risks on appropriate new technologies, and continuing to raise the standards of resource availability and user support. Current initiatives include a significant push to re-engineer the curriculum and put many complete courses or extensive course support materials online in WebCT and to implement a campus-wide portal strategy offering a single sign-on to all web-based materials and services.

CHARACTERISTICS OF THE UNIVERSITY AND THE PROGRAM TODAY

Drexel is a private university located in Philadelphia. It was founded in 1891 by visionary financier and philanthropist Anthony J. Drexel to provide a practical college education for working class children. Historically, Drexel has had a strong technical tradition and provided students with both education and knowledge for success in a variety of professions along with the opportunity to apply their learning in the workplace.

These remain Drexel's two distinguishing features—a technology-rich learning environment and a co-operative education program that is required for virtually all students. Drexel faculty have been leaders in integrating computing technology into the academic program across all disciplines. The technical skills students acquire through the academic program carry over into their co-op positions. Many students make significant innovative technical contributions at the companies that employ them, resulting in repeat co-op assignments and permanent positions after graduation.

Drexel has learned not only to be innovative but to respond quickly. The current president, Dr. Constantine Papadakis, has fostered an environment of rapid implementation and innovation with minimal administrative red tape. Now, rather than managing the details of selling and servicing computers and spending huge amounts of time debating what configurations should be recommended given pricing considerations, the university concentrates on maintaining a robust and stable infrastructure and supporting the technological innovation that is occurring. Departments and colleges have expended extensive energies in putting several masters degree programs online and fine-tuning them in response to student feedback. The provost's office just offered eight $7,000 stipends for rapid development and deployment of traditional courses across the disciplines. The computing department works to transform faculty's curricular modifications using video, audio, and other media.

Drexel was the first university to have a totally wireless high-speed network on campus, inside and outside. The wireless network has enhanced the meaning of ubiquitous computing. It now means access to electronic resources anytime, anyplace, under just about any circumstances. The wireless network has enticed more students to bring laptops to campus to take advantage of this newly defined ubiquity. The underlying premise remains the same even with this relatively new technology. We have not dictated or developed a curriculum requiring or dependent upon this technology. Rather, the university acted on the assumption that we "build it, and they will use it." Faculty are free to integrate wireless into their teaching in whatever way and to whatever extent makes sense for them.

Early on, there were no laptops to choose from, so students all had desktop computers. As laptops were introduced, some students purchased them but not many, given that the price was considerably higher. In addition, many students preferred the larger screens and greater expandability of a desktop model. However, the presence of wireless computing has increased the number of students bringing laptops to campus. Many students now have two devices, one in their residence and one to carry with them.

While the initial microcomputing program was more structured and standardized and emphasized expectations for faculty use of technology, over time, the strategy has changed to provide a rich infrastructure to support innovative, creative uses of technology in teaching, learning, and research. The upgrade of the campus network to a 100 Mb backbone with an OC 48 Sonet Ring connecting the three main campus sites provided the bandwidth and speed required for more online courses, greater use of audio and video on the network, and expanded research and development projects. The university became an early member of Internet II, again providing a rich and robust infrastructure to support academic pursuits. Now, the environment and the technology program are more open and inclusive, and faculty and students have a fertile field for their initiatives.

Throughout the process, computing support has been provided to the entire community. Initially, teaching people how to use these new tools was crucial. Regardless of how technologically savvy and astute our students and faculty have become, the demand for support has remained the same or increased. As software becomes richer and more complex, electronic administrative transactions are more prevalent and mission-critical, communications and file transfer of all kinds are more in demand, and the overall fragility of the entire enterprise increases the demand for effective user support. The need for education increases as well. User support has changed over the years— previously, it was more face-to-face and personal and, now, it relies more on the web and multimedia support materials. User demands are more sophisticated, requiring support staff to be much more than just a couple of pages ahead in the documentation.

Today, the university concentrates on technology choices that are more macro than micro, such as what kind of computer to recommend and how to structure a program. The university considers how much disk space to allow individuals for email and web hosting, what new software tools should be licensed for the campus and how best to distribute them, and how faculty can be supported in moving courses onto the web. Topics, such as standardizing an online course development architecture and establishing a single-login to all web resources, are currently getting a great deal of attention, and the electronic processing of administrative transactions supporting the academic enterprise is increasing daily.

Educational Rationale

The microcomputer requirement was established both for the promise that this new technology held for all of our students and because the decision would draw attention and distinguish the university from other similar institutions.

However, the greater goal of the program was to enhance the academic program and to transfer the skills learned in courses to the workplace. The microcomputer promised greater facility in the production and refinement of academic work. It meant students could edit, revise, and rework papers and projects and that research would be freed from the production drudgery of the typewriter. It meant faculty could quickly analyze different approaches to problems, easily incorporating timely responses to student questions into lectures. It meant that faculty could produce articles and research more quickly and work collaboratively with colleagues more easily. The microcomputer promised to extend the classroom, the laboratory, and the library into each student's dorm room or home. It promised to eliminate much of the manual labor of writing research papers and solving problems, enabling students and faculty to concentrate on analysis, inquiry, creativity, deduction, critical thinking, and all the other significant aspects of learning.

Competence with computing technology also had significant implications for our students' professional development and success. Each Drexel student completes 18 months of co-op work for graduation. This co-op experience provides Drexel graduates with a distinct advantage in finding attractive positions upon graduation and in being successful in those positions. Competence with a microcomputer only makes them more competitive and more unusual in their organizations.

Examples From the Classroom

Dr. Doug Chute has taught neuropsychology at Drexel since 1984. He immediately saw that the Macintosh had the unique potential to create a portable psychology lab to teach students how to do psychological testing. He created MacLaboratory as an extension of his university lab. He gave each student a disk containing tests in perception, eye-to-hand coordination, reaction time, and other quantifiable factors. Using their disks, they could conduct the tests and gather data in their dorms or the computer labs or classrooms. Later versions added multimedia components and were distributed by CD. MacLab was hugely successful. Chute's students loved it, and colleges, universities, and professional psychologists all over the world purchased MacLab for use in teaching, research, and treatment.

As the technology grew and changed, so did Chute's ideas for MacLab. Some parts evolved into research grade software, and some components were developed into online courses created by Drexel University and the National Academy of Neuropsychology. Dr. Chute has capitalized on the capabilities of the technology as it has evolved to create materials that have enriched both research and teaching in psychology.

Governance Issues

The microcomputing program was established by a university policy that stated, "Each incoming freshman will be guaranteed personal access to a microcomputer." A Microcomputing Policy Committee (MPC) was established to guide the development of the overall program. The committee was composed of a faculty member from each of the university's five colleges and had members of the Office of Computing Services as nonvoting resources. Committee members were expected to provide input from colleagues on support needs, hardware recommendations, software needed, and other related issues. They were to report back to their colleagues and keep the lines of communication open, providing a forum for anyone to comment and make recommendations regarding the course being charted. They were charged each year with recommending the computers that students would purchase—how many models, at what price points, and what software applications should be site licensed. The MPC was a subcommittee of the faculty senate.

Another major function of the committee was to allocate resources for the development of courseware applications. The Pew grant supported developing computer-based academic applications to further the innovative new microcomputing program. Faculty members submitted proposals describing applications they wanted to develop for use in classes. The MPC evaluated proposals, and those chosen were given programming time and expertise.

As computing became more essential throughout the university, many larger issues emerged—acceptable use, mass email policies, support for new administrative systems. To review these larger issues, the Computing Advisory Committee (CAC) reports to the Vice-President for Information Resources and Technology in an advisory and policy-making capacity. This committee has faculty representation from each college and school within Drexel, is chaired by a dean, and connects with the faculty senate through their Committee on Academic Support. The MPC has been disbanded.

One of the major political issues the university grappled with from 1983 to the present is the role that faculty technological innovation and integration would have in the tenure and promotion process. Technology integration projects, whether class simulations, online materials, or graphical support, required a significant investment of time and effort, and many felt it was not in junior faculty's best interest at the expense of writing and research. However, the junior faculty were generally more motivated to exploit these new resources. The passage of time and growth of technology have diminished this debate, because technology has become an accepted tool for all faculty to use in greater or lesser degrees in all courses.

The issue of intellectual property emerged almost immediately as faculty developed academic courseware. The university established a policy stating that the copyright for software remained university property, but royalties from its sale were shared by the faculty member and the university. The faculty member received 60% of all royalties up to $100,000, and then they were shared equally.

The development and ownership of online courses has not yet been resolved by a policy.

Financing Issues

The cost of the microcomputers in the Drexel program has always been borne by the students. From the program's inception, students were required to purchase their computers. At one time, Drexel had an arrangement with a local bank, which established a low-cost financing program that students could use to purchase their computers or to pay for any other Drexel expenses, including tuition, books, and supplies.

One significant cost to the university was setting up computer classrooms and public access areas that students could use between classes, especially upgrading the labs on a regular basis. There was never an upgrade plan with accompanying funding, so it has been done on an ad hoc basis. Now that approach is adequate because resources have become available, but when resources were tighter, labs and classrooms were neglected, and faculty and students were dissatisfied.

Another major expense was the distribution and repair center. While warranties covered the cost of parts, staff, training, and operational costs were significant, and contracting with a third party was found to be cheaper and more practical. The center was eliminated in 1996.

Equipping classrooms throughout the university with adequate display and projection systems and, later, the Internet connectivity to enable a professor to easily use microcomputer-developed materials and examples in class was a significant associated cost. While all computer classrooms were well equipped, regular classrooms were not. Faculty had to check out carts with projectors and computers, wheel them to class, set them up, and then return them. The process was simplified with the advent of smaller projectors and laptop computers. Within the past couple of years, the university has devoted more attention and resources to creating multimedia classrooms, but it remains a problem for faculty in many areas of the university. They feel it is not worth the effort to create technology-based classes and curricula if there is no adequate way to display and implement those materials.

Currently, costs associated with supporting the microcomputer program are costs that any university now includes among its capital and operating expenses to support the educational program. The robust campus network is required, regardless of any computing requirement or program—it's integral to research, administrative transactions, and communication. Staff are necessary to support faculty and other staff and to help students make effective use of communications applications, online business functions, and to produce high-quality presentations, projects, and papers. Today, it would be difficult to identify any costs specific to the microcomputing requirement, as they are an integral part of doing educational business.

Operational Issues

Our current program is one based on choice supported by recommendations. Students choose a laptop or desktop computer based on their academic program and their needs. They choose to bring a machine from home or purchase a new one. They choose the vendor offering the most attractive configuration at the best prices. President Papadakis takes pride in the fact that Drexel University is still a leader in academic technology integration, not only with a ubiquitous computing program but with robust infrastructure and outstanding resources to support all research, academic enrichment and professional development.

Just as our original program made sense in the mid-1980s, our current program makes sense today. It leverages resources students own and adds value where it has the greatest impact, in the overall technological structure of the campus. While students are generally more technically experienced and savvy than they were 15 years ago, they still require recommended standards, uniformly available licensed software, concise documentation and directions, clear and certain policies of conduct and procedures for use of resources, and help and training on using resources, both their own and the university's. The success of our program has been its ability to change and be modified as time goes on and the climate changes. Our program has endured the test of time as a result of modifications which have kept it practical and sensible to implement, cost-effective to manage, and academically sound for students.

A major strength throughout the development and growth of the microcomputing program has been the strong commitment to supporting computer use on campus with high-quality, easily accessible, full-time professional computing consultants. Drexel recognized the need for support early on and has maintained and expanded a support group that is available to assist all computer users with all questions and difficulties they may have.

During the difficult time of enrollment declines and financial constraints, it was impossible to maintain the number of staff needed to meet demands. However, the quality of support remained high as staff exploited new online and web technologies to provide information and education and leverage their resources. Open access areas were staffed by professionals and trained students during all hours of operation (about 80 hours per week). Phone assistance was also available. Off hours, users could send email to a special address to register a problem or request assistance or information.

While the focus and computing issues have changed over the years, the Instructional Technology Support Group has remained integral to the successful implementations and academic initiatives on campus. At first, the support group was more involved in training users on applications and motivating them to use the applications in creative and productive ways. Now problems and questions are related to configuring computers for connectivity from home using modems and DSL, configuring email clients, and publishing web materials. Drexel recognizes that regardless of how technologically sophisticated the community becomes, support remains necessary to assist users as the complexity of their tasks increases.

Another related benefit gained from the microcomputing program and the accompanying technological developments is the success of our students in their professional experiences as a result of their computing and technology skills. First in their required cooperative education experience and second in permanent placements, Drexel students have distinguished themselves professionally through technological contributions and innovations on the job. They have a competence and comfort with technology different from most students, and for the most part, they have a broad understanding of many roles technology has in business and industry. They are able to exploit technologies available in the workplace with ease and confidence and many times are technology innovators in spite of their junior status.

Finally, others have benefited from our microcomputing program as we have shared what we have learned with other organizations helping them to integrate technology. In many areas we paved the way, did the research, and in some cases made mistakes that others could avoid and benefit from. We have worked closely with the School District of Philadelphia to help them with various academic technology initiatives. Our "pioneering" enabled us to help them to move ahead with technology more easily and quickly in many areas than we did. We worked extensively with the Mayor's Commission on Literacy in Philadelphia and with several homeless shelters and community centers to assist them in integrating computers into their programs and services. Our assistance helped them transform the way they did business and provided services, assistance, and opportunities to the community. More recently we have worked with small colleges in the area to "raise the bar" and improve the efficiency and effectiveness of the way they offer computing services and support on their campuses. Our role as mentor and advisor is a great advantage to a small school in that they don't have to learn and develop everything on their own but can apply the template of policies, procedures, and standards we have developed and tested.

Lessons Learned for Mature Institutions

1. Recommend standards for computers.

2. Define and publicize what you support and to what extent.

3. Make use of electronic resources to leverage people resources.

4. Document policies and procedures and publicize them to create a mechanism for dealing with infractions or special requests, demands, etc.

5. Provide users with information, training, and documentation to empower them to become independent, skilled, and more confident in solving their own problems and answering their own questions.

6. Provide extensive training and supervision to student employees to expand staff resources.

7. Recognize the different needs of administrative and academic users and assign staff accordingly.

8. While all staff should have a common base of knowledge, beyond that level, allow them to specialize according to their interests, knowledge, and skills and assign them to roles and responsibilities compatible with their specialties.

9. Provide a forum for regular and open communication with support staff, so everyone is equally aware of changes in infrastructure, software licensing, policies and procedures, and operations.

10. Ensure a forum for support staff and infrastructure staff to communicate and to work together to upgrade, improve, and modify systems.

11. Provide support targeting specific groups, particularly faculty, to enable them to increase their use of technology.

12. No matter how sophisticated users are, they will never outgrow the need for support.

13. Publicize, promote, and advertise support services available to the community—redundancy is necessary and good—and communicate any changes to be made in labs, etc.

14. Involve faculty and users in the process of making changes in everything from classroom arrangements, policy, and resource procurement.

15. Reach out to administrative and academic departments to promote services, determine needs, and enlist support.

16. Provide regular training for staff, both from external sources, when necessary, and from internal personnel on a regular basis.

17. Automate as many functions as possible on the web—classroom reservations, picking up and managing accounts, submitting problems, checking grades and transcripts, etc.

18. Make use of help-desk software—commercial or home-grown—to assign and track problems. It improves efficiency, effectiveness, and accountability.

19. Purchase site licenses whenever possible to ensure access to the same tools for everyone.

20. Create committees of lab managers on campus to ensure departments are making technology purchases and decisions in concert with standards established by the IT department.

CONCLUDING INSIGHTS

While many were skeptical of the microcomputer at first and suspected it to be just another educational gimmick, time has proven it to be educationally effective, enriching, and here to stay. Colleges and universities should recommend and expect that students will bring computers to campus and should publish this expectation in all admissions collateral. Parents and students expect to bring their computers to class or purchase one upon entering, and they demand a technologically rich environment regardless of the size or type of school they choose. It is important to recognize that one size does not fit all and the lasting, practical program is based on choice within reason and standards. Provide recommended standards, provide extensive support, and provide the best infrastructure you can afford and students will use their computers whenever and wherever they are able. Faculty and students will exploit the resources you provide to expand, enhance, and enrich the educational experience on your campus and thus will be better prepared to succeed and compete in the professional workplace.

Contact Information

Janice Biros
Associate Vice President
Office of Information Resources and Technology
IRT/Instruction
Drexel University
Korman Center 6-112
Philadelphia, PA 19104
Phone: 215-895-2667
Fax: 215-895-6777
Email: biros@drexel.edu

SUNY Morrisville Unplugged

Jean L. Boland
Raymond Cross
Jessica A. DeCerce
Anne Englot

"IT REALLY WORKS!"

When students at the State University of New York at Morrisville arrived on campus in August 1999 to begin the new school year, they found some things had changed over the summer.

"What are these little black boxes attached to the walls? Has the college installed speakers in the dorm hallways? Is it surveillance equipment?" they wondered.

They soon understood the little black boxes when they were given wireless cards to insert in their laptops. These cards, they were told, are your tickets to freedom. You no longer require cords to access the network or the Internet.

Wireless technology was a somewhat foreign concept to most students, and some were skeptical of its abilities. Though they understood in theory how the technology worked, it seemed unlikely to succeed in a rural setting like Morrisville. Skeptical or not, all students were excited to try it out.

Residents of East Hall were the first to get wireless cards. As Jean Boland, the college's assistant vice-president for technology services, stood outside the residence hall talking to a colleague, she noticed a young man walking down the glass-enclosed hallway, open laptop in hand, staring intently at the screen. After taking a few steps, his face broke out into a huge grin. "It works! This is awesome!" she could hear him say.

Word of the new technology spread quickly, and by the end of the day, students could be seen surfing the Net and checking email in their dorm rooms, the hallways, the dining hall, and even outside in the quad. So began "wireless fever" at SUNY Morrisville.

HISTORICAL BACKGROUND AND FUTURE PLANS

SUNY Morrisville has been synonymous with technology since its inception as a college of agriculture and technology in 1908. The college has evolved with the definition of the word "technology" over the past 93 years, changing its programs and methods of teaching, learning, and working to fit the technological changes in society and the workplace.

Acknowledging the fluidity of technology and its effects on society at large, we must alter what we do to accommodate them. Specifically, we identified five societal paradigm shifts that would have a dramatic impact on our institution:

1. Connectivity—the shift away from a specific location or geography to connect electronically where convenient

2. Mobility—the ability to move technology from place to place

3. Portability—shrinking in size but increasing in capacity

4. Mass Customization—the individualization of products at mass production prices

5. Velocity—high speed and instant gratification

We also assessed changes in the workplace:

1. Workers are changing jobs and occupations much faster than in the past, causing a dramatic need for workforce upgrading and retraining.

2. Workers are shifting from being employed by a company to being self-employed.

Concurrent changes in the educational world reflect paradigm shifts in society and the workplace.

1. Distance learning or, better yet, distance-free learning accommodates workplace mobility and permits individuals to pursue careers that previously would have required them to take time off from their jobs to learn.

2. Information in libraries is becoming more accessible, with many catalogs and journals searchable electronically.

3. Learners' expectations are changing. Students look for relevance, real-world applications, and realistic experience in the learning process. They ask questions like, "Why is it important?" and "Where will I use it?" and want to be shown how.

4. Students' access to faculty and staff has expanded. Mobile and nomadic learning technologies allow students to work and learn anywhere at any time.

Given this backdrop, SUNY Morrisville has designed a technology-focused environment, an entrepreneurial learning community, and a business-oriented institution. Our goal is to make technology transparent to the user so it becomes a more effective tool in the pursuit of learning within a specific discipline. More than that, we want to give students tremendous comfort with technology and entrepreneurial and business principles so that they will have the confidence and practical knowledge to start their own businesses. When they graduate from SUNY Morrisville, students leave with a laptop in one hand and a business plan, ready to present to a venture capital group, in the other. We have developed a four-phase technological strategy to accomplish this goal.

Phase I: Mobile Computing

Mobile computing, as defined by the SUNY Morrisville strategy, meant placing technology in students' hands. We began Phase I in 1998 as a beta test, giving laptop computers (IBM ThinkPads) to students in four programs. All faculty members in each program committed to integrating laptop use into the course curricula. The laptop was to be used as more than a word processor. For example, our architectural technology department utilized the laptop for computer-aided design and modeling techniques.

The institution had to build a new infrastructure, which included making classrooms and common areas laptop-compatible. Specialized laptop classrooms were built to include a data and power port for each seat. Laptop lounges and a laptop café provided students with access to the Internet and the campus network away from their dorm rooms, classrooms, and the library. Students, faculty, and staff could now take the technology with them, connect from varying locations, use it at a high speed, and customize it to fit their needs. Mobile technology on campus soon moved from pervasive to transparent as it became part of the students' day-to-day lives. This fall, our fourth year in mobile computing, 2,000 students will be using laptops in 42 different curricula.

Phase II: Nomadic Learning

While students found increased mobility with laptop technology, they were still tethered by a network cord. Total mobility, with students accessing the campus network and the Internet from anywhere on campus at anytime, required a complete wireless network. Only one other campus in the nation had undertaken this task but without incorporating the laptop. The solution was to develop a partnership with a corporate expert, in this case, Raytheon.

Wireless transmitters were installed in all residence halls, academic buildings, and "hang spaces" such as lounges, the dining hall, and snack bars, and students were given wireless cards to insert in their laptops. Wireless transmitters were placed so that no matter where students were on campus, they would remain within a 500-foot radius of a transmitter, allowing for totally seamless wireless use.

This nomadic learning environment allows students to move freely, thereby promoting collaboration, which, as part of the overall vision of SUNY Morrisville, better equips students to enter the workforce.

Phases III and IV: Continuous Communications and Totally Digital Environment

We are currently engaged in Phase III of our technology strategy, termed "Continuous Communications." Our goal is to replace all phones in the residence halls with cellular phones and provide our students with a digital communications tool that we hope to build future applications around.

Our proposed Phase IV, which we're calling a "Totally Digital Environment," involves the blending of our cellular and wireless network systems into what we call a mobile commerce environment. The system will allow business transactions to occur smoothly in the cafeteria, bookstore, business office, and even off campus. We believe this process will eventually lead to the total integration of access tools from cellular phones to personal digital assistants (PDAs) to other, similar devices.

BASIC CHARACTERISTICS OF SUNY MORRISVILLE

The State University of New York at Morrisville is located in rural central New York, 35 miles southeast of Syracuse. The campus's nine residence halls house approximately 70 percent of the college's students. More than 75 two- and four-year programs in diverse majors, such as architectural technology, agriculture, and automotive technology, are offered.

Forty-two different curricula with a total of 2,000 students are participating in the laptop program. Each program integrates the use of laptops in a different way, but all have one thing in common: The laptop is an integral part of the curriculum and not simply a word-processing tool.

The college was ideally suited to increase its integration of technology. President Raymond Cross had launched a laptop program as the CEO of Northwest Technical College in Minnesota. He knew the benefits and could provide the leadership and vision to make the project successful. His commitment gave our college faculty and staff the energy, enthusiasm, and financial support to implement the project. Without the president's unwavering support, which included his understanding that we were going to make mistakes, we would not have been able to successfully implement ThinkPad University.

The college's existing physical infrastructure played a large role in the decision to fully implement wireless technology. The institution had been moving toward a very robust network for a number of years. However, given the cost and the extensive need, keeping up was difficult. The college decided to develop a complete gigabit Ethernet backbone, expand it to the academic areas, and integrate it with a wireless capability. We built the wireless network to foster easy collaboration of teams of any size at any location with laptops and Internet connectivity. Additionally, it reduced the cost of wiring all residence halls.

EDUCATIONAL RATIONALE

Taking Phases I and II of our technology strategy from theory to reality required intense planning, attention to detail, and constant communication with stakeholders. The changes in infrastructure were a perfect mirror for the changes in campus culture—we had to start from the ground and build upward to the user.

From the moment our campus decided to become a laptop university, we formed a working committee representing all the stakeholders. Their support and involvement were critical to success. We generally defined stakeholders as any campus group whose job function would change as a result of the implementation of the laptop program. Administrators and faculty with diverse interests and knowledge developed a project plan, including action plans to deal with implementation tasks and issues to be resolved. A responsible individual was assigned to each task and regular status-reporting meetings were held. For example, the director of financial aid was responsible for determining if and how the student laptops could be covered by available financial aid. Each committee member took responsibility for completing action items for his or her area, which resulted in a buy-in to the whole laptop university concept. Everyone had a vested interest in a successful implementation.

The faculty were perhaps the most crucial group. Without their resounding support, the laptop program would surely fail. We believed that faculty readiness, which is a part of institutional readiness, can be measured by evaluating the number of faculty in three groups. The first group is commonly referred to as the "zealots." They are generally very enthusiastic about adopting and using technology. In fact, they may be so zealous that they scare off other potential adopters, and their enthusiasm may also prevent them from making appropriate decisions to integrate technology. The second category of faculty is called the "resistors." They act on the belief that the use of technology will overwhelm the discipline and/or cause faculty to avoid discussions related to the discipline. The third group, called the "indifferents" or "neutrals," can be divided into two subcategories. Some may be indifferent but receptive with guidance. The others align with the resistors because they believe that technology is intrinsically inappropriate for the classroom.

At SUNY Morrisville, the zealot group was rather large and composed of faculty who were very serious about their academic disciplines. Conversely, there were very few resistors. The indifferents predominantly wanted to understand how to integrate their classes with technology better and what benefit it would be to their students.

Given the unusual level of faculty readiness, the integration of technology into the academic culture would be straightforward once the infrastructure was in place. Our faculty are very supportive of ThinkPad University because their participation is not mandatory. Every fall, the vice-president for academic affairs sends out a request for proposals (RFP) to all faculty. The RFP memo clearly states that all faculty in a curriculum must agree to participate in ThinkPad University before an RFP can be submitted for that curriculum. The memo asks each proposal to address the following questions:

- What is the program of study and which faculty will be involved?
- How will the program use laptops?
- How many laptops will be required for incoming freshman?
- How many laptops are needed for faculty?
- How will computer skills and applications be integrated into the curriculum?
- What is the extent of the participating faculty's computer expertise?
- What computer skills are currently required of students?

- How will this project affect student admissions, retention, and outcomes and contribute to the overall fulfillment of the college's mission/vision?

- How will laptops be handled for part-time students?

- Can an existing laptop classroom be used or will additional facilities be needed?

A committee composed of administrators, faculty, and deans representing each of the schools reviews the proposals and selects which curricula will become part of ThinkPad University starting with the following fall's freshman class. From then on, all communication to prospective students in those curricula includes information on their involvement in ThinkPad University. Each faculty member in a new ThinkPad University curriculum receives a new laptop, which will be the same model as their incoming freshmen will receive. Overall, the faculty have been very supportive and anxious to participate in ThinkPad University. We typically receive more proposals each year than we can effectively implement.

CHANGING THE WAY WE TEACH AND LEARN

Currently, 86 of our 165 faculty teach in laptop curricula. Making the switch from a traditional to a laptop curriculum requires a great deal of work by faculty, both on the individual and the departmental level. Anne Englot, assistant professor of architectural technology, was one of the first faculty members on campus to integrate laptop technology.

> Reflecting upon how the integration of computer technology has affected my teaching, I realized that it has allowed me to employ a more consistent pedagogy. I am now able to use methods intrinsic to the teaching of architectural design—cooperative learning, dialoging, and student presentations...

> One of the biggest advantages of digital presentations is the ease with which they can be made available to students for repeated viewing. Both my presentations and those the students create can be housed on the campus network or the Internet, where students can use them to study for quizzes and exams. The presentations can be made to be interactive—posing questions and then providing answers, in many different formats—in words, images, sounds, or hyperlinks.

In the design studio not much has changed in terms of method, rather, the computer is used to increase efficiency and communication: drawings once printed for students to share for design projects are now CAD (computer aided drawing) files residing in a shared network folder. The picture boards showing the site of the projects are now digital and accessible by all students simultaneously. Student-student dialog and student-professor dialog can now take place across time and space.

Perhaps the greatest improvement in efficiency can be seen in the creation of the architectural portfolios critical to the student's job search or application to continue their education at a professional school of architecture...

...Colleagues in architecture firms have called to tell us they were wowed by our students bringing laptops to their interview. Not only were they able to show their portfolio on the computer, but they were also demonstrating their acuity with the computer.

To help faculty to become comfortable with, and proficient in, both the hardware and software used by the laptops, the Teaching and Educational Change (TECH) Center was created. Staffed by a full-time faculty member, the TECH Center gives faculty and staff access to a wide variety of hardware and software. The center director and other faculty and staff members provide instruction and training in topics, such as desktop publishing, online course management, instructional design, and software, such as Excel, PowerPoint, and Photoshop. Without offering training and support for faculty and other stakeholders, the campus buy-in and high morale would have crumbled.

Another important support component was the help desk. Staffed by two full-time professionals and a cadre of work-study students, the help desk is open to students, faculty, or staff members who have a question about, or problem with, their laptop. The help desk is open every weekday, and problems can also be discussed by phone or email. If a problem cannot be fixed immediately and the computer has to be sent out for repair, the help desk will provide a temporary replacement to ensure the student has a laptop at all times.

FINANCING THE PLAN

Being a part of the State University of New York system, it was necessary to be cognizant of the many financial regulations in place. For example, if state budget money was used to buy the laptops, then students could not own the computers in the end. That was counter to our vision and goals; using the laptop and the technology associated with it was to become a part of the students' lives that would continue with them after they left SUNY Morrisville. Reclaiming it after graduation would be equal to taking away their class notes.

Therefore, we worked with Morrisville Auxiliary Corporation, a not-for-profit company chartered by the state of New York, whose primary function is to provide nonacademic services to the campus, to develop a plan where students could lease-to-buy the computers from the college. At the end of the payment plan, the students would own the computers. Since the laptops are required for courses of study, financial aid could be used to help cover the cost. The laptop would appear as a line item on the student's tuition bill and usually would be paid in four semester payments.

Before each fall and spring semester, the number of new laptops needed is calculated. The auxiliary corporation then negotiates a price based on specifications determined by the technology services department. Additional costs associated with the laptop program (software, wireless cards, carrying case, virus protection software, insurance, extra year of warranty) are factored in, and a final cost to the students is calculated.

The auxiliary corporation purchases the laptops with funding obtained through its local bank. This option provides flexibility, since the corporation and bank have an established relationship.

One suggestion we have for institutions that are considering a laptop program is to properly evaluate the loss of laptops due to early withdrawals and attrition. This should be factored into financial issues.

TO GOVERN OR NOT TO GOVERN?

We worked hard to operate within existing computing practices. The infusion of technology into students' lives was designed to open doors, not to close them. Laptop policies would require college faculty and staff to spend time policing students, not encouraging them to practice.

For example, many colleges and universities limit the space students may use on the college network. In order to encourage rather than limit student laptop use, network file space at SUNY Morrisville is not limited. We simply ask each student to keep no more than 100 MB of web space and no more than 100 MB of personal network file space. Students can actually save as much as they want. We periodically monitor network file space and have written some software that identifies students who have used more than a specific allotment of web space or personal network file space. The software automatically sends them an email asking them to reduce their space utilization to 100 MB or less by a certain date. The number of students who receive this email is usually no more than two dozen. If a student doesn't reduce his or her space allotment by the given date, then we turn off access to the network. When students come to see us because they no longer have access, we talk to them about reasonable disk space utilization and their options for burning CDs. Interestingly, the outcome is usually a unique, positive, personal relationship with each student, many of which have resulted in some excellent student suggestions, which we have implemented.

CONSTANT APPRAISAL

Evaluation at each step of the process is just as important as planning. We will discuss six successful outcomes of our strategy.

Laptop-inspired student collaboration

Collaboration encourages students' social development, exposes them to a diverse population, and prepares them for the working world, where more and more companies function in a team-task environment. The integration of laptops into academics made it easier for students to collaborate by giving them mobility, and wireless technology has freed them to collaborate wherever and whenever they choose. Our technology strategy has given students a common denominator.

Unconscious use of the laptop

Students require little training on how the laptop computer and wireless network function. This allows them to immerse themselves in the technology, quickly using it unconsciously. It's not a novelty or a toy for them; it is a way of life.

Changing college image

Though SUNY Morrisville has always been a college of technology, until the advent of the laptop program in 1997, the college image was primarily agriculture-focused. Our technology strategy and the resulting positive publicity has rapidly expanded the college's image to include high technology. We are now mentioned in the same sentence with exclusive, well-regarded technical schools, which has had a positive effect on enrollment.

Marketability of students and readiness to enter the workplace

Our graduates leave SUNY Morrisville with something besides a degree—they leave with expertise in technology that many of their peers from other institutions do not have. This expertise makes them infinitely more marketable to employers and gives them a leg up when it comes to initial productivity.

Faculty and staff technical development

The adoption of a laptop program and wireless technology made it necessary for faculty to quickly become experts in an area where many were uncomfortable. The laptop and wireless technology gave the faculty a common ground. The TECH Center is an integral part of faculty and staff development and helps them learn both general and curriculum-specific programs.

CRITICAL FACTORS FOR SUCCESS

The adoption of a department-by-department, curriculum-by-curriculum laptop program, coupled with the integration of wireless technology, has transformed the college and all who are connected to it. For readers who are considering such a program or have just begun, we offer these three critical success factors:

Significant faculty endorsement. The faculty is the front line in this program. Their interface with the end-users (students) must be enthusiastic, prepared, and supportive.

Executive vision and leadership. The implementation of such a comprehensive program absolutely requires leadership and vision at the highest level. In our case, it was Dr. Raymond Cross, our president, who developed a clear technology strategy for the college and encouraged faculty and staff to experiment and to ask questions.

Campus stakeholder involvement. Getting stakeholders involved early and throughout the implementation process aided development in two ways: First, the participation of stakeholders from different areas ensured that concerns or necessities for each would be addressed, and second, the stakeholders became the unofficial technology ambassadors to the rest of the campus and community.

LESSONS LEARNED

Lessons Learned for Beginners

1. Faculty ownership and buy-in is a critical success factor.

2. Never underestimate the power of teamwork.

3. Involve all stakeholders in decision-making and implementation.

4. Presidential support is crucial.

5. Financial commitment and creativity are needed to build the supporting infrastructure.

6. You can never have enough bandwidth to the Internet or network disk space.

7. Involve parents as early as possible and explain the details of the program to them.

8. A laptop inventory tied to your student information system is the most accurate way to forecast need and the most efficient means of inventory control.

9. Laptop distribution is a major production. Define each step and automate everything possible to reduce time in lines.

10. Encourage, don't limit, student and faculty/staff use.

11. Support faculty development for the integration of technology in the classroom.

Lessons Learned for Mature Institutions

1. Campus-wide wireless connectivity adds another dimension to ubiquitous computing.

2. The academic dynamics of the campus will change, and students will be working and learning everywhere.

3. Students will begin to use the laptop as a tool intuitively rather than consciously.

4. The image of the college will change.

5. Develop strategic partnerships versus buying from vendors.

6. The biggest financial challenge is what to do with laptops used for a semester or two and returned when a student withdraws or is academically dismissed.

7. Students will become more attractive to businesses, both after graduation and for summer employment and internships.

8. Help desk support provided by individuals with student-focused, service-minded attitudes is imperative.

9. Personal attention to detail is a critical component of an accurate laptop inventory.

10. The help desk must be close to most college classrooms.

Contact Information

Jean L. Boland
Assistant Vice President for Technology Services
SUNY Morrisville
P. O. Box 901
Morrisville, NY 13408
Phone: 315-684-6053
Fax: 31- 684-6453
Email: bolandjl@morrisville.edu
Web Address: http://www.morrisville.edu

Raymond Cross
President
SUNY Morrisville
P.O. Box 901
Morrisville, NY 13408
Phone: 315-684-6044
Fax: 315-684-6109
Email: crossrw@morrisville.edu
Web Address: http://www.morrisville.edu

Jessica A. DeCerce
Public Relations Officer
SUNY Morrisville
P.O. Box 901
Morrisville, NY 13408
Phone: 315-684-6041
Fax: 315-684-6041
Email: decercja@morrisville.edu
Web Address: http://www.morrisville.edu

Anne Englot
Assistant Professor of Architecture
Galbreath Hall
SUNY Morrisville
P.O. Box 901
Morrisville, NY 13408
Phone: 315-684-6281
Fax: 315-684-6679
Email: englotas@morrisville.edu
Web Address: http://people.morrisville.edu/~englotas
            http://academics.morrisville.edu/architecture

Ubiquitous Computing at Drew University

Alan Candiotti

In the winter of 2000, 16 years into its ubiquitous computing program, Drew University undertook a marketing study to assist college admissions. Prospective and current students were asked which aspects of the college were most important to them, including technology and ubiquitous computing. Some of us were a bit skeptical: How would ubiquitous computing be ranked against small classes, strong majors, and good faculty? The result: Among prospective students, laptops were "the third most frequently cited asset of the university." Current students were found to be "more appreciative of their laptops than prospective students are. In fact, only their small classes and close contact with the faculty receive more praise." It is hard to imagine that the program's designers could have wished for a better response.

HISTORICAL BACKGROUND AND VISION

The Drew ubiquitous computing program, known since its inception as the Computer Initiative, always had a dual vision: to support teaching and learning and to prepare students for careers in a sophisticated technological world. At different times, one or the other of these visions has predominated, but both have always been important.

The idea for the program arose from doing something else. In the early 1980s, the university's only academic computing facility was a multiuser minicomputer for programming courses. Students soon discovered a line editor that included rudimentary word processing features and began using it to write papers, causing excessive demand on the facility. The university equipped a room with personal computers, mostly to accommodate the word processing demand and relieve the other system. A few creative faculty members saw the value of a personal computer for each student, launched the idea of including a personal computer with the price of tuition, and won the support of the college faculty and administration. Not only would the computer be valuable to students, but it would distinguish the college among all other liberal arts colleges in the country during a demographic downturn in admissions. In September 1983, the college faculty voted 63 to 2 to initiate the program with the 1984 incoming class. Faculty received personal computers in the spring of 1984 and new students in the fall. Despite some skepticism, the program was an immediate success, and it was quickly obvious that it would continue.

Along with using the computer for word processing and spreadsheets, we imagined that we would easily write software for use in many academic courses. Some efforts included programs that traced the digestive and circulatory systems for biology and taught grammar for first-year English. We soon learned that writing software usable by others was extremely difficult and time-consuming, and that little was available for purchase. We tried authoring system software and funded students to program grammar and statistical analysis software in the summer. By and large, the software, especially the user interfaces, was too primitive to have a major classroom impact. Productivity tools, word processing in particular, were very widely used, and a host-based email culture developed. In 1988, the university installed a system that gave everyone access to text email, the Internet, and the library catalog. That year, for the first time, students received laptop computers, after a survey indicated a great preference for portability. The end of the 1980s witnessed heavy use of productivity tools and universal connectivity but not too much academic application outside such areas as computer and social science, which had previously used computing facilities. While word processing and email had indeed created a revolution, the university wanted more.

In the early 1990s, emphasis shifted to academic applications. A formal faculty development program was initiated, reaching well over half of the faculty with intensive workshops. Classroom computing and projection facilities were installed, and professional staff who focused mainly on classroom and faculty support were hired. Academic applications, using commercially available software, began to proliferate and reached most departments.

Because of the early installation of the host-based email system, the university was late in installing a true network. Some people thought we already had one, and others were not convinced that we needed one. The rapid emergence of the World Wide Web and the increasing universality of networks convinced the university to install one in the mid-1990s. By the late 1990s, every student had a standard notebook computer and a network connection in his or her residence hall, and the Internet and web pages were accessible to everyone.

Each year, more faculty use technology in their courses, whether web pages, presentation tools, email or other online discussions, Internet-based research, shared course files on the network, or course-applicable software. Students also use their computers independently—developing web pages and using the Internet and the computer to enhance their productivity. In general, they adapt to new technology faster than the faculty do. We are launching a wireless component to the campus network that will eventually enable ubiquitous connectivity. We still envision that all students will use their computing devices to learn from all available sources, to enhance their productivity within and outside of their academic courses, and to engage in two-way communication within and outside of the university. The university will provide this facility to all students, regardless of their financial means or other circumstances, and support it for the length of the four-year liberal arts curriculum. We will also try to supply a baseline level of services to all students, faculty, and staff without requiring special requests and to keep that baseline level as high as possible. We believe this environment creates a culture that encourages students to make the most of it.

BASIC CHARACTERISTICS OF THE COLLEGE AND THE PROGRAM

Drew University comprises three schools. It was originally founded as a Methodist seminary in 1866. A nonsectarian liberal arts college was founded in 1928, and a small graduate school was added in 1955. The liberal arts college enrolls about 1,500 students, about 80% of the university's full-time-equivalent students, and is the original and primary home of the Computer Initiative. The seminary, now called the Theological School, has been participating in the program for its three-year, major degree program since 1995, and its faculty also participate in the faculty development program. The graduate school has been in and out of the program and is currently not participating.

The College

The college is nationally ranked in major publications but below the highest tier of liberal arts colleges. Student SAT scores average just over 1,200. About half of the students are from New Jersey, another third from New England and the Middle Atlantic states, and the remainder from most of the other states and several foreign countries. Over 90% live on campus, and almost all the rest commute from family homes nearby. The university endowment is about $200 million, with significant fractions restricted to the college and the Theological School. Tuition, largely from the college, provides about three-quarters of the university's operating budget. Drew has one of three Phi Beta Kappa chapters in the state of New Jersey (along with Princeton and Rutgers). The college has no peer schools within the state but quite a few in neighboring New York and Pennsylvania.

The college offers 26 majors in liberal arts disciplines, including computer science, but not business or education, although it does support nonmajor programs in those areas. In the last decade, the most heavily enrolled majors have been biology, economics, English, political science, and psychology. Faculty number about 115 and have a venerable tradition of excellent teaching and supportive relations with students. Although faculty research has recently been more emphasized for promotion and tenure and the faculty are well published, the strong teaching tradition continues. The spirit of cooperation in the educational enterprise was described a decade ago, in a decennial report from an accrediting agency, as "a love affair between faculty and students."

The Computing Program

All full-time students in the college receive a notebook computer, inkjet printer, and standard software configuration whose cost is covered by four years of tuition. The computers are purchased in bulk, after competitive bidding, in the summer before the students arrive and distributed during orientation week. A CD-ROM, including the software configuration, the network client software, the supported email reader software, and initial settings for the hardware, is created, duplicated, and distributed with the computers, so that after a few minutes all the new students are able to use the campus network. Students use the same computer for four years and keep it upon graduation. Those entering late or leaving early can buy in or out by paying a fixed amount for each semester less than eight of their attendance.

Although vendors bid independently each year, we have purchased student computers from only five in eighteen years and have generally remained with a vendor for several consecutive years. Our current vendor is Compaq. In order to obtain the most current model possible within our budget, we buy as late as possible in the year but still early enough to secure late August delivery.

Services provided with the computer include a warranty for four years of hardware support. The computer center provides diagnostic services, maintains records, and ships the computers back and forth to the vendor for repair when necessary, at no cost to the student as long as the repair is within the standard warranty. We attempt to obtain favorable prices for students in the event of user damage and also represent them if their computer is a "lemon." A student-staffed desk provides comprehensive help to students, faculty, and staff for supported software, which includes an office suite, browser, email reader, virus protection, and web-development software. Some faculty have one of the notebook models provided to students, but most have desktop computers, and about a dozen classrooms are also furnished with desktop computers attached to the network and projectors.

The campus network includes connections in every faculty and staff office and classroom, a port-per-pillow in the residence halls, and ports in such public areas as the library, student center, and residence hall lounges. After receiving a nightly data feed from the administrative computing system, a service developed by Drew professional staff and known as ATTIC (Academic Technology Tools for Instructional Computing) automatically assigns drive space to the faculty and students in each academic course. This space is used for shared data files, email lists, electronic reserves, discussion and chat, submission and return of assignments, and course web pages. All students have network access, university email, and access to the Internet while on campus at no additional charge. ATTIC and email are heavily used and have become basic campus utilities. Web-based interfaces to both email and network files allow off-campus users with Internet service providers to obtain access.

Faculty make heavy use of classroom presentation tools, including software and image databases, course web pages, and Internet-based information resources. A continuing development program and a special lab provide them with support services. Outside of a few courses such as English writing, statistics and science labs, students are not observed bringing their computers to class very frequently. The reasons are not fully clear, but an important factor is that the ubiquitous computing program predates the availability of most academic software and the campus network, so student and faculty usage patterns developed accordingly

The heavily residential nature of the college, proximity of commuting students, and the tradition of close contact between faculty and students mitigate against distance education. Although many courses have online components, the Internet is used in both learning and general communication, and many faculty members and students have web pages, not all shared information is web-based. Many services, including shared network space and licensed software, are designed first for on-campus use, with secondary web interfaces developed when possible.

Educational Rationale

In the beginning, the primary educational rationale was that having a personal computer would increase student productivity enormously and also prepare them for work in the modern world. The idea was so novel that no one really knew who the stakeholders were. Faculty and university administration had to be convinced that the idea was educationally sound and logistically and financially feasible. The faculty quickly approved the idea by a huge vote. Proponents had credibility and, aside from some concern that computers would change the liberal arts college into a technical school, no one really saw any downside. Personal computers were new and exciting, and no one was yet invested in them, so standardization was not an issue. For the administration, the concerns were financial and logistical. The financial concern was met by increasing the annual tuition by 25% of the cost of the equipment in addition to the normal annual increase. The university was able to raise the cash for the purchase, and the tuition increase would eventually cover equipment costs. A team of faculty, administration, and technical support staff created a schedule, and, as they met its milestones, the community saw that the logistics were feasible.

The decision to change from desktop computers to laptops was made in 1988, based on a student opinion survey that was over 90% in favor of laptops, even though discussion brought out that processing power and other features would have to be sacrificed in order to obtain laptops within the budget. For some time, we offered a desktop option, but interest waned until we discontinued it.

By 1990, personal computers were no longer a novelty, and the true educational rationale—providing 24-hour, universal access without having to operate all-night labs sized for peak demand—had surfaced. By that time, trustees and others were beginning to question whether productivity applications, such as email and word processing, which had become universal, were sufficient to justify the program. We hired an energetic new director of academic computing, who increased the pace of classroom applications by installing mediated classrooms and starting a strong faculty development program that attracted significant government and foundation grants. Now, faculty and students use their computers in every academic department, and electronic communication is the fabric of daily life. The fact that all students, regardless of financial resources or other circumstances, have a supported computer gives them enough access and ownership that they learn how to manage and use it. Generally, when new technology appears, students lead the faculty in adopting it. Many students had their own web pages on our system before the faculty, and students also adapted instantly to using shared files on the network. Although by now most students would bring computers without a ubiquitous computing program, the high-profile program undoubtedly adds incentive to use their computers creatively and effectively.

In 1996, the administration questioned whether the program limited the university's ability to charge market tuition rates and compete with other schools that did not include a computer in tuition. At the next college faculty meeting, faculty from all areas made positive comments, and the faculty voted unanimously to continue the program. Then the student newspaper endorsed a tuition increase to raise the annual budget for the computers. After 13 years, the program had been reaffirmed by both faculty and students.

Initially, standardization was not an issue: No one had a personal computer in 1984, so providing one model to all faculty and students was not controversial. The rationale for uniformity was clear—the faculty would know exactly what the students had, and standards would facilitate hardware support. The issue remained uncontroversial through the 1980s because just about everyone at Drew was trained on our standard systems. Entering students seldom had laptops of sufficient power to compete with the Drew issue, and most had already factored the Drew program into their planning.

The challenge arose with faculty who arrived since the late 1980s, had experience on the Macintosh, and questioned the all-Windows environment. Others countered that the faculty should use what the students use and that the Macintosh's 1980s software advantages had largely vanished. A recent survey of operating system preferences indicated that about 15 faculty members prefer the Macintosh, but only about 3% of students and 3% of staff share that preference. Nevertheless, the issue of standardization still causes some tension as it conflicts with complete faculty autonomy.

Governance Issues

Although the program is in its 18th year, governance structures are anything but clear. After securing initial faculty approval, the university has been content to leave most decision-making about the program to information technology staff and administration. Interest in reviewing contenders for the next year's system flagged as few faculty wanted to commit time in the summer, and quick decisions were frequently necessary at the 11th hour. A standing Academic Computing Advisory Committee, including elected faculty, a student representative, and academic and IT administrators, reviews major decisions, and ad hoc committees have formed to deal with major changes, particularly two changes in the supported office suite. Recently, a

University Technology Committee has been formed to consider all technology issues facing the university.

Financing Issues

Reckoning the program's cost is complicated. By now, even in the absence of the program, most students would probably purchase and bring their own computer. Including 25% of the equipment cost as an add-on to tuition then merely replaces an existing expense, and the only added expense the university would bear is the price of four-year financing. About two full-time staff positions are occupied with computer procurement and distribution and hardware support, and increased use of computers in teaching demands extra support personnel. Thus, the program costs three or four staff positions and the four-year financing. On the other hand, if one assumes that, even without this program, tuition would remain the same, including the increment, then the cost of equipment for 2,000 students is about $1 million per year.

There are some savings. Most liberal arts colleges in our peer group provide about one public computer—in the library, computer center, or departmental labs—per 10 students, even though a high percentage of their students bring computers. Some students do not have computers; others have computers that cannot run the software for assignments; and, in the absence of standards, some departments may require PCs and others Macs, and no students have both. Because all of our students have computers whose capabilities we know, we provide approximately one public computer per 20 students. On the other hand, we operate a special faculty lab with computers and other facilities, so we may not realize all of the savings that come from fewer public computers.

Considering all of these factors, the program is affordable, provided the university has the cash flow to manage the financed purchase and the tuition capacity to include the cost of the computer without restricting other programs.

Operational Issues

Anyone who talks to Drew students cannot fail to observe how much computer technology is integrated into the fabric of life. During the history of the program, the library catalog was automated and a web interface constructed; student and faculty web pages proliferated; faculty incorporated classroom presentation tools; electronic mail became the dominant mode of communication; academic resources were placed on the campus network; and use of digitized images and sound in fine arts and music courses increased. While these changes have occurred elsewhere, at Drew they occurred simultaneously

and are assumed as a matter of course. Indeed, because of ubiquitous computing, the dominant student culture uses the computer thoroughly. A telling
indicator is the pressure students exert when their computers are not working;
we have developed a web-based system that looks like the FedEx tracking system to inform students of the status of computers under repair. Computers
are simply necessary. Students learn to use their computers effectively, to
manage them, and to use networks and the Internet to an extent that serves
them well when they enter the workplace.

Computer use in the academic program is quite broad, with applications
in every department. In a few areas students bring their computers to class,
but in most cases the use is more subtle. When a shared drive was set up on
the network, files appeared quickly in hundreds of courses. If, suddenly, faculty could not assume that every student had full access to a computer, the network, and the Internet, literally every course in the college would be significantly altered, some drastically. When asked recently how student life would
be without the ubiquitous computing program, student government leaders,
none of them science or technology experts, responded that this was one program that really helped them.

Finally, the program provides a very strong platform for adopting new
technology. Students and faculty were quick to adopt email, create web pages,
and use the network. Now, we are piloting wireless networking, and, if the
pattern continues, it will undoubtedly take hold quickly, without any need
for carts full of notebook computers. The program creates an atmosphere that
encourages students to focus their creativity on using their computers.

SOME PROBLEMS TO AVOID

Little mistakes that might have seemed big at the time are easy to remember:
trying to share one university-owned printer between two first-year students
rather than providing each with a printer. Over the longer term, our largest
mistake was in not establishing the Computer Initiative as a regular academic
program, with the same reviewing and budgeting mechanisms as all other
academic programs. While the program may have boosted college admissions
and may still and while it could be viewed as simply a technology service, the
real reason for having this program is to facilitate teaching and learning, and
the questions that should be asked about it concern whether students are
learning more. Because the program does not have a regular academic reporting channel, university administrators and trustees sometimes view it as an
isolated program or even as part of college admissions. Too often, we hear references to "free computers" or questions about whether the program "gets us

more students" or is "worth the money." Although these questions might be asked about the English or chemistry departments, they would be answered in an academic context, and the same should be true for the Computer Initiative.

Further, the budget should be handled like other academic budgets, with provision for growth when needed. We lived with the original per-student dollar allocation from 1984 to 1996, achieved a 25% increase then because it was impossible to procure adequate computers for less, and have been at that level since 1996. It is now very difficult for students to use the same computer for four years, and seniors have the oldest computers but the heaviest software demands. While some technology committees have recommended a two-year refreshment or a midterm upgrade, the budgeting channel is not regularly established, and we have not yet achieved it. Despite the rigors of establishing new academic programs and all the reviews entailed, the Computer Initiative should be treated as such.

CONCLUDING INSIGHTS

A ubiquitous computing program will change a school's character and it will have a very high profile. There is every reason to believe that the change induced by such a program will be beneficial and that students will receive a better education because of it. To succeed in such a program, it is important to do the following:

1. Be clear about the way the program integrates with the school's mission.

2. Obtain a clear faculty buy-in and establish the same mechanism for periodic academic review as every other academic program.

3. Know what you are trying to accomplish and be wary of goals that are not within reason—enhancing education and preparing students for work in today's world but not magically transforming education.

4. Know that no single course or faculty member will be able to accomplish the whole program's goals and that effective use of broad technology systems—word processing, electronic mail, the Internet—are, by themselves, revolutionary.

5. Establish a regular budget and a means for changing it when necessary.

6. Provide faculty training, support, and recognition, including arrangements for training part-time faculty.

7. Arrange for program leaders with the right vision and competence and include them in academic councils.

After 18 years, our students and alumni have very good things to say about our program, and they are undoubtedly the best judges.

LESSONS LEARNED

For New Programs

1. Establish the program as an academic program with academic review structures.

2. Establish a clear financial plan and budget and a mechanism for revising the budget annually.

3. Understand the role of standards, and obtain agreement from faculty and administration.

4. Coordinate the program with faculty development and training.

5. Have reasonable expectations for the effect of ubiquitous computing on the academic program. Pay attention to general applications as well as those for individual courses.

6. Pay attention to the logistics of equipment distribution. It's harder than you think.

7. Sign procurement contracts with major vendors specifying their responsibilities for delivery and equipment that fails initially or repeatedly.

8. Have a structure for repair of student computers.

9. Don't accept a vendor's first bid. The market is competitive, and vendors will improve their bids to get your business.

10. Models and prices change fast. Don't buy too early in the year and then be forced to deliver a discontinued model to your students, while they read newspaper ads for models at fire-sale prices.

For Mature Programs

1. Remember that the students are the center of the program. Everyone else is important, but the program serves the students directly.

2. No matter what equipment you buy, it gets old faster than you think, so consider how third- and fourth-year students will run current applications.

3. Keep your admissions office informed, and help them review their literature so that it is accurate.

4. Keep language describing the program in university publications and web sites as consistent as possible.

5. Make sure your upper administrators get the same view of the program as your students. They might not look at that view unless you show it to them.

6. Encourage the faculty to take advantage of the fact that 100% of students have computers.

7. Have a good system for repair of student computers and try to keep turnaround time as low as possible.

8. Coordinate the program with your campus network. If 100% of students have computers, they should all have network accounts, and network applications should affect all of them.

9. Provide enough faculty training and support and continue as the technology changes.

10. Because of the campus standards, students can be excellent support personnel, which is good for them and good for the university.

Acknowledgment

I would like to acknowledge the assistance of Neil Clarke, director of Academic Technology at Drew University, in discussing this article, as well as his inestimable help in operating the program for these many years. I also acknowledge Richard Detweiler, now president of Hartwick College, for his formative work and early leadership of the program.

Contact Information

Alan Candiotti
Professor of Mathematics
Assistant Vice-President, University Technology
Drew University
36 Madison Ave.
Madison, NJ 07940
Email: acandiot@drew.edu

The Virtuose Program at L'École des Hautes Études Commerciales de Montréal

Paul Mireault

A NEW DAY!

Dear Sir:

I have a complaint about Professor Jones. I sent him an email two hours ago, and he hasn't answered it yet. How do you expect us to learn when we can't get help when we need it? Can you please instruct Professor Jones to check and answer his email more often. Thank you.

Martin Smith

Things have changed since I was a student. I may have gone to a professor's office less than 10 times during my whole undergraduate study. As a professor, I used to see some students very often, the "regulars," but never see most students outside the classroom. Now, however, with increased use of the Internet and email, specifically, I find that I communicate with many more of my students on a one-to-one or a one-to-many basis.

ABOUT HEC MONTREAL

L'École des Hautes Études Commerciales (HEC) is a French-speaking business school affiliated with the University of Montreal but functionally independent. In fact, it can be viewed as a small, specialized university with a single, self-contained faculty; it has its own economics department, mathematics department, sociology department, and so on. Being self-contained greatly simplified the implementation of the instructional technology initiative. We did not have to consider sending our students to other faculties that were not using laptop computers or take care of students from other faculties in our laptop classes.

The largest among HEC's 30 management programs are the Certificate program (5,000 part-time students), the BBA program (3,600 full-time students), the MSc in Management program (400 full-time students), and the MBA program (250 part-time and full-time students). In all, more than 10,000 full-time and part-time students, including 950 foreign students from 60 countries, are enrolled in day or evening courses.

About 4,000 students are in programs requiring a laptop. They must commit to the Virtuose Program, whereby all participants use laptop computers loaded with standard software. The computers are most conveniently and inexpensively available for purchase through the student coop, although students may buy independently.

THE DECISION TO REQUIRE LAPTOP COMPUTERS

Since his appointment as dean of HEC Montreal in January 1995, Jean-Marie Toulouse has been convinced that information technologies should occupy a growing place in business schools. His understanding of the business world indicated that the use of technology as a daily tool is a constant concern for companies and that business schools must offer cutting-edge technology training to the decision-makers of tomorrow. If HEC were to compete internationally, incorporation of technology into both the pedagogy and curriculum would be essential.

Early discussions with IBM, which promoted the ThinkPad University concept, led to a vision of each and every student equipped with a portable computer. The students would be able to use their computers whenever they had time and wherever they were located. Faculty, assured of having a classroom of network-connected students, could experiment with, and develop new, pedagogical methods.

Laptops Versus Desktops

In the workplace, there are two kinds of employees. "Sedentary" employees have an assigned work area equipped with the usual business tools, like a telephone, a desktop computer, a nearby fax machine, and so on. "Nomad" employees either have no assigned work area or are out of the office for most work hours, usually equipped with a mobile telephone and a laptop computer. But whether sedentary or nomad, all employees must communicate and have access to all their computerized business tools.

While most of our students will be sedentary employees when they graduate, as long as they are students, they have all the characteristics of nomad employees: out of their "office" most of the time and no assigned work area. The main difference is that the nomad worker may have to circulate in a wide geographical area, like a city, and the student is usually confined to the campus or a few buildings on the campus. The smaller area, however, still doesn't make a desktop solution feasible. Our students commute. They don't go home or to a dorm between classes; they stay in the building. Even if we could afford to give everyone a desk, the student would be away from it most of the time. So nearly 200 four-station worktables were placed throughout our two, very large campus buildings—in the corridors between classrooms and in public areas. Each of these worktables has four electrical outlets and four network connections. In the library, another 200 single-station worktables were installed in designated areas, each with an electrical outlet and a network connection. Almost all the classrooms have all their seats supplied with an electrical outlet and a network connection—over 3,500 in total.

In the long run, we expected that we would have three to four thousand students in the Virtuose program and realized that we would not be able to give them adequate support if we had multiple brands. The drivers from brand to brand and even within the same brand are different, and each computer manufacturer has its own way of distributing them. So we were contemplating maintenance and support hell unless we standardized on one specific manufacturer and model. That was a quick decision. We decided to go with Microsoft Windows, because all the software used by faculty run on this platform. Macintoshes and Unix machines are not prevalent in business schools.

LAPTOPS AND LEARNING

Some faculty members have found innovative ways to use technology in their classrooms. Some methods could have worked in a computer lab but would have occupied the lab for a full class period even when the students would use the computers for only 20 or 30 minutes. The laptops can transform a fully wired classroom into a lab when needed.

For example, an economics professor, in his federal budget course, presents an Excel worksheet simulating how some key decision-making variables, such as income tax and subsidies, have an impact on key results, such as the national debt and the GNP. He then divides the class into three sections and has students work with the spreadsheet, by themselves, with different objectives: reduce the debt, increase the GNP, etc. The students send their results by email, and the professor chooses two or three to present their solution to the class.

In a marketing course, when they talk about brand recognition, all the students participate in a survey about a contemporary product, like a brand of beer. The results can be shown immediately, and the professor can lead students through a cooperative analysis. The best part of this course is when the professor shows the results of the same survey from a neighboring classroom and then another and another. The results are almost always similar, and finally, the students understand what we teach them in statistics: A sample size of 30 to 50 is often good enough, and an increase does not add much more information. For many students, it's an epiphany, a lesson they will never forget.

FINANCING ISSUES

Running a program like Virtuose is expensive. The support team has two full-time and about 25 part-time student employees, with an annual budget of close to $400,000 (Canadian) for salaries and other expenses. The Virtuose assistants are assigned to a teaching department, which allows every department to develop personalized contact with their assistants, who become their technological reference. During the summer months, they work with faculty, helping them develop their courses' web sites and experimenting with different technologies. During the regular semesters, they help faculty to develop and maintain their courses' web sites and investigate new uses of technology.

Since the program began four years ago, we have added an average of 1,800 network ports and electrical outlets each summer. At the moment, we have 7,200 ports, and the total investment has been around C$4 million.

OPERATIONAL ISSUES

One of the most positive impacts of the Virtuose project has been the increase in student quality. In the province of Québec, the Education Department has a central database of all students and their R-Score, which is a calculation comparing each student's grade to the class average. One might not agree that the R-Score is a valid indicator of a student's ability, but it is a surrogate measurement that is well accepted. The R-Score has been used, at HEC, as a cutoff for admission offers.

However, in the first year that Virtuose was implemented in the BBA program, we thought that the sudden cost increase would lower the number of students accepting our admission offers, so we lowered the R-Score cutoff point, thus extending admission to more students. To our surprise, the acceptance percentage increased. This double increase brought more students than we expected, and we had to open more sections of the core courses. It was a nice problem but a problem nonetheless. Since the introduction of Virtuose in the BBA, the lowest R-Score has risen steadily, indicating that the quality of the students has increased each year.

Another phenomenon that we recently observed was a decrease in applications. When it happened, it caused some consternation: Had the popularity of the program been tarnished without our knowing it? We imagined such headlines as "Costly program spurned by students." The final analysis showed that the overall number of applications decreased only because potential applicants knew what the required R-Score was, and those who were below did not bother to apply, thereby saving the application fee. The number of applicants who were above the last year's R-Score increased.

We also noticed a significant improvement in students' technological ability. In a survey, students answered self-assessment questions regarding their ability with different computer tasks and programs both before their admission and two semesters later. A majority indicated an important increase in their overall ability.

Virtuose has introduced a major change in the work habits of the entire school. Email has become the official means of communication within HEC, and all the administrative units now communicate via email, including students who are not in a Virtuose program.

LESSONS LEARNED AND CONCLUDING INSIGHTS

Embarking on a laptop project is risky, because you cannot afford to fail and you have to make significant investments, but when it succeeds, you will find it is worth it. Students love it, even though a few don't like the extra cost and don't think it contributes to their education. Faculty members are divided: Some don't like it, because they find that students get distracted during class. Some like it a lot, because they can now try out pedagogical ideas that they would not have dreamed of before. The next big challenge is to encourage more faculty to become part of the latter group. From our experience, important lessons include the management of expectations, especially stressing that all professors will not use laptops in all classes. Prepare for the worst. Provide support and plenty of it.

Contact Information

Paul Mireault
Director of Technologies
École des Hautes Etudes Commerciales de Montréal
3000, Chemin de la Côte-Sainte-Catherine
Montréal, Québec, H3T 2A7
Phone: + 514-340-6492
Fax: + 514-340-6899
Email: paul.mireault@hec.ca
Web Address: http://www.hec.ca/en

A Faculty Perspective on Ubiquitous Computing: Clayton College & State University

Donna Wood McCarty
Elliott W. McElroy

Clayton College & State University (CCSU) is not a privileged private institution for affluent students with high entrance test scores. It is part of the public University System of Georgia and composed of many first-generation college students from blue-collar or rural backgrounds, approximately half from a minority group. Many entering students are less than fully prepared for college and have relatively low scores on entrance tests. The average student age is 28, and a large number are working adults, returning to school to further their educational goals. CCSU is a commuter campus in a metropolitan Atlanta suburb and currently serves just under 5,000 students each semester.

THE INFORMATION TECHNOLOGY PROJECT (ITP)

During the 1996–1997 academic year, the Georgia university system's Board of Regents adopted mission guidelines for institutions in each sector. The following component was included for institutions in the state university sector: "technology to enhance educational purposes, including instructional technology, student support services, and distance education." CCSU faculty responded by drafting a new mission statement: "Clayton State is dedicated to placing a major emphasis on technologically advanced access to information and to ensuring that all students acquire a working familiarity with the uses, limitations, and ethical implications of modern informational technology."

Online teaching and learning were then established as priorities for the Academic Affairs section of the university's Strategic Plan (1999). The emphasis on instructional technology has been continued as part of the university's Strategic Planning Themes for 2000–2001.

In keeping with the goals of the university system and its own institutional mission, CCSU implemented a rather bold educational experiment in the fall of 1997. The Information Technology Project (ITP) was intended to achieve a total infusion of information technology into instruction. In preparation for the program's implementation, all faculty as well as students in the Honors Program were equipped with laptop computers and unlimited Internet access both from campus and home and received an array of training in the applications that were to be common to all students and faculty. At the beginning of fall quarter 1997, faculty were issued upgraded notebook computers, and in late fall 1997 into early 1998, all students were issued university-owned notebook computers. The Microsoft Office suite of applications, identical to those of the faculty, were part of a technology package that included unlimited Internet access from home and campus, a help desk for support and repair, and training. The package was financed by a student technology fee of $200 per quarter ($300 per semester beginning fall 1998).

All involved certainly wanted to prepare students for careers in the next century, but the major concern was that the project have a positive impact on the quality of student learning. Such educational outcomes as the ability to communicate in writing and to think critically are of primary importance to CCSU's faculty and administration, and everyone wanted to be sure that ITP was enhancing these overriding goals. While grades, standardized test scores, and other indices are of use in ensuring that a program like ITP benefits students, these measures cannot capture the faculty's and students' rich experience. Furthermore, standardized measures cannot provide the detailed information useful for improving the program and sharing with other institutions considering an infusion of technology.

THE ITP EVALUATION STRATEGY

A strategy for examining ITP's impact on teaching and learning was established to answer the major question: Will the systematic use of information technology enhance learning productivity? "Learning productivity" was defined as the effectiveness of instructional approaches, the efficiency of resource use, and the satisfaction of faculty, students, and employers. "Information technology for instruction" was defined as student and faculty use of notebook computers, the Internet, and other educational technology. Students were to be given surveys and standardized tests, but a method of data collection that would provide more detailed and contextual information about the project's impact was still needed.

Two CCSU faculty members developed a qualitative study called the Chronicles of Change (McCarty & Robinson, 1999), based on the premise that an infusion of technology at a university will succeed only if the faculty believe that these tools and methods can help students learn. For this reason, the chronicles collected faculty journal entries that responded to prompts, such as teaching and learning effectiveness and efficiency, campus culture, and communication.

Just prior to fall quarter 1997, volunteers were solicited for the project through faculty meetings and email. No tangible rewards, such as stipends or release time, were offered. Initially, 23 faculty across all four schools volunteered. The proportion from each school roughly mirrored the proportion of full-time teaching faculty across schools. Participants also represented a range of attitudes toward ITP from extremely supportive to quite skeptical. Since they were volunteers, whether their experiences were typical of the faculty-at-large is unclear. However, their profile, their attitudes toward ITP, and their disciplines suggest that their observations are likely to represent other faculty.

After three months, it became apparent that 18 of the volunteers were committed to the project and would participate long-term. Fortunately, the loss of five volunteers did not skew results in favor of any one school or attitude toward ITP.

Data analysis was facilitated by a widely used software program for the analysis of qualitative data, Non-Numerical Unstructured Data Indexing Searching Theorizing (QSR NUD*IST). Data were imported into the software and coded by topic. Each concept could be reported under as many topics as appropriate. The journal data were then examined for patterns and their exceptions.

The examination revealed that time was an extremely important factor in the events following ITP implementation. Patterns suggested that implementation occurred in a three-phase process, with each phase exhibiting unique characteristics. Periodic examination of the data enabled the administration to modify implementation strategies. The data suggest that these alterations were critical to ITP's success.

Phase I

In Phase I of the project, optimism and enthusiasm ran high. Both faculty and students anticipated that ITP was going to have a very positive impact on teaching and learning at CCSU. In a pre-ITP survey, 89% of faculty and 71%

of students were moderately to entirely positive when asked how they felt about students having their own notebook computers. Similarly, 97% of faculty and 91% of students believed that technology would enhance the students' learning experience (Clayton College & State University, 1999). Clearly, most faculty and students had faith in technology as a change-agent and that ITP would enhance learning. In the words of one faculty chronicler:

> I believe that students' critical thinking skills will be strongly enhanced as a result of ITP, beginning at the moment that they first use the laptop. Getting an email account, learning to connect from remote locations, using the Internet, and generally learning to use the computer are just the beginning of the critical thinking and problem-solving skills that will be required of students. As they become more experienced users, critical thinking will be a natural part of using the Internet more efficiently. Students will be encouraged to work independently and to discover the vast array of information that is at their fingertips. Also, as they learn to use Microsoft Office, their problem-solving skills will develop. I think this will be one of the major accomplishments of ITP.

The optimism expressed in the survey results and some of the Chronicles of Change was tempered by a healthy sense of realism about the impact of ubiquitous technology. Another faculty member stated:

> Critical thinking skills will be greatly improved if classes engage in activities based on interactive tasks. Learning how to type with a word processor or to complete exercises on the computer will not move students to think more critically. If activities are designed to stimulate thinking on several levels, however, the students will think more critically. In other words, if they combine reading, discussion, and writing with the power of the computer to generate group discussion, research, and peer evaluation, they will improve their critical thinking skills.

Yet another expressed cautious optimism about the project's impact:

> I do not believe that ITP by itself will enhance the teaching/learning process. The teaching/learning process will be enhanced if teachers and students regard the program with

enthusiasm and put it to good use. The process will be degraded if teachers of students get so bogged down or caught up in the technology that the process gets away from them. It is completely up to the humans involved to use these tools as such in creative ways.

A very small subset of the chroniclers were not at all optimistic about ITP's benefits and predicted that the technology would not have any major impact on teaching and learning. One faculty member expressed this view as follows:

To date there is no recognized diet pill that really works and allows people to lose weight, yet millions of people try these pills every year. We constantly look for the "quick" fix to problems. I think the computer is the new diet pill in education. We hope (expect, think, etc.) that this will cause students to be better critical thinkers, more educated, use more resources, study longer, harder, more thoroughly. I do not think this will be the case...

Very early in project implementation, the faculty expressed a great deal of optimism about the ways in which ITP would enhance the efficiency of their instructional efforts. An analysis of the Chronicles of Change data supports the notion that ITP had a dramatic effect on efficiency. Innovations, such as the ability to send messages to entire classes at once via a listserv and to place class materials on a faculty member's web site added greatly to the efficiency of both teaching and learning.

Faculty were also quite concerned about how the project would affect communication skills. Virtually everyone associated with the project noted a rapid escalation in communication between faculty and students and between students. Most of the comments submitted to Chronicles of Change in Phase I focused on the joys and frustrations of burgeoning email use. The extent to which writing skills were actually improving as a result of all of this communication was unclear; while some faculty seemed to use the technology to enhance writing, others seemed to focus almost entirely on sharing information. The potential to enhance writing skills was apparent, however, as faculty commented on students sending in successive drafts of assignments and being more likely to try different kinds of sentences, development patterns, and word choices because of the ease of word processing.

However, the ability to communicate with students made teaching an around-the-clock job, and the volume was rapidly becoming burdensome.

The rapidity with which the project caught on led to huge demand on the supporting infrastructure, which persistently hampered reliability. Students turned out to be less technologically savvy than expected, and much time and energy was expended in assisting them with basic skills, like saving and managing files. While the project produced many positive effects early on, the negatives created frustration and somewhat diluted the benefits.

Phase II

Phase II could be summed up as a time of reality-checks and midcourse corrections. By early Phase II, the project's novelty had diminished, and faculty chronicle entries were characterized by a heightened sense of realism and, in some cases, frustration. Making ITP a success required a very steep learning curve; faculty skill levels at the use of technology for instruction were building rapidly, and so were their concerns over the difficulties of implementation. However, when asked whether they would continue with ITP, the chroniclers unanimously expressed their desire to continue.

As the faculty's comfort with technology increased, their frustration at the difficulty of using technology effectively for instruction increased. Highly creative and adventurous faculty seemed to find solutions to problems. Others became blocked during Phase II and mired in frustrations. Technical support and many workshops on technological skills were provided on campus; however, support that targeted faculty desire to use technology effectively for instruction was not provided in any formal sense. The huge time commitment required to produce instructional technology seemed to discourage the faculty chroniclers.

Phase II was an interesting part of the implementation process, because it encompassed both extremely positive experiences of faculty and students, who were getting more and more proficient with technology, and extremely negative experiences, as their expectations of reliable access were not being met. Underlying the growing frustration was the sense that substantive improvements in the quality of teaching and learning could be made if faculty support and system reliability could be improved.

Some midcourse corrections were needed. While faculty development surveys were also of great use, the Chronicles of Change proved particularly useful in determining strategies for program improvement. The chroniclers expressed many ideas that were useful in formulating a plan to enhance the effectiveness of ITP support. The observation that instructional technology support belongs in Academic Affairs as opposed to the Office of Information Technology Services was extremely valuable. One chronicler clearly stated the key concern: "I wonder why instructional technology doesn't fall under the oversight of the VPAA like everything else connected with curriculum."

Based on the Chronicles of Change as well as responses to a faculty development survey, the Faculty Development Coordinating Committee devised a set of recommendations (Clayton College & State University, 1998) for the improvement of support, including an instructional technology center that would provide:

- The hardware and software to produce instructional materials

- Careful staffing by academically oriented professionals with strong instructional design expertise (not "techies")

- A faculty mentoring program, where faculty with expertise in instructional technology can assist their peers in a collegial atmosphere

- Workshops, online information, and other instructional materials for beginning, intermediate, and advanced-level faculty that would be designed, taught, or distributed through the center

- Student assistants to work with faculty on projects

- A pleasant, collegial, stimulating environment for faculty to discuss instructional issues and work on projects of mutual or individual interest.

The data persuaded the administration to find the resources necessary to implement the faculty committee's recommendations. A conveniently located center, the HUB, administered by the Office of Information Technology and Services (OITS), continued to offer hardware and operating system support. Support for software use, however, was transferred to new units in Academic Affairs: a Center for Instructional Development (CID) and a Faculty Instructional Development Lab (FIDL). Once these targeted improvements were implemented, it remained to be seen whether satisfaction with ITP would improve.

Phase III

Faculty comments during Phase III were strikingly different from those of the previous phases. They indicated that ITP had become a fully integrated part of CCSU, even for those who were initially resistant. One chronicler stated, "...ITP is part of our culture, for better or for worse. Personally and professionally, I think we are the better and our students in the long run will benefit greatly." The faculty also expressed satisfaction at what they described as an increased student acceptance of, and confidence in, their use of technology:

"Student acceptance is way up ... as they become more familiar with the tool they are using it more and in more ways. It would be hard to go back to the old way of doing things."

These observations are supported by a follow-up survey. When asked how they felt about students having their own notebook computers, 84% of the faculty were moderately to entirely positive after almost two years of project implementation; this figure is only slightly down from the 89% who expressed such positive responses prior to implementation. On the same item, 75% of the students reported that they were moderately to entirely positive about having their own notebook computers. Students were slightly more positive than they were pre-ITP, when 73% reported positive feelings. When asked to what extent technology had enhanced the CCSU student learning experience, 91% of the faculty and 84% of the students still had faith in the technology's benefits after two years. These figures are down slightly from the 97% and 91%, respectively, who responded positively before implementation.

One aspect of the project that was controversial from the beginning was the use of laptops during class. Both faculty and students were much less positive about this prospect before implementation, with only 52% of faculty and 65% of students expressing moderately to entirely positive feelings. Following almost two years of implementation, these figures were down to 47% of faculty and 53% of students. For many faculty and students, computers are best used between and after classes as an enhancement to preparation. Before implementation, 99% of faculty and 88% of students believed that students would use their computers for coursework outside of class; these figures were 96% for faculty and 76% for students after two years of implementation (Clayton College & State University, 1999). These results suggest that both faculty and students remain very positive about ITP but became more realistic about the challenges as they gained experience.

The survey results are consistent with the Chronicles of Change data. The faculty express continued satisfaction with ITP, and the expressions of frustration that characterized Phase II steadily decrease. Throughout Phase III, faculty consistently note the increased reliability of email, the web server, and other infrastructure-related aspects of the project. Faculty unanimously praised the newly established CID and FIDL. These comments are typical: "The FIDL is providing excellent support for a myriad of functions"; "has been a lifesaver ... always available if I need help"; "The CID is the best thing that we could have done for the faculty"; and "[FIDL] continues to provide wonderful classes, which improve our comfort level and our expertise." Faculty mentoring provided additional stability and collegiality to the faculty support effort.

In Phase III, the frustration provoked by unreliable systems and inadequate faculty support is channeled into a new area: the challenges inherent in harnessing technology's power for true pedagogical improvement. In a positive trend, the faculty noted that ITP was beginning to enhance instructional effectiveness in significant ways. For example, one faculty member noted, "I think that ITP has caused me to reassess the way I teach, and the materials I have created as a result of technology have, for the most part, been improvements over my previously used class materials." Technology was being used more and more selectively.

Classroom sessions have had to be rethought with the new system. All of this work has made a good number of them prioritize what is important to education and to dump things that are stylish, but provide no substance. Hence, many of them have dropped the grandiose to use the computers for all aspects of their teaching. They are beginning, instead, to go with those few things that are proving to be useful, like email for communication after class and the web for delivering documents they used to hand out.

The faculty journal entries reflect a significant shift in focus from mastering the technology itself to striving to find the proper pedagogical uses of the technology. This shift seems part of a natural process, as the faculty become comfortable with the technology. As with any complex activity, the basic processes become more automatic with time, allowing greater attention to more sophisticated aspects. Throughout Phase III, many of the chroniclers expressed the desire to achieve a balance between time expenditure and instructional efficacy.

However, time and experience were not eliminating all concerns regarding the use of technology for instruction. What began as relatively simple problems of learning to use technology and to adapt existing instructional materials to new formats were evolving into difficult pedagogical issues. For example, one faculty chronicler noted an unintended consequence in developing a web site:

> Making so much of the course material available on the web causes students who are prepared for class to be bored when I review the material. I'm having to think of ways to create discussion points and classroom activities to augment the material. It is difficult, as it has always been, to design instruction that meets the needs of all types of students.

The faculty also expressed concern about a tendency on the part of some students to become too dependent on technology. One chronicler feared she might be creating more dependent students, although that was clearly not her intention:

> At the same time that I am assuming increased understanding of the software, I find students accepting the availability of the technology as if it has always been here. They commonly ask, "Will this be on your web site?" or "Will you email us these class discussion notes?" In one way, this is good because it shows familiarity with the computer technology, but in another way I see these questions as foreshadowing of my becoming an enabler for a lack of notetaking or listening in class. They might become too dependent upon my having everything posted on the web or upon my willingness to save discussion notes and save as an attachment to a class email.

Phase III is an interesting time in which both the benefits and the limitations of technology become better understood and accepted by the faculty. It is an exciting time, as substantive improvements in pedagogy become common. The faculty are acquiring a sophisticated understanding of how to enhance the principles of good instruction through the application of technology.

ITP CHOICE

Ubiquitous computing is now standard at CCSU. However, because so many students have access to powerful computers through employers and family and so few are using computers during class, the university no longer issues computers or requires students to pay a $300-per-semester technology fee. Instead, each student is required to provide his or her own notebook computer and Internet service provider. Each student computer must meet campus specifications, and some majors require students to have a computer that meets additional specifications.

The Office of Information Technology and Services continues to maintain the campus infrastructure, 25 model classrooms with power outlets at all student stations, and 21 classrooms with data ports at all student stations. It also provides hardware and operating system support at the HUB, including repair of in-warranty computers from four preferred vendors. OITS also provides staff and supervision for the new Student Software Support Services

Center, where campus-licensed software is installed on student computers and students receive initial training in its use. OITS also maintains a server to provide each student a campus mailbox.

The newly expanded Center for Instructional Development assists in technology-enhanced instruction, and the Center for Learning Enhancement supports students engaged in online learning. Both centers report through Academic Affairs.

KEYS TO SUCCESS: OPERATIONAL ISSUES

The success of Clayton State's Information Technology Project is, in our judgment, a result of several operational features: the change strategy, faculty development activities and support functions, and a focus on accomplishments valued by the faculty.

1. The project's change strategy followed these basic assumptions:

   - The availability of user-friendly technology itself is a powerful change agent. Efforts to make the technology user-friendly included providing distribution lists to the instructor of each class, 24-hour turnaround on repair or replacement of dysfunctional computers, and easily accessible hardware and operating system support at the HUB.

   - Faculty are committed to helping students learn. If they are provided a tool which will enable them to be more effective in helping students to become active learners, this commitment will motivate faculty to discover ways to maximize its effectiveness.

   - Students who have paid for a service and found it effective in some classes will develop expectations for its use in other classes. Student expectations for a positive learning environment powerfully motivate faculty.

Based on these guiding assumptions, faculty were encouraged to find their own comfort levels in using the technology. The administration set no minimum expectations for computer use in each class because, in our judgment, it is vital to allow natural processes like faculty concern for students drive the project rather than artificially imposed rules and sanctions.

2. Faculty support developed in response to their needs as identified and expressed in the Chronicles of Change, faculty surveys, and informal discussions. Administrators learned early on that their efforts to develop the

faculty were doomed. Administrators had to become active listeners and to work continually to provide ways for faculty to communicate and then let the administrative response be guided by further listening to faculty leaders.

3. Keeping the project focused on accomplishments that are valued by the faculty was and is essential. When faculty indicated discomfort with the development of external degree programs offered at a distance entirely by online instruction, the university dropped the plan. Success can be realized only when all the major players feel that their participation and support are consistent with their values, principles, and beliefs.

As illustrated in the Chronicles of Change excerpts, the university's most significant blunder was the delay in realizing that support for faculty in using technology as a tool for teaching should be under the aegis of Academic Affairs. Faculty and student expectations regarding instructional technology could have been managed more effectively. While the rewards have been great, the challenges have been significant and beyond what many administrators, faculty, and students anticipated.

CONCLUSIONS

Implementing the Information Technology Project has been a fascinating journey. While countless conclusions can be drawn, the following are among the most important:

- Despite the natural tendency for faculty and students to become obsessed with the technology itself, keeping the focus squarely on the teaching/learning process and on improving pedagogy is important.

- The expectation that technology will transform teaching and learning virtually overnight is unrealistic; adapting to the challenges of using instructional technology takes time and is a multiphase process.

- Given sufficient time, effectively infusing technology into instruction can yield significant benefits for students, faculty, institution, and community.

- As faculty become more sophisticated technology users, they become increasingly selective about when and where to apply each tool. They need support services to assist them in learning to use technology effectively for instruction. Faculty colleagues can be valuable in providing such support.

Future analyses will be undertaken to understand the impact of the evolving Information Technology Project at Clayton College & State University. We hope that improved teaching and learning will continue to be the focus of this adventure in technology.

REFERENCES

Clayton College & State University. (1998). *Recommendations, spring 1998.* Faculty Development Coordinating Committee, Internal Document.

Clayton College & State University. (1999). *Faculty and Student Satisfaction Survey Data.* Academic Effectiveness Information, Vice-President for Academic Affairs web site, http://adminservices.clayton.edu/vpaa/academiceffectiveness.html

McCarty, D., & Robinson, K. (1999). *The chronicles of change project, a qualitative study—Summary of results.* Unpublished Report. Academic Effectiveness Information, Vice-President for Academic Affairs web site, http://adminservices.clayton.edu/vpaa/academiceffectiveness.html

Miles, M., & Huberman, A. (1994). *Qualitative data analysis* (2nd ed.). Thousand Oaks, CA: Sage.

Contact Information

Donna Wood McCarty
Professor of Psychology
School of Arts and Sciences
Clayton College & State University
5900 N. Lee St.
Morrow, GA 30260
Phone: 770-961-3467
Fax: 770-960-4335
Email: donnamccarty@mail.clayton.edu

Elliott W. McElroy
Vice President for Academic Affairs
Clayton College & State University
5900 N. Lee St.
Morrow, GA 30260
Phone: 770-961-3485
Email: elliottmcelroy@mail.clayton.edu

Ubiquitous Computing at Seton Hall University

Stephen G. Landry

What is honour? a word. What is that word, honour? Air. A trim reckoning! Who hath it? He that died o' Wednesday.

William Shakespeare, *King Henry IV,* Pt. 1, V. i, 136–38

In the early morning hours of Wednesday, January 19, 2000, an intense fire swept through Boland Hall, the six-storied freshmen dormitory at Seton Hall University. Within minutes, the third floor was engulfed in flames, and, in its wake, the fire claimed the lives of three young men and injured 58 other students.

The tragic event not only devastated the suburban community of South Orange, New Jersey, it also stirred debate among campuses about the public safety of residence halls. For weeks and then months, Seton Hall was thrown into the national limelight. Everything was scrutinized, from the investigation conducted by the Essex County Prosecutor's Office to the school's sprinkler and smoke-detection systems. The local and national media camped out at the library for the first week to report on the story as it unfolded. The debate on the sprinkler system became a national issue concerning all campuses nationwide.

While this may not at first appear to have any connection to ubiquitous computing, having a strong technology infrastructure in place would prove vital in providing information and support to the university community and the community at large. The public's primary source for information was the main Seton Hall web site, http://www.shu.edu, which was accessible at all times. For the concerned student or parent, the site provided information about the school's closing and reopening. News briefings were posted as soon as they were relayed to the press. The site also became a way to reach out to the public. A plea for blankets and the announcement of a blood drive were both posted on the site, and the community responded at once. From January 19 to February 9, the main site received over seven million hits.

This tragic event disrupted the school's academic calendar. Students who had just returned from Christmas break were now asked to return home for another five days while the university reorganized. However, since all undergraduate students were equipped with laptops—the university had just completed its four-year laptop initiative—they were able to log onto the Internet for the latest news. All students, from freshmen to seniors, had connectivity and could readily get assignments and notes from their professors while on forced sabbatical. Chat rooms were set up to provide grief counseling. Within days of the fire, replacement laptops were offered to all residents of Boland Hall whose machines had been damaged.

Senior account managers with the school's Public Relations Department consider ubiquitous computing essential for today's colleges and universities, because it provides 24/7 accessibility and the immediate posting of current information, something that allows institutions to keep the lines of communication open both with the public and the members of their own community. A tragedy like the one that occurred on that Wednesday morning in January would not usually be an occasion for citing the success of ubiquitous computing, but had it not been in place, the ability to communicate with, and provide support for, our students, faculty, staff, and the public would not have been as swift or true.

First Stirrings

Ubiquitous computing at Seton Hall University officially began in August 1995, when 12 faculty and two administrators embarked on a flight to Raleigh, North Carolina. The university had just committed to pilot ubiquitous computing for freshman honors students in the School of Business. The 20 or so freshmen attended the bulk of their courses, including core courses in both business and arts and sciences, as a cohort. At the same time, the Business School was in the process of redesigning the college's core curriculum, which offered the university a tremendous opportunity to observe the impact of ubiquitous computing in the classroom. The 12 faculty from business and arts and sciences teaching these core courses were attending the Institute for Academic Technology (a joint venture between the University of North Carolina and IBM Corporation) to learn about technology in teaching and learning. The delivery of the IBM ThinkPad computers used in this pilot project was delayed (a situation that would occur several times in subsequent years), and so in true "just-in-time" fashion, the faculty's laptop computers were handed to them at the airport as they boarded the plane.

Seton Hall's ubiquitous computing program was planned and implemented with one goal in mind: to serve the university's mission in preparing students to be leaders in a global society. The integration of technology into the curriculum was a means to achieve this mission, not an end in itself. In implementing its vision for the management and use of Information Technology in preparing future leaders, Seton Hall also won distinction: the 1999 EDUCAUSE Award for Excellence in Campus Networking and honorable mention in the 2000 EDUCAUSE Award for Systemic Progress in Teaching and Learning competition. For the past three years, Seton Hall has ranked among the 50 most wired universities in the annual Yahoo! Internet Life Survey of the Most Wired Colleges and Universities.

Yet seven years ago, Seton Hall had many of the same technology problems that seem endemic to higher education: obsolete computer labs, unstable networks, lack of professional support services, disparate and disorganized allocation of technology resources, little integration of technology into teaching, and inadequate plans and resources to deal with the rapid obsolescence of technology. Seton Hall's technology achievements came about as a result of careful planning and the commitment of time and resources by the university's faculty and executive team. A certain amount of good fortune was also needed.

Seton Hall University is a private, midsized, Catholic-affiliated university located in suburban South Orange, New Jersey. The university has a Carnegie classification of Research/Doctoral II. Its 58-acre campus is located 14 miles from New York City, which can be reached by direct train from South Orange. Founded in 1856, Seton Hall is the oldest and largest diocesan university in the United States. It has 4,400 full-time undergraduate students, about half of whom are residents. Approximately 30% of undergraduates are minority students. The university has a total enrollment of 10,000, including the Law School and the School of Graduate Medical Education.

In 1993, Seton Hall University had just completed re-accreditation with the Middle States Association of Colleges and Universities. Two issues highlighted in the process were the lack of a strategic plan and the need to improve the technology infrastructure. As a result, the university began a strategic planning initiative. By the fall of 1994, "providing a technologically advanced learning environment for students and faculty" was identified as one of the university's strategic goals. In December 1994, the Computing and Information Technology Planning and Policy Committee (CITPPC), composed of six faculty members and five administrators, was established to assess the existing computing and technology environment and to recommend a long-range technology plan and budget.

Planning committees are often convened to address issues in higher education but with markedly mixed results. CITPPC and the resulting IT long-range plan were successful for a number of reasons. First, both the vice-president for academic affairs and the vice-president for finance served as co-executive sponsors, directly involved in the planning process. Their participation ensured that the plan could and would be implemented. Second, the planning committee included both faculty leaders and key administrators who were responsible for implementation. Third, the committee was given significant resources. In addition to a significant budget for travel, workshops, and consultants, committee members were given 50% release time for the spring 1995 semester. Since the full committee met 20 hours a week, this time for members to focus on technology issues and trends in higher education was one of the most valuable resources provided by the university. Fourth, the university engaged a technology planning facilitator. Finally, the committee sought a wide range of input. Over 140 faculty, staff, administrators, and students attended focus groups aimed at identifying technology needs. The committee administered surveys to faculty, staff, and students, and the 40% response rate indicated that technology was an important issue to the community.

In addition, the committee sought to create a compelling vision for how technology would enhance teaching and learning and improve administration. The report states, "This is the committee's vision for the future of Seton Hall University. It predicts the evolution of a learner-centered educational environment, a network-centered mobile computing environment with the digital library as the focus of network services, and a more efficient and responsive administrative structure" (Division of Information Technology, 1995).

As part of the planning process, CITPPC had a good deal of contact with the concept of ubiquitous computing. One of the papers read by the planning team on technology trends was by William Graves, then Interim Chief Information Officer (CIO) at the University of North Carolina at Chapel Hill. It outlined the case for ubiquitous computing. While we all recognized the value of technology to the education process, we were at first very skeptical of the cost of implementing ubiquitous computing. We hosted a team of faculty and administrators from the University of Minnesota at Crookston, the first "ThinkPad University," who had just implemented ubiquitous computing on their campus. We also sent a small delegation, including four committee members and the vice-president for academic affairs, to Wake Forest University, which was at the time piloting ubiquitous computing with the intention of making it mandatory for all freshman the following year. Another consideration was our School of Business's clear desire to require laptop computers for all business majors. The technology planning committee believed that the reasons to require laptops applied equally to all academic programs, while the value of a laptop initiative would be diluted if it were not ubiquitous. These experiences convinced us that it was possible for a university to successfully implement ubiquitous computing. How could Seton Hall University implement ubiquitous computing?

Seton Hall's strategic technology plan was completed in June 1995 and included a number of recommendations, including:

- Piloting ubiquitous computing, with planned expansion to a laptop requirement for all incoming freshmen by fall 1999

- Piloting fully online graduate degrees and professional certifications in order to expand the university's market for graduate and professional programs

- Making key student services available online via the web

- Upgrading the campus network, public computer labs, and other technological infrastructure

- Standardizing most campus technology, placing all computers and equipment on a regular replacement cycle, and, in particular, providing all full-time faculty with a laptop computer that would be replaced every two years

- Expanding and reorganizing technological services for students and faculty in support of these objectives, including support and incentives for faculty to use technology to enhance teaching and learning and, in particular, centralizing the support for campus core technologies (desktop and laptop computers, networks, email, etc.)

The technology plan and budget requested $15 million in new spending over the period from 1995 to 2000 to achieve these objectives. Approximately $5 million was a one-time infusion of capital from the university's quasi-endowment, approximately $5 million was raised through a new technology fee, and $5 million was obtained through internal reallocation (including the annual tuition increases).

The next challenge was to obtain support for the technology plan and budget from the university's executive team and Board of Regents. In this, we were fortunate in timing. The university's Board of Regents was very supportive. Father Peterson, chancellor of the university, was ailing, and Monsignor Robert Sheeran, then vice-chancellor for planning, was assuming the role of chief operating officer. In January 1996, he was appointed president of the university. As its architect, Msgr. Sheeran embraced and promoted the strategic plan, including the long-range technology plan and budget.

Adoption of the university's strategic plan dramatically changed the budget process for the next few years. Objectives from the strategic plan were funded, while other initiatives were deferred, and operating budgets remained flat or were reduced. Adoption of the long-range technology plan and budget changed the way technology was funded at Seton Hall, shifting most technology expenditures from capital to operating budgets. As a result, most computer and network equipment is now leased rather than purchased.

Obtaining wide buy-in to the technology was another challenge. Implementing the plan would mean a significant change in the way technology was funded, acquired, and supported. For example, departmental networks would be consolidated into one campus network, resulting in some local loss of control. Standardization of hardware and software would also result in some local loss of control. Here, the lack of technology on campus was actually a benefit. A large number of faculty lacked access to any computer or network. In particular, the university had a relatively small number of Macintosh computers, so we were able to largely sidestep the PC versus Mac debate.

The most powerful arguments for centralization and standardization came from the student focus groups and surveys. For example, while faculty in some departments were quite proud of their unique lab and network services, students found the array of hardware and networks quite confusing. Students wanted a single network account that would give them access to all possible network services from any lab. They wanted all computers to behave the same. This contrast was repeated for any number of technology issues: Faculty, who generally work within a single academic department, valued choice and customization, while students, who are generally academic nomads moving through multiple departments every day, valued standardization and predictability.

The technology planning committee made the case that hardware standardization might actually increase the instructional options available to faculty.

Consider, for example, a mathematics instructor who wishes to use a computer algebra system as part of her coursework. Compare the software options available when all students have a two-year-old IBM ThinkPad as opposed to a variety of platforms ranging from a brand-new Mac to a four-year-old PC. Paradoxically, more instructional options are available to the faculty when hardware for her students is standardized. Constant communication of these messages was critical in obtaining broad consensus across the university for adoption of the technology plan.

Implementing the Plan

Ubiquitous computing was one of the most visible changes brought about by the university's technology plan. For Seton Hall, ubiquitous computing is intended to be an innovative academic initiative involving three components: access to a laptop computer, access to a rich array of network services and support, and integration of technology to enhance teaching and learning.

From fall 1995 to spring 1997, the university's ubiquitous computing initiative grew to include approximately 50 faculty and 70 students. Based on the success of this small pilot, the university's executive team decided in late fall 1996 to expand in fall 1997 and to make the program mandatory for all incoming freshman in fall 1998. The academic council determined that freshman biology, business, and honors students (approximately 350 students or one-third of the freshman class) would comprise the fall 1997 large-scale pilot.

The long-range technology plan saw the need for a quality infrastructure and support organization to serve both academic and administrative users and to support ubiquitous computing. The plan, therefore, called for the consolidation of academic computing (reporting to the vice-president for academic affairs) and administrative computing (reporting to the vice-president for finance) under a CIO. The author was appointed to this position effective January 1997. After several cabinet reorganizations in the period 1997–1999, this position now reports to the vice-president for finance and technology.

Recognizing that the demand for technological support would increase dramatically as a result of ubiquitous computing, one of the first tasks undertaken by the new IT management team in 1997 was the reorganization and expansion of support services. Existing staff were reorganized according to the types of services they provided rather than the type of client they supported. Thus, the PC technicians and network technicians from the former academic computing and administrative computing areas were consolidated into PC support services and systems support, respectively. A professionally staffed technology help desk was established. Media services, formerly reporting to the dean of university libraries, the instructional technologists and trainers from academic computing, and the technology-oriented staff and programs from the teaching center were consolidated into a teaching, learning, and technology center (TLT Center). Ten new support positions were added in summer 1997 and ten more in summer 1998, increasing the size of the staff by more than 40%. The number of student technology assistants more than tripled, from 40 to over 120.

The teaching, learning, and technology center established a number of initiatives promoting and supporting faculty adoption of technology in teaching and learning. Core TLT center services include professional instructional designers, technology trainers, digital media specialists, and traditional media services (delivery and support of media equipment in the classroom). The TLT center's curriculum development initiative (CDI) provided significant multiyear funding to academic departments that integrated technology into required core courses. This initiative provided $250,000 per year in incentives to academic departments. Other initiatives provided incentives and support for small projects and individual faculty.

Vital to the success of ubiquitous computing were faculty training and curricular integration. To ensure incoming students would see the value of ubiquitous computing early in their academic careers, two curriculum development initiatives targeted freshman English and mathematics courses. At the TLT Center Summer Institute (a.k.a. Faculty College), faculty were immersed for a week in the uses of instructional technology. Thirty faculty participated in June 1997, expanding to over 80 in June 1998.

Faculty require significant support, if they are to use technology effectively in teaching and learning. Along with the increase in student technology assistants (STAs), IT work-study students, their role was expanded in 1997 to include technical support for the faculty and management of the STA program. In addition to digitizing materials, developing course-related web pages, and other traditional faculty support services, the STAs can be available during classes to provide technical assistance and training for students in the course. Innovative aspects of this program include an emphasis on student management as well as "intellectual barter," whereby faculty mentoring of STAs is included as part of the contract between students and faculty.

The infrastructure needed major improvements in anticipation of ubiquitous computing. Prior to 1996, networks were installed and maintained by individual academic or administrative departments, with little central coordination or support. While some departments had excellent network access, faculty in the humanities generally lacked it. In 1996, the university implemented two large Novell servers to provide network file services and email to all students, faculty, and staff. The campus residence halls were wired "port-per-pillow" (approximately 2,000 ports in total), and all faculty offices were wired. In 1997, the campus network backbone was upgraded to ATM, running between 155 megabits per second (Mbps) and 620 Mbps between buildings, and pilot Lotus Notes and Lotus LearningSpace servers were installed. The same year saw the opening of a new academic building with 24 state-of-the-art classrooms, featuring a port-per-seat and built-in media projection systems. In 1998, the university's network servers were replaced, including the campus email system and the administrative mainframe.

The initial ubiquitous computing pilot projects in 1995 and 1996 highlighted the need for stronger project and budget management. A preliminary assessment of the pilot noted that, while overall satisfaction with the project was high, faculty and students were often frustrated by minor hardware and software bugs, including burnt-out bulbs in the data projectors, bad network ports, problems connecting to printers, and other technical issues that should have been addressed relatively quickly and easily. In addition, we were facing significant logistical issues as we prepared to distribute and track laptop computers and perform major upgrades to the campus infrastructure. In response, the Technology Project and Budget Office was created in early 1997. Initially staffed with one full-time Seton Hall administrator and one full-time professional project manager contracted through IBM Corporation, this office's primary purposes were to develop effective policies and procedures and comprehensive plans for the ubiquitous computing program and infrastructure upgrades and to transfer project management skills to university staff.

Project management was a discipline new to Seton Hall University. From early 1997 through the end of 1998, cross-functional project teams, co-led by the director of the Technology Project and Budget Office and the IBM project manager, and including representatives from Academic Affairs, Enrollment Services, IT, Public Relations, and Student Affairs, met weekly to develop and to refine project plans, policies, and procedures for ubiquitous computing. The importance of this planning effort was clearly demonstrated during the first distributions of laptop computers in fall 1997 and fall 1998. Execution of the plan was nearly flawless; every problem that did arise had been considered, and a plan was already in place to address it. This system worked so well for ubiquitous computing that it has been subsequently implemented for many other IT projects.

The IBM Alliance

Consider for a moment the challenges the university faced in early 1997. It had publicly mandated that a third of the incoming freshmen would be required to participate in a ubiquitous computing pilot program as would all incoming freshmen beginning fall 1998. The university did not yet have in place a plan for laptop distribution, support, or asset management. Major infrastructure upgrades were necessary. Significant faculty support and training initiatives were started. At the same time, the university had a greenhorn CIO, just promoted from the faculty, charged with reorganizing and expanding IT services to support ubiquitous computing. While significant funds were allocated to implement the university's technology plan, ubiquitous computing and the surrounding technology initiatives were broad and resource-intensive, and it was clear that the budget must be used wisely and somewhat sparingly.

Fortunately, IBM Corporation was ready to deal. After nearly a year of meetings, Seton Hall signed a strategic alliance with IBM in April 1997. The agreement identified IBM as the university's preferred vendor for computer and networking equipment and services. IBM committed to price its products and services competitively with other Tier 1 providers. The university would showcase IBM products and solutions for higher education, and IBM would make substantial contributions of equipment and services.

The contributions turned out to be invaluable. In particular, the IBM project manager and the university's adoption of project management were important factors in the success of ubiquitous computing. Other services, such as network planning and design and technology implementation, would have been out of the university's reach without this alliance. Technology implementation services were especially critical, as the university was reorganizing IT services. The resulting staff turnover could have been catastrophic without the services provided through the alliance.

This alliance was not without controversy. Faculty were concerned about aligning with a large, multinational corporation. While the alliance did minimize the total cost of ownership for laptop computers, the campus network and servers, and other infrastructure, some departments felt constrained by IBM's preferred vendor status and felt they were paying more than necessary for computer equipment. In addition, some technologies adopted as a result of the alliance were not entirely successful. Early versions of Lotus Learning-Space and wireless networking were implemented at Seton Hall before they were ready for market. Overall, however, the alliance was a success, providing important services at critical times and the lowest total cost for the array of technologies the university implemented.

PAST THE STARTUP: PRELIMINARY RESULTS OF UBIQUITOUS COMPUTING

When Seton Hall launched the initial ubiquitous computing pilot in 1995, handing out 14 IBM ThinkPads in one of the departure lounges in Newark airport, the university was well aware that it was embarking on a bold educational experiment. It felt a responsibility to assess the program's success and impact on the learning environment. Consequently, a cross-functional ubiquitous computing assessment team was formed in early 1996 to begin gathering baseline data on the university's learning environment and to develop and implement an assessment plan. The team had two overarching objectives: 1) to gather data regarding the strengths and weaknesses of the program and recommend improvements and 2) to gather longitudinal data on the long-term impact of ubiquitous computing on the learning environment.

Some feedback allowed immediate correction of problems. For example, early in the program, students complained that the six-foot Ethernet cable provided with their laptop computers did not reach their beds from the ports (naively installed near their desks). We immediately began offering longer Ethernet cables.

In planning for ubiquitous computing, planners had three main fears about making the program mandatory for all incoming freshman in 1998.

1. The added burden of the technology fee ($500 per semester in 1998) would result in lower enrollments.

2. Faculty would not use the technology.

3. The loss rate for student laptop computers would be unacceptably high, a very understandable concern when you consider that, in 1998, approximately $3.5 million in university assets were wandering around the campus in students' backpacks.

None of these fears were realized.

As part of the university's overall strategic plan, the number of scholarships available to incoming freshmen was increased to offset, in part, the additional cost. As a result, enrollments actually increased by 9% over the previous year, resulting in Seton Hall's largest freshman class. At the same time, average SAT scores increased by 4%. Faculty in targeted CDI courses, particularly freshman English and mathematics, adopted technology into the curriculum faster than expected.

One of the biggest surprises, however, was in the area of laptop loss. In order to minimize the university's risk, student laptops were insured for full replacement value. Faculty laptops were insured by a less expansive policy with a significant deductible. In the 1998–1999 academic year, student laptop loss was under 2%, while faculty laptop loss was nearly 10%. The difference between faculty and student work habits turned out to be a key factor. Faculty were used to leaving their offices to visit colleagues, make copies, get coffee, and the like. Most faculty losses were from unsecured offices. Students, on the other hand, travel the campus with their backpacks. The following year, faculty laptops were also insured for full replacement value; however, their greater awareness of security has significantly reduced the loss rate.

Some other notable lessons learned include:

- Begin with a quality technology plan that is informed by and supports the institution's strategic plan. It should articulate a compelling vision for how ubiquitous computing will help achieve the university's strategic goals. Be sure the plan has strong executive sponsorship and community input. Ensure strong project management for implementation of the plan.

- Standardization of hardware greatly eases support requirements. Technicians in PC Support Services are certified to perform warranty repairs on IBM ThinkPad computers. With this ability, most hardware problems are resolved in 15 minutes by swapping the user's hard drive into a new machine. Because all the laptops have a standard software load that keeps all users' data in a convenient location, software problems can, if necessary, be resolved by copying user data to a server and replacing the standard software image.

- A quality network infrastructure is necessary for the success of ubiquitous computing. While the technology plan envisioned the laptop computer as a platform for instructional software, this role has been overshadowed by its roles as a communication and research tool. Communication and research require a reliable network and Internet connection. As a result of implementing ubiquitous computing, Internet bandwidth has been increasing nearly exponentially, from 1.5 Mbps in 1995, 3 Mbps in 1997, 6 Mbps in 1999, 10 Mbps in 2000, to 20 Mbps in 2001.

- Students require significant training to make effective use of their laptop computers. Initial planning assumed that most incoming students were computer savvy and that a combination of computer-based training and optional, classroom-based technology training would meet their needs. This plan worked during the initial pilot projects from 1995 to 1998. However, when we expanded the program in fall 1998 to include all incoming freshmen, faculty reported that a large minority of students were frankly lost when it came to making effective use of the technology. Analysis indicated that the students who participated in the early pilot projects (business, biology, and honors students) were probably more technically literate than the typical Seton Hall student. In response, we incorporated six hours of mandatory technology training for incoming freshmen as part of their orientation and studies skills course.

- Web-enabled student services. In implementing the university's strategic and technology plans, Seton Hall made significant efforts to enhance student services. In 1998, the offices of admissions, the bursar, financial aid, and the registrar, previously in separate locations and reporting to different parts of the organization, were combined into a single office of enrollment services, providing one-stop shopping for most student services. In 1999, the university web-enabled its legacy administrative systems, allowing web-based application, registration, drop/add, access to academic progress and financial aid information, and the like.

- Wiring public spaces and residence halls is more important than wiring teaching spaces. Nearly half of the university's 80 classrooms have a port for each seat. However, the use of laptops in the classroom is relatively low. On the other hand, use of network connections in public spaces, such as the library, study lounges, and the Pirates' Cove coffee bar, is quite high. In 1998, the university pulled power, data, and voice to the University Green in order to support events. We provided power and data connections at a number of benches. These ports are constantly in use during good weather.

- Classroom presentation equipment is more important to faculty than wiring the classroom. The most desired classrooms are those with built-in projection equipment and an Internet connection for the instructor. While faculty do not often ask the students to use their laptops in the classroom, they often use their laptops for presentations and demonstrations.

- Use of the public computer labs continues to be high. The technology plan originally assumed that, with the implementation of ubiquitous computing, the demand for public computer labs would go down. Quite the opposite occurred. In 1998, we began to see lines, and in response, the university created two new public computer labs. With the emphasis on freshman courses in 1997 and 1998 and the incentives to incorporate technology into their teaching, the faculty naturally also incorporated technology into their upper-level and graduate courses. In addition, we noted that students in the ubiquitous computing program did not always carry their laptops around with them but wanted to check email, print assignments, and the like between classes using the computer labs.

- Asset management is more challenging and complex than anticipated. While distribution and refreshment (that is, replacing the computers after two years) are well planned and well executed, hundreds of students, faculty, and adjunct faculty leave each year without returning the university's computer. While nearly all of these computers are eventually recovered, tracking them down is time consuming. We began the program with one administrator handling asset management on a part-time basis. We now have two full-time positions. In addition, we supplement the asset management staff during laptop distribution. To assist in this process, our technology team has developed computer inventory management system (CIMS), a Lotus Notes–based asset management system integrated with our student information system and human resource system. CIMS is invaluable in determining which students and employees have left the university without returning the university's computer asset.

- Continual assessment is vital to improving the program and demonstrating its value to faculty, senior executives, and governing boards. A well-planned and executed assessment plan should gather data not only on ubiquitous computing's long-term impact on the learning environment but also provide immediate feedback regarding what is working and what needs improvement. Assessment should involve a cross-section of the university community, including academics, student affairs, enrollment services, and other groups in frequent contact with the students.

Faculty, Curriculum, and Governance Issues

One of the biggest lessons learned in implementing ubiquitous computing at Seton Hall concerned faculty adoption. The university has had tremendous success as well as difficult challenges in this complex area. By announcing that the ubiquitous computing program would integrate technology into the curriculum, we publicly committed to students using their laptops in their coursework. This commitment set the bar very high and increased the risk of failure. One way to avoid this risk is to sidestep the issues of faculty use and curricular integration altogether and focus on ubiquitous computing as a tool for learning, research, and communication.

Nevertheless, Seton Hall was in a position where faculty adoption and curricular integration were vital to our own perception of success. These issues were quite easily addressed in the pilot projects from 1995 through 1998. The number of students participating increased from 20 to approximately 400 during this period, but faculty volunteers and incentive programs like the curriculum development initiative provided enough core course sections using laptops to meet our self-imposed high standard of success.

We knew the next challenge would come when ubiquitous computing became mandatory for all incoming freshmen in fall 1998. In order to achieve our goal of curricular integration, we developed a number of strategies. Several projects were targeted to high-enrollment core courses typically taken by freshmen, including freshman English, introductory statistics, and the general education biology course. Sections of these courses were restricted to students in the ubiquitous computing program. A group of faculty developed guidelines specifying acceptable levels of technology use in course sections designated "ubiquitous" and "technology-enhanced."

Preliminary assessment data from the 1998–1999 academic year showed that these strategies were initially successful in that students reported high satisfaction with the program as well as significant use of technology as a learning tool. This trend continued for freshmen in fall 1999; however, at the same time, sophomores reported a significant drop in both use and overall satisfaction. We had evidently not paid sufficient attention to faculty training, support, and incentives for upper-level courses. Beginning in 1999, we focused several new CDI projects on high-enrollment core courses typically taken by upperclassmen.

Were these initiatives successful? In the latest assessment surveys from fall 2000, overall student satisfaction with the program remains high. More than two-thirds of students report they are either satisfied or very satisfied with the ubiquitous computing program. However, lack of faculty use of technology in teaching is one of the most frequently cited problems students report with the program.

On the faculty side, nearly all [faculty] now report they use email regularly to communicate with students, a dramatic rise from 1995. A majority report they use the web as part of classroom demonstrations, student research projects, and the like. However, just under half report that they use the university's course management system (formerly Lotus LearningSpace, now BlackBoard) or have an active web page with interactive components, such as an online discussion forum. After dramatic increases from 1996 to 1998, faculty adoption of course management systems and active web pages slowed considerably.

Fortunately, faculty confronted and resolved these issues. Since 1996, a TLT Roundtable has advised the university's technology initiatives. Following a model developed by the American Association of Higher Education's TLT Group, it brings together faculty, administrators, and IT professionals to address ways in which IT can enhance and, ultimately, transform teaching and learning. The TLT Roundtable has had a key role in ongoing planning in support of ubiquitous computing. Small teams of the TLT Roundtable reviewed and recommended an upgraded campus mail system and a new course management system.

In 1999, the TLT Roundtable successfully worked with the Faculty Senate and Office of the Provost to implement guidelines to recognize the development of technology-based course materials as evidence of teaching excellence, research, and service to the institution. The TLT Group also hosts several "best practices" showcases each semester, highlighting the work of Seton Hall faculty in developing effective ways of using technology to enhance teaching. Beginning fall 2000, the TLT Roundtable began development of the next IT Long-Range Plan and Budget.

Ubiquitous computing galvanized the university community, sparking serious faculty debates on the use of technology in teaching and learning. In 1999, a faculty member observed, "In the 11 years I've been here before [ubiquitous] computing, there were rarely discussions about teaching. I would talk to my colleagues frequently about literature, current events, and the weather, but never about my own teaching or what happened in the classroom that day. Since we began the computing program, it seems that teaching is all we talk about."

Several lessons learned in the area of faculty and curricular development include:

- Faculty engagement is essential for the program's success. Faculty need formal mechanisms to provide input into the planning and implementation of a ubiquitous computing program.

- Faculty require time, support, and incentives to make effective use of technology in teaching and learning. Faculty cannot feel that their considerable investment of time and talent in using technology will go unrewarded or, worse, place them at a disadvantage for tenure and promotion.

- Carefully manage expectations, especially when promoting a ubiquitous computing program to incoming students and parents. Expecting all faculty to use technology or the laptop computer a great deal in the classroom is not reasonable. Expecting many faculty to use the technology as a communication tool and for course enrichment is reasonable but takes time, support, and incentives.

- To this end, focus on the laptop computer as a communication and research tool rather than as a teaching tool.

- Remember that technology is a lever for change not an end in itself. Provide opportunities for faculty to share and to reflect on the teaching and learning issues that ubiquitous computing will bring to the fore.

Financing Ubiquitous Computing

The most frequently asked question about ubiquitous computing is "How much does it cost?" There is no simple answer. Ubiquitous computing was implemented as one component of a comprehensive strategic plan. The university's central technology budget was increased significantly, but so were other strategic budgets, including the financial aid budget. As technology services were centralized, the departmental budgets for technology were not captured, so not all the central budget increases for technology represented new spending. On the other hand, not all technology expenses are funded from the central technology budget. Academic Affairs, Enrollment Services, Freshman Studies, Public Relations, and Student Affairs all provide critical support for the university's ubiquitous computing program. Nevertheless, it is useful to examine the budget for the Division of Information Technology.

In fiscal year 2001, the university had a general and education (G&E) budget for the South Orange campus (excluding the Law School, Seminary, SetonWorldWide, and Graduate Medical Education) of approximately $115 million. The Division of Information Technology had a budget of just under $15 million, or 13% of the university's G&E budget. This figure included the cost of leasing the IBM ThinkPad computers and a portion of the library's technology costs. It did not include technology funded from grants and other external sources, the library's operating budget, technology for SetonWorldWide (the university's online graduate and professional degree programs), or the technology expenditures for the Law School. Table 14.1 outlines how the Division of Information Technology's $15 million operating budget was allocated.

Table 14.1

**Summary of the Division of
Information Technology (DoIT) Budget, FY01**

	Amt ($000)	% of Budget	%
SALARIES AND WAGES	$5,831	39%	
Major Subdivisions in IT			
Office of Technology			5%
Applications Support			5%
Systems Support			6%
Operation Support			2%
Telecommunications			4%
PC Support Services			10%
TLT Center (Faculty and Classroom Support)			7%
OPERATING BUDGETS	$4,668	32%	
Major Operating Expense Categories			
Computer Leases (Faculty)			4%
Computer Leases (Staff/Admin.)			3%
Library Automation System (Lease/Maint.)			1%
Network Server Lease/Admin. Sys. Maint.			2%
Maint. SP2 & S/390			2%
Computer Leases (Public Labs)			2%
ATM (Network) Equip. Leases			2%
TLT Center (CDI, Media Equip., etc.)			4%
Telecommunications			7%
Computing Operations			3%
Other Noncategorized Expenses			2%
UBIQUITOUS COMPUTING BUDGET (student laptop computers)	$4,283	29%	29%
TOTAL	$14,782		100%

It is clear from Table 14.1 that a large part of the technology budget goes toward personnel. Personnel costs (excluding fringe benefits) represent 39% of the central technology budget. Of the personnel budget, nearly half goes to PC Support Services and the TLT Center. Maintaining the university's inventory of laptop and desktop computers (including the ubiquitous computing program budget, laptop computers for faculty, and desktop computers for staff, administrators, and public computer labs) consumes nearly two-thirds of the nonpersonnel budget (62%). Maintaining the university's voice and data networks and related services (including the administrative and library systems) consumes 28% of the nonpersonnel budget.

The technology budget was not always funded at this level. For example, in 1994, before the implementation of the strategic technology plan, the central technology operating budget was approximately 2.8% of the G&E budget. Significant additional funds were spent from capital funds and the operating funds of other academic and administrative units; nevertheless, there is little doubt that the overall technology expenditures of the university have increased significantly. These increases came about through careful planning and were implemented over several years. Funding for these initiatives came from a variety of sources, including:

- *Reallocation:* Before implementing the technology plan, technology budgets were highly decentralized. The technology plan called for central funding of basic infrastructure, including centralization of network funding and regular replacement of computer stock. The development of the central technology budget was achieved, in part, by reallocation of these formerly decentralized technology funds.

- *Tuition and fees:* Seton Hall University is a tuition-driven institution; that is, the bulk of the expense budgets are funded from student tuition and fees. To fund the technology initiatives, Seton Hall implemented a $650 per semester Mobile Computing Technology Fee for undergraduate students. In addition, a significant portion of the university's tuition increases over the past several years have gone toward the central technology budget.

- *One-time infusion of capital:* Seton Hall recognized that an initial investment in the technology infrastructure was needed to begin the ubiquitous computing program. To jump start implementation of the technology plan, the Board of Regents allocated $5 million in capital from the university's quasi-endowment to provide laptop computers for all faculty, upgrade the campus network, and begin funding faculty and curriculum development.

- *Cost cutting in nonacademic areas:* During implementation of the technology plan, the university also reengineered the campus procurement process and negotiated preferred vendor relationships, which somewhat reduced operating costs. To recoup those costs, all nonacademic operating budgets (excluding personnel) were reduced by 5%.

- *Partnerships with vendors:* As part of a comprehensive strategic alliance with Seton Hall, IBM Corporation made significant investments in the campus infrastructure.

The most significant change in the technology budget is the shift of almost all technology funding from capital to operating budgets. Shifting funding from capital to operating budgets has significant benefits. It has allowed Seton Hall to lease, rather than to purchase, most of the equipment used on campus and to plan regular refreshment cycles for various technology components.

The importance of leasing cannot be overemphasized. The technology plan called for a $1 million upgrade to the campus fiber-optic backbone in 1997. It was funded by the long-range technology budget beginning at $300,000 per year, starting with the 1997–1998 fiscal year. As a result, the university leased a state-of-the-art, high-speed campus backbone. The three-year lease dramatically reduced the entry cost of implementing such technology.

Leasing from operating budgets recognizes the rapid obsolescence of technology. In early 1999, University Computing Services noted network congestion at the core of the network backbone. Network traffic between academic buildings in 1999 had grown beyond the capacity of 1997 state-of-the-art equipment. In response, University Computing Services negotiated an early end to the lease and replaced the core network equipment after only two years. Not only did this allow the university to upgrade to state-of-the-art 1999 equipment, but the monthly lease payments on the new lease were actually lower than the 1997 lease.

Despite the concerns of many that Seton Hall could not afford its technology plan, other areas of the campus, particularly the academic area, also experienced significant growth during implementation of ubiquitous computing. In particular, strategic initiatives aimed at reducing the average class size, increasing incoming students' average SAT scores, and new programs were also funded. For example, the number of full-time faculty increased by 15% during this period. Average undergraduate class sizes were reduced, in part allaying faculty concerns that implementation of ubiquitous computing would result in their replacement by computers. Seton WorldWide was launched, and new programs were initiated in diplomacy and international relations and graduate medical education.

NEXT STEPS

Seton Hall now has an evolving, technologically rich learning environment, including a mature and highly successful ubiquitous computing environment. It developed and implemented bold, innovative strategic and technology plans. What are the next steps?

Beginning fall 2000, Seton Hall began a large-scale wireless network pilot project with Symbol Technology. Access points were installed in a number of classroom and public spaces, including the library and student center. Faculty and students in pilot sections of biology, education, and English were provided wireless network cards. The faculty reported that wireless networking increased their ability to use laptops in class for student research, team projects, collaborative writing, and other learning activities. Wireless brought network connectivity into the large lecture halls and wet labs, which were difficult to wire. Based on this pilot project, the university adopted an IBM ThinkPad i-series computer with built-in wireless capability for the 2001 ubiquitous computing model. Additional access points were installed, providing wireless network access from most classrooms and public spaces on campus.

Along with implementation of wireless, the campus network backbone is being upgraded. This fall, the existing IBM ATM-based campus backbone is being replaced by a Cisco gigabit Ethernet backbone.

An unexpected result of Seton Hall going wireless was the first on-campus student demonstration in over 10 years. A vocal minority of sophomores who were having their IBM ThinkPad model 390E computers replaced with the wireless IBM ThinkPad i-series computers in April 2001 did not see the value of wireless and correctly noted that they could have gotten a larger screen and a larger hard drive if the university had chosen a model without built-in wireless networking. After several meetings of the Student Senate, 50 students demonstrated in front of the administration building with banners, drums, and bagpipes. The issue settled down quickly once the wireless access points were deployed in August 2001. A walk through any of the public spaces around campus will find dozens of students using wireless laptop computers. This issue did highlight the need for more communication with student governing bodies. In addition, it highlighted a potential problem with deploying wireless devices before the infrastructure is ready to accommodate them.

Another important part of the evolution of the ubiquitous campus is the development of a quality web portal for faculty and students. Until last year, Seton Hall had a first-generation web site that was relatively static and designed around university organization. Users had difficulty navigating and finding the resources they were looking for. In January 2000, the web site was completely overhauled. Information was organized around constituencies (current students, prospective students, faculty and staff, alumni, parents, etc.), rather than the university's organizational units. Interactive elements, such as discussion databases, job postings, and community announcements, were added. Media-rich online presentations and newsletters were developed, including streaming video and slide shows. With the implementation of BlackBoard this past summer, the university began implementation of a true portal that users can customize to receive information based on their user profile.

The university recognizes that technology planning is an ongoing process rather than a discrete event. The strategic technology plan and budget must be upgraded on a regular basis. The original 1995 long-range technology plan underwent a major revision in 1997. Another revision was begun in 1999. The Boland Hall fire in January 2000 delayed that process, while the university recovered and focused on fire safety. Beginning fall 2000, the IT2 Planning Task Team of the university's TLT Roundtable began development of the next major revision of Seton Hall's technology plan. The task team was aided by planning facilitators from Eduprise, Inc. The task team delivered a preliminary plan to the university's executive team in June 2001.

Although this plan is still under development, some highlights include:

- Expand the CDI with a focus on large-enrollment undergraduate core courses.

- Enhance the university's administrative system. Expand use of the technical infrastructure to enable the redesign of administrative processes, including online processing of employment forms, time sheets, curriculum adjustments, and requisitions. Expand the data warehousing pilot project to a full decision support system. Establish a task team to begin planning for the implementation of a new administrative system.

- Expand the wireless network to the entire campus. Pilot the use of wireless handheld computing devices. Pilot the use of wireless access protocol (WAP) to expand access to core web-based university services.

CONCLUSION

The mission statement for the ubiquitous computing program states, "Seton Hall University is a community of scholars dedicated to the creation and dissemination of knowledge and the preparation of future leaders in a global society. Seton Hall's Computing Initiative is designed to break down the barriers of space and time and ensure that all learners we admit into our community have access to the tools and learning. Through the effective use of information technology, Seton Hall University will ensure that every student masters a critical body of knowledge and meets standards of performance."

The university took what appeared at the time to be enormous risks—financial, institutional, and pedagogical—in implementing ubiquitous computing. In the end, the program was successful in many ways. Through implementation of ubiquitous computing, the university achieved a certain amount of recognition. Many aspects of the university have changed, including our budget and planning processes. A campus dialog regarding teaching and learning was sparked. Our self-perception has changed, and we are proud of our accomplishments in technology-enhanced teaching and learning.

Seton Hall's ubiquitous computing program will continue to evolve. The community will tackle what's next with the same aplomb it has always exhibited in the face of challenges. This attitude is exemplified by the university's motto, *Hazard Zet Forward*, which, translated from the Norman French and English, means "advance despite difficulties." This attitude led the university to venture into ubiquitous computing and sustains everyone involved.

LESSONS LEARNED

- Align the campus-wide technology plan with the institution's strategic plan. The technology plan should support teaching, learning, and administration and focus on the student experience with technology. It should deal with issues surrounding hardware and software standardization and central technology planning, funding, and support.

- Executive sponsorship is critical. The president, chief academic officer, and chief financial officer must all be on board.

- Faculty engagement is equally critical. Encourage faculty input into planning. Provide multiple ways of supporting faculty innovation, including both "top-down" and "bottom-up" strategies. Establish an effective advisory committee. Consider implementing an AAHE/TLT Group Teaching, Learning, and Technology Roundtable as this advisory group.

- Create cross-divisional consensus for ubiquitous computing. Involve student affairs and enrollment services in planning and implementation.

- Phase in implementation. Pilot new technologies, including ubiquitous computing, extensively. Remember that building infrastructure, teams, and support organizations takes time.

- Implement quality project management.

- Establish long-range budget models. Funding ubiquitous computing is likely to require a combination of tuition increases and/or fees, internal reallocation of resources, and external investment. Deal with the rapid obsolescence of technology by placing all technology on a regular replacement cycle and shifting technology expenditures from capital to operating budgets. Explore leasing options.

- Seek partnerships and alliances. The lowest overall cost is more likely to come through a long-range relationship with a vendor than a series of individual transactions. Explore the lowest total cost of ownership models to make this case.

REFERENCES

Division of Information Tecchnology. (1995). *Information technology plan.* Available: http://technology.shu.edu/techplan/

Contact Information

Stephen G. Landry
Chief Information Officer
Seton Hall University
400 South Orange Ave
South Orange, NJ 07079
Phone: 973 761 7386
Fax: 973 761 9300
Email: landryst@shu.edu
Web Address: http://www.pirate.shu.edu/~landryst

Assessment of the Impact of Ubiquitous Computing

Ross Griffith
Heather Stewart

Editor's note (from David G. Brown): Friends and skeptics repeatedly ask: Is the investment in ubiquitous computing yielding returns through increased learning? In the August 2000 Syllabus, *I argued that "the jury is in." That column is, with permission, reprinted here:*

> *I speak about computers to a lot of college and university audiences. Body language usually provides an early alert. Whether it's a seminar with 200 faculty on "how to enhance teaching through computers" or a private session with the university's president, from every audience comes the inevitable question: "What proof do you have that all this money spent on technology increases student learning?"*
>
> *My first answers convinced no one. I cited how grades in basic chemistry increased at the University of Virginia, how failure rates declined at Virginia Tech, how end-of-course test scores jumped at the University of Central Florida, and how much higher rates of approval Wake Forest students gave to computer enhanced versions of similar courses. But, for every study I cited the interrogator-searching-for-an-answer would reference a counter-conclusion from the "no significant difference" movement. Few, if any, minds were changed!*
>
> *I guess I would have the same skepticism about studies "proving" that blackboards and chalk, or five-color textbooks, or*

million volume libraries, or newly purchased electron micro-scopes, or the implementation of Bloom's taxonomy was the sin-gle factor among many that increased learning. Classrooms are not sterile laboratories. Students are not guinea pigs. Rigorous studies tracing the change of a single variable are not possible.

On almost every campus, opinion surveys of both faculty and students involved in face-to-face courses reveal that they think computer enhancements increase learning. They know they pre-fer such courses. Professors who have once incorporated com-puter enhancements, keep them. Students who have once enrolled in a computer enhanced course tend to seek out another one. But, the skeptics argue, both students and faculty have something of a vested interest and are therefore not fully rational. Opinion polls are not enough.

Recently I've approached the inevitable question in another way. It seems to work. Some minds have been changed. The new approach is more logic than empiricism.

From studies that have nothing to do with technology we know that learning increases when

(1) there is more interaction and quicker feedback between students and their professors, between parents and their chil-dren;

(2) students (and siblings) help each other learn (collaborative learning); and

(3) students are redundantly provided the same material in multiple formats (different strokes for different folks).

We also have hard evidence that in computer enhanced courses

(1) communications between faculty and students is more fre-quent and timely,

(2) more collaboration occurs among students, and

(3) students have access to a broader range of materials and people.

Computers enable more interaction, collaboration, and cus-tomization. As a result, there is more learning. The jury is in, on the benefit side!

> *Feeling somewhat cornered, the skeptics, who have not yet changed body language, ask: "Wouldn't the same money be better spent on more professors? Wouldn't the effort be better invested in learning grammar and the theory of relativity?"*
>
> *Perhaps! Let's think a moment, however, about the cost. By a computer enhanced course we mean a course taught on the assumption that all students have appropriate access to the Internet and sufficient knowledge to use the access. Now that students learn how to use a computer in order to play games, listen to rock concerts, buy T-shirts, and routinely exchange emails with friends, the additional cost of using the computer for school purposes is nil! Students are learning to use web browsers on their own time, not study time! Access is first sought for ".com" purposes. The add on or marginal cost of using computers for their studies is insignificant!*
>
> *High benefit. Low cost. The jury is in! Computer enhanced instruction leads toward increased learning! Is it possible that the body language will change?*

My column has not, however, put the issue to rest. All are still looking for hard data. An appropriate conclusion to this collection of case studies is a focused examination of the state of existing research. This concluding chapter includes a bibliography of the assessment research and highlights two very different approaches to the measurement challenge.

ASSESSMENT AT WAKE FOREST

Implementation of the 1995 Strategic Plan "will allow Wake Forest students to compete in this new era.... All teaching should proceed from the premise that students have personal access to and routinely use computers.... Computers have a profound effect on modern education. We need to ensure that computers play an integral role in education at Wake Forest. The reason for this is twofold. One, faculty must be efficient users of technology to enhance their teacher/scholar role. Two, students must leave Wake Forest with the needed skills to succeed in the modern, highly technological world" (Plan for the Class of 2000, 1995).

Six years later, to what extent has this goal been achieved? An evaluation committee consisting of eight faculty members and two administrators is assessing the strategic plan. To encourage *use* of assessment data, the evaluation committee members serve as liaisons with different committees and administrative offices throughout the university. They provide these groups with survey results and other data, with analyses as appropriate (Griffith, 1999).

The fundamental goals of the plan, which includes our move to ubiquitous computing and 36 other recommendations, are listed as follows:

- Recommit to the whole person—reason, faith, and service

- Strengthen student-faculty relations, especially one-on-one

- Encourage greater student engagement with ideas

- Improve the effectiveness and efficiency of learning and teaching inside and outside the classroom

- Prepare students for the information age

- Increase recognition of our world's diversity in students, faculty, and programs

- Increase the quality/quantity of scholarship (Griffith et al., 1999)

To monitor progress toward these goals, the evaluation committee tracks 27 key measures in the following areas: quality upon entrance, quality of activities while in attendance, quality upon exit, and opinions concerning quality (Griffith, 1999). "Examples of key measures being monitored are freshman retention rates, student-faculty ratio, percent of graduates receiving degree credits abroad, graduation rates, alumni giving rates and academic reputation as measured in *U.S. News & World Report*" (Griffith, 1999).

INSTRUMENTS OF MEASUREMENT

The 27 key measures are, for the most part, drawn from general purpose, nationally normed questionnaires. Primary among them are the following nine:

1. *College Student Experiences Questionnaire (CSEQ).* The survey was administered to freshmen, sophomores, and juniors in the spring of 1996, 1997, 1998, and 2000. One of the CSEQ's strong features is that it determines how students use their time. Comparative data with other schools is also available. Wake Forest's CSEQ results were highlighted in *Change* (Banta and Kuh, 1998).

2. *Cooperative Institutional Research Program (CIRP)* Freshman Survey. The survey has been administered to the freshmen in different years since 1980. Trend analysis has enabled the school to learn about demographic

changes of the entering freshmen. Comparative data with other schools is available.

3. *Freshman Essay.* Effective 1996, freshman classes were asked to respond to questions about their college expectations. A follow-up essay questionnaire is administered to the respondents upon their graduation, so that the university can compare the two responses and determine how students changed while in college.

4. *Higher Education Data Sharing (HEDS)* Consortium Alumni/ae Survey. The survey was administered to the classes of 1989 and 1993. Results enable the institution to assess the effects of undergraduate education on graduates' lives five years later. Comparative data with peer institutions is also provided by HEDS.

5. *HEDS Senior Survey.* The survey was administered to the graduating classes of 1993, 1994, 1995, 1996, 1997, 1998, and 2000. Results enable the school to assess graduating seniors' overall experiences based primarily on satisfaction and experiential ratings in a number of different areas. Comparative data with peer institutions is also provided by HEDS.

6. *Higher Education Research Institute (HERI) Faculty Survey.* The survey was administered to the undergraduate and MBA faculty in 1998 and was scheduled to be administered to the undergraduate faculty in fall 2001. Comparative data from other institutions is provided by HERI and HEDS.

7. *In-House Faculty Computer Survey.* The survey was developed by communication department faculty to assess faculty use of computers. It was administered to undergraduate faculty from 1996 to 2000.

8. *In-House Faculty Survey.* The survey was developed by the evaluation committee to assess the effectiveness of all portions of the strategic plan and was administered to the undergraduate faculty in 1995, 1998, and 2001.

9. *In-House Student Computer Survey.* Faculty in the communication department developed the survey to assess student use of computers. It was administered to the students from 1996 to 2000.

FINDINGS: COMPUTER USAGE

The CSEQ, HEDS Senior Survey, In-House Faculty Survey, In-House Student Computer Survey, and In-House Faculty Computer Survey were administered to students and faculty before and after the strategic plan was implemented.

Utilizing .05 as the level of significance, the institution has been able to demonstrate changes in computer usage (McCoy, Griffith, and Gu, 1999). CSEQ results show that, under the strategic plan, students' scores rose significantly in the following items: use of computers, courses using computers, use of computer in doing research, and discussion of computers (see Figure 15.1, Griffith et al., 1999).

Figure 15.1

College Student Experiences Questionnaire (CSEQ)

Mean Responses

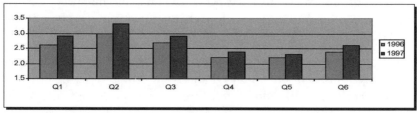

Q1: Use of computers   Q4: Computer training
Q2: Courses use computers   Q5: Discuss computers
Q3: Computer skill   Q6: Research: card catalogue & computer

Subsequent administrations of the CSEQ to freshmen, sophomores, and juniors in 1998 and 2000 resulted in more increases. Figure 15.2 represents the sum of nine computer usage items for the 2000 Wake Forest students as compared to 1998 Wake Forest students as well as national norm groups. These norm groups included results from undergraduate students at research universities (RU), doctoral universities (DU), comprehensive colleges and universities (CCU), selective liberal arts colleges (SLA), and general liberal arts colleges (GLA). As expected, the 2000 Wake Forest results are higher than 1998 Wake Forest results. Both 2000 and 1998 Wake Forest results are higher than the results for each of the norm groups. The CSEQ results demonstrate that Wake Forest students are using computers more than students at other institutions nationally.

Figure 15.2

CSEQ—Quality of Effort: Computer and Information Technology Scale

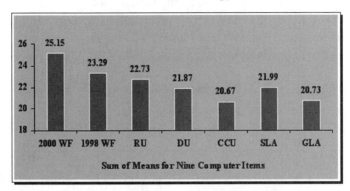

Sum of Means for Nine Computer Items

Similarly, the HEDS Senior Survey, which was administered to the 1998 and 2000 senior classes, provides results for the class that entered prior to the computing initiative as compared to the first class that entered with computers (the Class of 2000). Figure 15.3 shows the seniors' responses to the item "enhancement in the use of quantitative tools" during the course of their undergraduate study. As well as being significantly higher than the Class of 1998, the Wake Forest Class of 2000 is significantly higher than seniors from a preselected "College Peer Group" and "University Peer Group" for this particular item.

Figure 15.3

HEDS Senior Survey: Use of Quantitative Tools—Enhancement

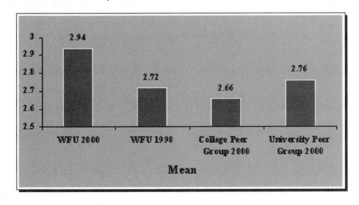

Mean

The Wake Forest Faculty Survey results indicated significant increases in 2001 as compared to both 1995 and 1998 in faculty use of computers for teaching classes and individualized instruction and student use in communicating, gathering information, and giving presentations. Faculty believed that they increased the effectiveness of their presentations in class, communication with students, access to resource materials, and approach to teaching through the increased use of computers (see Figure 15.4).

Figure 15.4

**Wake Forest Faculty Survey
Mean Response**

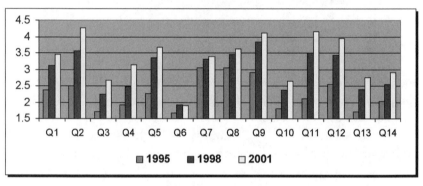

Q1: Computers in teaching

Q2: Computers in communication

Q3: Computers in individual instruction

Q4: Computers for presentations

Q5: Computers with information gathering

Q6: Computers for modeling/simulation

Q7: Computer knowledge compared to colleagues

Q8: Computer training & assistance

Q9: Students proficient with computers

Q10: Technology changed effectiveness of teaching

Q11: Effect of computers on communication

Q12: Effect of computers on resource material

Q13: Effect of computers on teaching/ presentations

Q14: Effect of computers on teaching approach Mean Responses

The HERI Faculty Survey, administered to Wake Forest faculty and other faculty nationally in 1998, asked questions on eight different computer use areas. Compared to a peer group of nine private institutions, Wake Forest results were higher in six of eight educational computer tasks used "at least twice a week" (see Figure 15.5).

Figure 15.5

Use of Computers: 1998 HERI Faculty Survey

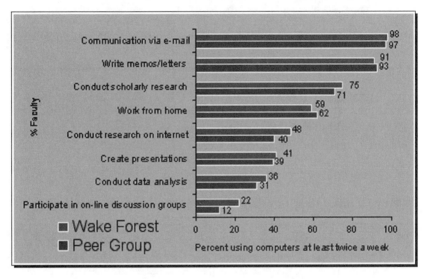

Results from the in-house student and faculty computer surveys have revealed different types of computer behaviors. For example, students under the computing initiative use email to communicate in general but prefer to communicate with faculty and other students face-to-face; faculty attitudes toward computing overall have become more positive; and the highly skilled faculty tend to use the computer for specialized purposes (Mitra and Hazen, 1999).

FINDINGS: ACADEMIC OUTCOMES

Evidence suggests that the Computer Initiative has had a positive impact on academic achievement. The retention rate of first-year students who entered in 1996 (the first year of the strategic plan) was higher than that in the previous three years. Also, the 94.3% retention rate of the 1997 freshman class was even higher than the 1996 freshman class retention rate of 93.4% (Griffith et al., 1999). However, the 1998 retention rate dropped to 91.0%, but the 1999 rate rebounded to 94.5%, highest of all (see Figure 15.6).

Figure 15.6

Freshman Retention Rate Following Year

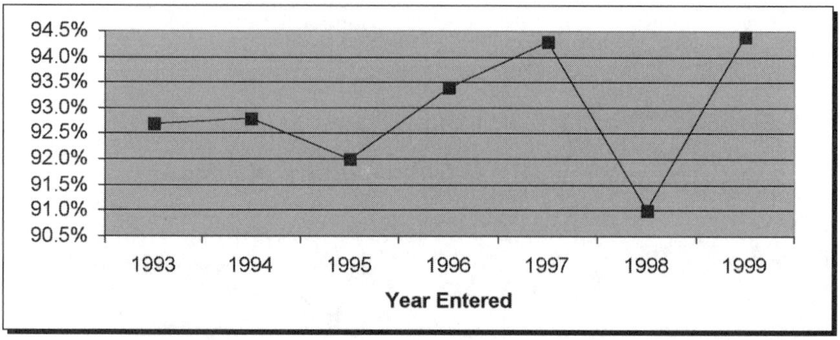

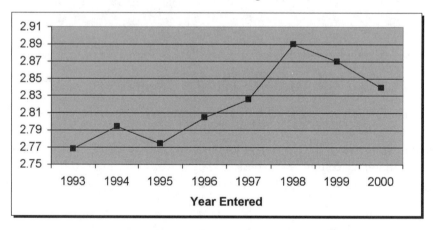

The mean grade-point average at the end of their first year was higher for the freshmen who entered in 1996 (2.81), 1997 (2.83), 1998 (2.89), 1999 (2.87), and 2000 (2.84) than for those in the years immediately prior to the implementation of the strategic plan (see Figure 15.7).

Figure 15.7

Mean Cumulative Grade Point Average End of Freshman Year

The academic quality of the entering freshman class, based on mean SAT scores and academic rankings in high school graduating classes, has not essentially changed since the computing initiative was implemented.

IMPLICATIONS

The assessment results indicate that the expected outcomes have been realized. Computers do play an integral role in education at Wake Forest. Both student and faculty survey results show that use in a number of areas has increased overwhelmingly since the computing initiative was implemented. Students are leaving Wake Forest with the skills needed to succeed in the modern, highly technological world, as evidenced by the survey results that compared them with different college and university peer groups. Similarly, faculty survey results indicate that their efficient use of technology enhances their teacher/scholar role.

Freshman retention rates and mean freshman GPAs have increased since the implementation of the Plan for the Class of 2000, implying that Wake Forest students are achieving at a higher level academically.

ASSESSMENT AT SETON HALL

Measurement Strategy

Seton Hall University has refined a set of metrics that are now being used at more than a dozen institutions. The project, known as the Technology Assessment Data Repository, now provides access to survey design, administration, and data collection for colleges and universities that want to use it. It includes a web-based interface, Java code, and DB2 database storage and retrieval features and is housed on a designated, secured Linux server. Institutions are assigned unique URLs and can either use surveys that are already developed or develop their own. Although comparative results are not yet available, it is instructive to note the results at Seton Hall.

In the fall of 1996, Seton Hall implemented a strategic, long-range information technology plan composed of a series of teaching, learning, and technology integration initiatives. In parallel, the university received an external grant to understand technology's impact on teaching and learning. A number of research techniques were used to explore the topic including self-report journals, internally and externally developed surveys, focus groups, interviews, and case studies.

Seton Hall elected to measure the impact of technology on teaching and learning on three interacting components: the students, the faculty, and the institution as a whole (shown in Figure 15.8).

Figure 15.8

Impact of Technology

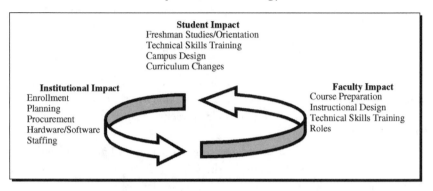

Because valid educational assessment is contingent upon asking the right questions, a team representing all university constituencies determined the appropriate questions, defined the key success indicators, evaluated the assessment process, and analyzed the results (see http://technology.shu.edu).

The mechanisms for collecting data were incorporated into routine academic operations, such as freshman orientation, residence hall programs, senior exit questionnaires, and faculty development and deans' surveys.

Our study focused upon the student-faculty relationship. The instrument used to collect the data from over 2,000 students had three sections: general satisfaction with elements of the ubiquitous computing program; types of technology used, including frequency and duration; and student learning outcomes. Items taken from the survey and subscales were developed for each of the three important elements of the student-faculty relationship: (1) the degree to which the relationship fosters student self-exploration; (2) the quality and frequency of contact between student and faculty member; and (3) the degree to which the relationship fosters the student's active engagement on academic projects.

FINDINGS

The preponderance of students from all groups reported that technology use had a positive impact on their capacity for self-exploration, contact with professors, and active engagement in academic projects.

Self-exploration. We determined that students were expanding their capacity for self-exploration if they reported an increase in their ability to 1) observe and record their own progress, 2) identify their strengths and weaknesses, 3) present their work in different ways, 4) reflect on what they learn,

5) make comparisons and associations of content and their lives' experiences, and 6) relate their experiences to course materials.

Using these measures, more than 82% of all respondents indicate that technology has either a positive or very positive effect on their capacity for self-exploration. Very few students (1%) reported any negative responses to the items, and 17% reported no difference. Figure 15.9 provides a visual depiction of frequency data for the subscale. The range for responses is 6–30, with 30 equivalent to a very positive response on all six dimensions.

Figure 15.9

Distribution of Responses for Self-exploration Subscale

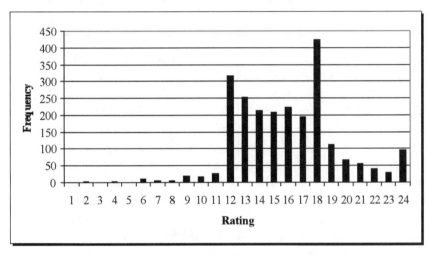

Student-faculty Contact. Three subscales were used to measure the quality and frequency of student-faculty contact: 1) Have contact with professors on course content, 2) feel a part of a community of learners, and 3) get prompt feedback from their professors on their performance. Using these measures, 84% scored positively or very positively. 1% were negative, and 15% reported that technology made no difference. Figure 15.10 provides a visual depiction of frequency data for the subscale. The range for responses is 3–5, with 15 equivalent to a very positive response on all three dimensions.

Figure 15.10

Distribution of Responses for Student-Faculty Contact Subscale

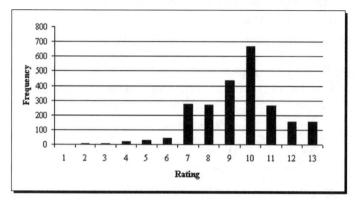

Active Engagement. In dealing specifically with educational technology use for students' active engagement on academic projects, four subscales were used: 1) be directly involved with discovering knowledge, 2) actively apply learned skills, 3) engage in activities beyond the classroom that enrich course activities, and 4) engage in a process of correction and improvement.

Eighty-two percent of responses were positive or very positive. Seventeen percent reported that the technology made no difference, and 1% felt that technology decreased active involvement. Figure 15.11 provides a visual depiction of frequency data, with 20 being the highest possible (or more positive) score.

Figure 15.11

Distribution of Responses for Engagement on Academic Projects Subscale

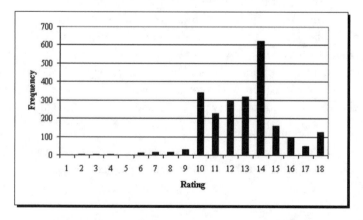

Types of Technology. Having established that technology positively affects self-exploration, student-faculty contact, and active engagement, the study went on to determine which types of technology were most effective with different subscales. Fifteen types of computer uses were identified: communicating, visualizing, experimenting, researching, testing, designing, modeling, automating a process, collaborating, editing, storing data, conferencing, computer-based training, practicing, and presenting.

Using Spearman's Rho at a .05 significance level and Hinkle's Rule of Thumb, no significant differences were found. In other words, "communicating" uses of the computer affected equally all three clusters of subscales. The same was true for the 14 other computer uses.

Conclusion. This study indicates is that something positive is happening between students and faculty through the use of technology. There *is* value in continuing to find ways to improve student learning through technology. Unfortunately, but not surprisingly, no particular type of technology is magic.

REFERENCES AND BIBLIOGRAPHY

American Association for Higher Education, American College Personnel Association, National Association of Student Personnel Administrators. (1999). *Powerful partnerships: A shared responsibility for learning.* Washington, DC: Author.

Angelo, T. A., and Cross, K. P. (1993). *Classroom assessment techniques.* San Francisco, CA: Jossey-Bass.

Astin, A. W. (1991). *Assessment for excellence.* New York, NY: ACE/Macmillan.

Banta, T. W. (1996). *Assessment in practice: Putting principles to work on college campuses.* San Francisco, CA: Jossey-Bass.

Banta, T. W. (1993). *Making a difference: Outcomes of a decade of assessment in higher education.* San Francisco, CA: Jossey-Bass.

Banta, T. W., and Kuh, G. D. (1998, March/April). A missing link in assessment. *Change,* pp. 40–46.

Banta, T. W., Lund, J. P., Black, K. E., and Oblander, F. W. (1988). Implementing outcomes assessment: Promise and perils. *New Directions for Institutional Research No. 59.* San Francisco, CA: Jossey-Bass.

Borden, V. M. H., and Banta, T. W. (Eds.). (1994). *Using performance indicators to guide strategic decision-making.* San Francisco, CA: Jossey-Bass.

226 *Ubiquitous Computing*

Boyer, E. L. (1987). *College: The undergraduate experience in America.* New York, NY: Harper and Row.

Brown, D. G. (2000, August). The jury is in!: Computer-enhanced instruction works. *Syllabus, 22.*

Centra, J. A. (Ed.). (1977). Renewing and evaluating teaching. *New Directions for Higher Education, No. 17.* San Francisco, CA: Jossey-Bass.

Chickering, A.W., and Gamson, Z. (1987). Seven principles for good practice in undergraduate education. *AAHE Bulletin, 87* (3).

Chickering, A.W., and Reisser, L. (1993). *Education and identity.* San Francisco, CA: Jossey-Bass.

Computer-enhanced learning initiative. Retrieved March 24, 1999, http://www.wfu.edu/CELI/

Courts, P. L., and McInerney, K. H. (1993). *Assessment in higher education: Politics, pedagogy, and portfolios.* Westport, CT: Praeger.

Davis, J.D., and Young, R.E. (Eds.). (1982). Students and faculty: Classroom and beyond. *Plantings, 3.*

DeLoughry, T. J. (1995, May 5). Mandatory computers. *The Chronicle of Higher Education,* pp. A37, A39.

Donovan, M.S., Bransford, J. D., and Pellegrino, J. W. (1999). *How people learn: Bridging research and practice.* Washington, DC: National Research Council.

Ehrmann, S.C. (1995, March/April). Asking the right questions: What does research tell us about technology and higher learning? *Change, 27* (2), 20-27.

Erwin, T.D. (1991). *Assessing student learning and development.* San Francisco, CA: Jossey-Bass.

Ewell, P. (Ed.). (1985). Assessing educational outcomes. *New Directions for Institutional Research, No. 47.* San Francisco, CA: Jossey-Bass.

Gaff, J. G. and Ratcliff, A. (1997). *Handbook of the undergraduate curriculum: A comprehensive guide to purposes, structures, practices, and change.* San Francisco, CA: Jossey-Bass.

Griffith, R. (1999, April). Connecting students and faculty through technology, collaboration, and globalization at Wake Forest University. *The Technology Source.* Available: http://horizon.unc.edu/TS/cases/1999-04.asp

Griffith, R., Gu, Y., and Brown, D. G. (1999, May). *Assessment of the impact of ubiquitous computing.* Paper presented to The Association for Institutional Research (AIR). Seattle, WA. (ERIC Document Reproduction Service No. ED433766)

Institutional Research Office. (1995). *The departmental guide and record book for student outcomes assessment and institutional effectiveness.* New York, NY: Agathon Press.

Katz, R. (Ed.). (1999). *Dancing with the devil: Information technology and the new competition in higher education.* San Francisco, CA: Jossey-Bass

Katz, S. N. (2001, June 15). In information technology, don't mistake a tool for a goal. *The Chronicle of Higher Education,* p. B9.

Landry, S. G. (2000). *Project planning for ubiquitous computing: A case study of ubiquitous computing at Seton Hall University.* Paper presented at the meeting of EDUCAUSE, Nashville, TN.

MacVicar, M.L. (1982). *College admissions and the transition to postsecondary education.* Testimony to the National Commission on Excellence in Education, Chicago, IL.

McCoy, L., Griffith, R., and Gu, Y. (1999). Assessment from multipurpose surveys and other sources. In D. G. Brown (Ed.), *Electronically enhanced education* (pp. 95–100). Winston-Salem, NC: Wake Forest University Press.

Mitra, A., and Hazen, M. (1999). Longitudinal Assessment of Computer Enrichment at Wake Forest University. In D. G. Brown (Ed.), *Electronically enhanced education* (pp. 101–6). Winston-Salem, NC: Wake Forest University Press.

National Research Council. (2000). *How people learn: Bridging research and practice.* Washington, DC: National Academy Press, Committee on Learning Research and Educational Practice.

Nichols, J. O. (1995). *A practitioner's handbook for institutional effectiveness and student outcomes assessment implementation* (3rd ed.). New York, NY: Agathon Press.

Office of Institutional Research. (2001, March). *Fact book.* Available: http://www.wfu.edu/Administrative-offices/Institutional-Research/OnlineFact-Book2000-2001/FBintro0.htm

Office of Institutional Research. (1998). *Faculty survey.* Available: http://www.wfu.edu/Administrative-offices/Institutional-Research/Faculty-Survey/1998Results.PDF

Office of the Provost, Wake Forest University. (1995, January). *Plan for the class of 2000.* Available: http://www.wfu.edu/Academic-departments/Program-Planning-Committee/Plan-for-the-Class-of-2000.txt.

Pascarella, E.T., et al. (1983). Student-faculty relationships and freshman year intellectual and personal growth in a nonresidential setting. *Journal of College Student Personnel, 24,* (5), 395–402.

Potter, D.L., et al. (1998). *Powerful partnerships: A shared responsibility for learning.* Washington, DC: A joint report of the American Association for Higher Education, American College Personnel Association, and the National Association for Student Personnel Management.

Ratcliff, J. L. (Ed.). (1992). Assessment and curriculum reform. *New Directions for Higher Education, No. 80.* San Francisco, CA: Jossey-Bass.

Terenzini, P. T. (1989, November/December). Assessment with open eyes: Pitfalls in studying student outcomes. *Journal of Higher Education 60,* 644-64.

Volkwein, J.F., and Carbone, D. (1991). *A study of research and teaching orientations in twenty-seven academic departments: The impact on undergraduates.* Paper presented at the annual meeting of the American Society for Higher Education, Boston, MA.

Contact Information

Ross Griffith
Director of Institutional Research
and Academic Administration
Wake Forest University
P. O. Box 7373, Reynolda Station
Winston-Salem, NC 27109
Phone: 336-758-5020
Fax: 336-758-5162
Email: griffith@wfu.edu
Web Address: http://www.wfu.edu/ir

Heather Stewart
Assistant Vice President for Finance and Technology
Seton Hall University
400 South Orange Ave.
South Orange, NJ 07079
Phone: 973-495-2602
Fax: 973-761-7942
Email: stewarhe@shu.edu

Bibliography

American Association for Higher Education, American College Personnel Association, National Association of Student Personnel Administrators. (1999). *Powerful partnerships: A shared responsibility for learning.* Washington, DC: Author.

Angelo, T. A., and Cross, K. P. (1993). *Classroom assessment techniques.* San Francisco, CA: Jossey-Bass.

Astin, A. W. (1991). *Assessment for excellence.* New York, NY: ACE/Macmillan.

Banta, T. W. (1993). *Making a difference: Outcomes of a decade of assessment in higher education.* San Francisco, CA: Jossey-Bass.

Banta, T. W. (1996). *Assessment in practice: Putting principles to work on college campuses.* San Francisco, CA: Jossey-Bass.

Banta, T. W., and Kuh, G. D. (1998, March/April). A missing link in assessment. *Change*, pp. 40–46.

Banta, T. W., Lund, J. P., Black, K. E., and Oblander, F. W. (1988). Implementing outcomes assessment: Promise and perils. *New Directions for Institutional Research No. 59.* San Francisco, CA: Jossey-Bass.

Belton, V., Johnston, B., and Walls, L. (2001). *Developing key skills at Strathclyde business school through the integrative core.* Innovations in teaching business and management. Birmingham, England: SEDA.

Borden, V. M. H., and Banta, T. W. (Eds.). (1994). *Using performance indicators to guide strategic decision-making.* San Francisco, CA: Jossey-Bass.

Boyer, E. L. (1987). *College: The undergraduate experience in America.* New York, NY: Harper and Row.

Brown, D. G. (2000, August). The jury is in!: Computer-enhanced instruction works. *Syllabus*, 22.

Centra, J. A. (Ed.). (1977). Renewing and evaluating teaching. *New Directions for Higher Education, No. 17.* San Francisco, CA: Jossey-Bass.

Chickering, A.W., and Gamson, Z. (1987). Seven principles for good practice in undergraduate education. *AAHE Bulletin, 87* (3).

Chickering, A.W., and Reisser, L. (1993). *Education and identity.* San Francisco, CA: Jossey-Bass.

Clark, B. R. (1998). *Creating entrepreneurial universities: Organizational pathways of transformation.* Tarrytown, NY: Pergamon.

Clayton College & State University. (1998). Recommendations, spring 1998. Faculty Development Coordinating Committee, Internal Document.

Clayton College & State University. (1999). *Faculty and Student Satisfaction Survey Data.* Academic Effectiveness Information, Vice-President for Academic Affairs web site, http://adminservices.clayton.edu/vpaa/academic effectiveness.html

Computer-enhanced learning initiative. Retrieved March 24, 1999, http://www.wfu.edu/CELI/

Courts, P. L., and McInerney, K. H. (1993). *Assessment in higher education: Politics, pedagogy, and portfolios.* Westport, CT: Praeger.

Davis, J.D., and Young, R.E. (Eds.). (1982). Students and faculty: Classroom and beyond. *Plantings, 3.*

DeLoughry, T. J. (1995, May 5). Mandatory computers. *The Chronicle of Higher Education,* pp. A37, A39.

Division of Information Technology. (1995). *Information technology plan.* Available: http://technology.shu.edu/techplan/

Donovan, M.S. et al. (1999). *How people learn: Bridging research and practice.* Washington, DC: National Research Council.

Ehrmann, S. C., & Milam, J. H. (1999). *Flashlight cost analysis handbook: Modeling resource use in teaching and learning with technology.* Washington, DC: The TLT Group (The Teaching, Learning, and Technology Affiliate of AAHE).

Ehrmann, S.C. (1995, March/April). Asking the right questions: What does research tell us about technology and higher learning? *Change, 27* (2), 20-27.

Erwin, T.D. (1991). *Assessing student learning and development.* San Francisco, CA: Jossey-Bass.

Ewell, P. (Ed.). (1985). Assessing educational outcomes. *New Directions for Institutional Research, No. 47.* San Francisco, CA: Jossey-Bass.

Gaff, J. G. and Ratcliff, A. (1997). *Handbook of the undergraduate curriculum: A comprehensive guide to purposes, structures, practices, and change.* San Francisco, CA: Jossey-Bass.

Granger, M. J. and Lippert, S. K. (1998). Preparing future technology users. *Journal of End User Computing, 10,* 27–31.

Griffith, R. (1999, April). Connecting students and faculty through technology, collaboration, and globalization at Wake Forest University. *The Technology Source.* Available: http://horizon.unc.edu/TS/cases/1999-04.asp

Griffith, R., Gu, Y., and Brown, D. G. (1999, May). *Assessment of the impact of ubiquitous computing.* Paper presented to The Association for Institutional Research (AIR). Seattle, WA. (ERIC Document Reproduction Service No. ED433766)

Hong Kong Housing Authority. (2000). *Housing statistics: Housing in figures 2000.* http://www.info.gov.hk/hd/eng/hd/stat_00/mid_f.htm

Igbaria, M. (1999). The driving forces in the virtual society. *Communications of the ACM, 42,* 64–70.

Institutional Research Office. (1995). *The departmental guide and record book for student outcomes assessment and institutional effectiveness.* New York, NY: Agathon Press.

Katz, R. (Ed.). (1999). *Dancing with the devil: Information technology and the new competition in higher education.* San Francisco, CA: Jossey-Bass

Katz, S. N. (2001, June 15). In information technology, don't mistake a tool for a goal. *The Chronicle of Higher Education,* p. B9.

Landry, S. G. (2000). *Project planning for ubiquitous computing: A case study of ubiquitous computing at Seton Hall University.* Paper presented at the meeting of EDUCAUSE, Nashville, TN.

Laurillard, D. (1993). *Rethinking university teaching: A framework for the effective use of educational technology.* New York, NY: Routledge.

MacVicar, M.L. (1982). *College admissions and the transition to postsecondary education.* Testimony to the National Commission on Excellence in Education, Chicago, IL.

McCarty, D., and Robinson, K. (1999). *The chronicles of change project, a qualitative study—Summary of results.* Unpublished Report. Academic Effectiveness Information, Vice- President for Academic Affairs web site, http://adminservices.clayton.edu/vpaa/academiceffectiveness.html

McCoy, L., Griffith, R., and Gu, Y. (1999). Assessment from multipurpose surveys and other sources. In D. G. Brown (Ed.), *Electronically enhanced education* (pp. 95–100). Winston-Salem, NC: Wake Forest University Press.

Miles, M., and Huberman, A. (1994). *Qualitative Data Analysis* (2nd ed.). Thousand Oaks, CA: Sage.

Mitra, A., and Hazen, M. (1999). Longitudinal Assessment of Computer Enrichment at Wake Forest University. In D. G. Brown (Ed.), *Electronically enhanced education* (pp. 101–6). Winston-Salem, NC: Wake Forest University Press.

National Committee of Enquiry into Higher Education. (1997). *Higher education in the learning society (The Dearing report).* London, England: HSMO.

National Research Council. (2000). *How people learn: Bridging research and practice.* Washington, DC: National Academy Press, Committee on Learning Research and Educational Practice.

Nichols, J. O. (1995). *A practitioner's handbook for institutional effectiveness and student outcomes assessment implementation* (3rd ed.). New York, NY: Agathon Press.

Office of Institutional Research. (1998). *Faculty survey.* Available: http://www.wfu.edu/Administrative-offices/Institutional-Research/Faculty-Survey/1998Results.PDF

Office of Institutional Research. (2001, March). *Fact book.* Available: http://www.wfu.edu/Administrative-offices/Institutional-Research/OnlineFact-Book2000-2001/FBintro0.htm

Office of Student Affairs. (2000). *A profile of new full-time undergraduate students 2000.* University of Hong Kong, Office of Student Affairs, Pokfulam, Hong Kong: SAR.

Office of the Provost, Wake Forest University. (1995, January). *Plan for the class of 2000.* Available: http://www.wfu.edu/Academic-departments/Program-Planning-Committee/Plan-for-the-Class-of-2000.txt.

Pascarella, E.T., et al. (1983). Student-faculty relationships and freshman year intellectual and personal growth in a nonresidential setting. *Journal of College Student Personnel, 24,* (5), 395–402.

Potter, D.L., et al. (1998). *Powerful partnerships: A shared responsibility for learning.* Washington, DC: A joint report of the American Association for Higher Education, American College Personnel Association, and the National Association for Student Personnel Management.

Ratcliff, J. L. (Ed.). (1992). Assessment and curriculum reform. *New Directions for Higher Education, No. 80.* San Francisco, CA: Jossey-Bass.

Schacter, J. and Fagnano, C. (1999). Does technology improve student learning and achievement? How, when, and under what conditions? *Journal of Educational Computing Research, 20,* 329–343.

Smye, R., and Greyborn, A. (2000). *Taming the wired classroom.* Montreal, Québec, Canada: IBM ThinkTank 2000, HEC.

Terenzini, P. T. (1989, November/December). Assessment with open eyes: Pitfalls in studying student outcomes. *Journal of Higher Education 60,* 644-64.

Volkwein, J.F., and Carbone, D. (1991). *A study of research and teaching orientations in twenty-seven academic departments: The impact on undergraduates.* Paper presented at the annual meeting of the American Society for Higher Education, Boston, MA.

Yi-zheng, L. (1998). Asian Society Asian Update Series: An economic roundup of post-handover Hong Kong. In J. Fischer, H. J. Ivory, L. Yi-zheng, & J. T. H. Tang (Eds.), *Hong Kong: The challenges of change.* http://www.Asiasociety.org/publications/update_hongkong_challenges.html

Index

by David Brown, 8
by Node Learning, 8
by Ray Brown, 8
by Ron Toll, 8
Lister, Brad, 62, 70
Literacy in IT
    Hong Kong's objective, 35, 45
    Acadia's compulsory course, 121
    basic course at Crookston, 92
    Strathclyde requirement, 77
Loaner pool
    Strathclyde, 81
Lonsway, Brian, 66
Lotus LearningSpace, 195
Low hanging fruit, 85
Lund, J. P., 225

M
Macintosh
    Dartmouth, 17, 23
    Drew, 161
    Drexel, 128
MacVicar, M, L., 227
Maintenance and repair
    Hong Kong Centre, 38
    Drew, 158, 163
    Drexel, 130, 136
    Rensselaer, 63, 67
Mandate use of computers
    Clayton, 183
    not at Dartmouth, 22
    not at Drexel, 132
    not at Wake Forest, 108
    Seton Hall, 201
Marketing
    Acadia, 120
    an application, 169
    benefit of portability, 8
    benefit of standardization, 7
    Drew, 156

Hong Kong, 44
    SUNY Morrisville, 150
    Wake Forest, 108
Mathematics
    an application, 55, 60
Matthews, Richard, 113
McCarty, Donna Wood, 173, 185
McCoy, L., 227
McElroy, Elliott W., 173
McGraw-Hill, 127
McInerney, K. H., 226
Measurement instruments, 214, 221
Methodology
    selection of authors, 3
Microsoft Office, 22
Milam, J. H., 51
Miles, M., 185
Mireault, Paul, 167
Mitra, A., 227
Mobile computing
    Dartmouth's Center, 24
Modem service
    Dartmouth, 27
Morrisville Auxiliary Corporation
    SUNY Morrisville, 149
Mullins, Lynnette, 93
Multimedia equipment
    access at Acadia, 121

N
National Association of Student
    Personnel Administrators, 225
National Committee of Enquiry
    Into Higher Education, 86
National Research Council, 227
Needy students
    Clayton, 173
    Rensselaer, 58
    Strathclyde, 81